OPPOSABLE THUMBS

HOW SISKEL & EBERT
CHANGED MOVIES FOREVER

MATT SINGER

G. P. PUTNAM'S SONS
NEW YORK

PUTNAM
— EST. 1838 —

G. P. Putnam's Sons
Publishers Since 1838
An imprint of Penguin Random House LLC
penguinrandomhouse.com

Library of Congress Cataloging-in-Publication Data

Names: Singer, Matt, author.
Title: Opposable thumbs: how Siskel & Ebert changed movies forever / Matt Singer.
Description: New York: G. P. Putnam's Sons, 2023. |
Includes bibliographical references and index. |
Identifiers: LCCN 2023027428 (print) |
LCCN 2023027429 (ebook) | ISBN 9780593540152 (hardcover) |
ISBN 9780593540169 (ebook)
Subjects: LCSH: Ebert, Roger. | Siskel, Gene. | Film critics—United
States—Biography. | Motion pictures—Reviews.
Classification: LCC PN1998.3.E327 S56 2023 (print) | LCC PN1998.3.E327 (ebook) |
DDC 791.43092/2 [B]—dc23/eng/20230802
LC record available at https://lccn.loc.gov/2023027428
LC ebook record available at https://lccn.loc.gov/2023027429

Printed in the United States of America
2nd Printing

Book design by Kristin del Rosario
Title page art: Camera © hugolacasse/Shutterstock.com

For Riley and Eloise
And for Eloise and Riley

(Like Gene and Roger,
they both wanted their names to be first.)

CONTENTS

INTRODUCTION
Coming Attractions 1

CHAPTER ONE
Ebert Before Siskel 15

CHAPTER TWO
Siskel Before Ebert 35

CHAPTER THREE
Opening Soon at a Theater Near You 57

CHAPTER FOUR
The First-Take Show 79

CHAPTER FIVE
Rompin' Stompin' Film Criticism 103

CHAPTER SIX
Two Thumbs Up 127

CHAPTER SEVEN
Across the Aisle 147

CHAPTER EIGHT
Hooray for Hollywood 165

CHAPTER NINE
Get to the Crosstalk   185

CHAPTER TEN
The Future of the Movies   201

CHAPTER ELEVEN
The Balcony Is Closed   217

CHAPTER TWELVE
Ebert & Roeper & Lyons & Mankiewicz &
Phillips & Scott & Lemire & Vishnevetsky   233

EPILOGUE
Until Next Time, We'll See You at the Movies   261

APPENDIX: BURIED TREASURES THAT
SISKEL AND EBERT LOVED   277

ACKNOWLEDGMENTS   297

NOTES   301

PHOTO CREDITS   331

INDEX   333

OPPOSABLE THUMBS

COMING ATTRACTIONS

If you want to learn about history you can find it in the most odd places. The patterns in the world will force themselves into other corners of the world. . . . Looking at it small, you can get more detailed.

—GENE SISKEL

When you ask someone for the truth about themselves, you may get the truth, or part of the truth, or none of the truth, but you will certainly get what they would like you to think is the truth.

—ROGER EBERT

ike a lot of what you're about to read, this story starts with a disagreement.

Everyone involved agrees on this much: the key moment that altered the course of American film criticism—along with the history of television, and even the movies themselves—took place at a diner in Chicago on a Saturday afternoon in early 1976. That's where two men who knew each other for six years before they ever engaged in a meaningful conversation met for the most important lunch of their professional lives.

Their names were Gene Siskel and Roger Ebert. They were

summoned to the Oxford Pub, a popular hangout for reporters on Lincoln Avenue, by a woman they had never met. Her name was Thea Flaum. She had a proposal for them.

Siskel and Ebert might have been curious to hear what Flaum had to say, but they were not thrilled to see each other again. From the first time they'd laid eyes on one another, Roger Ebert and Gene Siskel had known they had chemistry—the kind that causes glycerin to explode when it's mixed with nitric and sulfuric acid. When they were placed in close proximity, something could erupt at any moment. It often did.

The two had been locked in a bitter rivalry for more than half a decade. In the mid-1970s, there were four big newspapers in Chicago, each with its own film critic. Ebert, at the *Chicago Sun-Times*, was on good terms with David Elliott, his counterpart at the *Chicago Daily News*, and Mary Knoblauch at *Chicago Today*. But Siskel, at the *Chicago Tribune*, was a perpetual thorn in his side.

Ebert had become the *Sun-Times'* critic in 1967. Siskel followed at the *Tribune* in 1969, a development Ebert perceived as a deliberate attempt by the paper to compete with him head-on by bringing in their own young critic to cover the Chicago film scene. Shortly after Siskel got the job at the *Tribune*, he even started using stars to rate the movies he reviewed. Previously, Ebert had been the only critic in Chicago to use such a system.

These developments left Ebert certain: Siskel was explicitly hired to knock him off.

Siskel, for his part, needed no added motivation to view Ebert as a threat. Siskel's former roommate at Yale called him "the most competitive person I've ever run across—more so than Michael Jordan or Bill and Hillary Clinton." So if Roger viewed him as his adversary, that was just fine with Gene, who always loved a good contest.

Now he had one: destroy Ebert.

Gene Siskel and Roger Ebert saw each other as more than competitors; they were closer to mortal enemies. Each considered it an essential aspect of their job to beat the other: to write the best review, to land the biggest interview, to score the best scoops. And they took their jobs very seriously.

As the two men settled in for lunch, they sized each other up. The lanky Siskel, who was just about to celebrate his thirtieth birthday, was trying to compensate for his accelerating hair loss by growing out a painter's brush mustache and an enormous set of sideburns. The pudgy Ebert, thirty-three, had no such problem with male-pattern baldness; his hair was so thick it threatened to overtake his forehead entirely as it drooped down toward a pair of thick glasses. The two men were so at odds even their hairstyles were diametrically opposed to one another.

But Siskel and Ebert weren't strangers. In fact, this was a reunion of sorts. A few months earlier, the two men had set aside their mutual hostility long enough to shoot a pilot at Chicago's public television station, WTTW. While local newscasts in New York City had begun adding film critics to their lineup of reporters by the early 1960s, this pilot, titled *Opening Soon . . . at a Theater Near You*, represented a totally new concept for a TV series. Instead of a lone critic presenting themselves as a singular authority on a work of art, *Opening Soon* showcased *two* film critics—in conversation—discussing their respective reactions to the latest movies in town.

Here's another thing everyone agrees about: the pilot was a mess.

Roger and Gene had each worked in television prior to *Opening Soon,* but you wouldn't know it from their performance. Despite their experience, the pair hosted the pilot like they had never even watched a TV show before, much less appeared on one.

Ebert's enormous glasses reflected every light in the TV studio whenever he so much as glanced at his cohost, and in wide shots the camera occasionally glimpsed him nervously fidgeting with the cuff of his pants. For his part, Siskel flubbed the title of the show, calling it "Opening for Us at a Theater Near You" just before the closing credits. The unlikely partners didn't necessarily act like they hated each other on camera, but they both looked slightly miserable and intensely nervous, as if someone standing just off camera had trained a gun on them and forced them to discuss the 1975 Anthony Newley musical *Mister Quilp*.

A few weeks after the *Opening Soon* pilot aired, WTTW's head of programming, Dick Bowman, called Flaum into his office for a meeting. After helping create an award-winning PBS documentary on criminal courts and a successful series for parents titled *Look at Me*, Flaum had recently joined the WTTW staff.

"Do you like movies?" Bowman asked.

"I love movies," Flaum responded.

"What would you think about doing a show about movies?"

"I would *love* to do a show about movies."

Just like that, Flaum became the new producer of *Opening Soon . . . at a Theater Near You*.

Bowman wanted her to keep the basic concept: two critics debating recent movies. Beyond that, Flaum had carte blanche to rework the busted pilot—and even to replace either or both of its hosts if she saw fit.

Whatever the problems with the original *Opening Soon*, Flaum recognized the format had a lot of possibilities. In the mid-1970s, American movies were on a significant upswing. Five months before *Opening Soon* premiered on WTTW, a relatively unknown twenty-eight-year-old director named Steven Spielberg had shocked Hollywood by turning a B-level thriller about a police chief, a scientist, a drunken fisherman, and a great white shark into the highest-grossing picture in the history of the industry.

Spielberg's *Jaws* took the movie world by storm, and it was just one of dozens of landmark movies released during the decade. In the first half of the '70s, a slew of films pushed the boundaries of mainstream cinema with stories full of mature themes, shocking sexuality, and frank depictions of violence and drug use. In the second half of the '70s, other filmmakers, like Spielberg and a talented USC graduate named George Lucas, redefined what financial success in the film industry could look like, with massive hits that grossed hundreds of millions of dollars at the box office. The blockbuster was born.

Siskel and Ebert were part of a new generation of film critics raised on movies and just as in love with them as these young directors. It was their job to reckon with these new developments in American cinema. But a movie review in print could only *describe* its subject. On television, a critic could include clips, giving the audience a real taste of what the film looked and sounded like. And in the 1970s, footage from new films was very hard to come by outside of actual movie theaters. A TV show built around scenes from the latest motion pictures would have a powerful lure for cinephiles hungry for information about new releases—no matter which critics were responsible for discussing them.

But that didn't mean *any* two critics could host this show. Flaum did give some consideration to replacing either Siskel or Ebert, or both. (Decades later, she specifically remembers David Elliott at the *Chicago Daily News* as a possible candidate.) Still, even if Gene Siskel and Roger Ebert's innate charisma didn't leap off the screen in that *Opening Soon* pilot, Flaum sensed the duo had potential.

"There was *no* chemistry. They didn't even like each other!"

Flaum says. "But they had a style of relating to the movies, which both of them loved. They were very good critics, and very smart."

Siskel had been reviewing movies on camera at the local CBS affiliate since 1974, and his large profile in the Chicago media world made him an obvious choice. And Ebert, for all his awkwardness on camera, was an undeniable star in the field of film criticism. His reviews were already syndicated in almost a hundred papers around the country. A few months before the *Opening Soon* pilot premiered on WTTW, Ebert had become the first film critic in history to win the Pulitzer Prize for criticism. A film critic wouldn't win the award again for another twenty-eight years.

No one would give Roger and Gene an award for their performance in the *Opening Soon* pilot. But on closer inspection, the show wasn't a complete disaster. (A partial disaster, yes.) As Flaum notes, the men certainly knew their subject, and in brief moments they played off each other well. About nine minutes into the pilot, Ebert noted that 1975 marked the eleventh year of the Chicago International Film Festival.

"I can remember when it could have been held in a hotel room, so few people turned up," he quipped.

Without missing a beat, Siskel shot back, "*I* can remember when some of the films they showed deserved being *shown* in a hotel room."

"Probably were photographed there, too," Ebert replied with equally adroit timing.

The way the two spontaneously built off each other's comments suggested that while Siskel and Ebert didn't like each other, they *did* understand each other. It showed Flaum that with the right guidance and enough training, they could develop an on-air rapport.

It wasn't much, but it was something; enough to convince

Flaum that Siskel and Ebert deserved a second shot at hosting the show. And that was why Flaum asked Gene and Roger to meet her for lunch at the Oxford Pub.

After they arrived and ordered some hamburgers, Flaum made her pitch. They would try *Opening Soon . . . at a Theater Near You* again. This time, they'd do it her way.

She would rework the show's presentation, from the look of the set to the style of the hosts' wardrobes. She would help them improve their on-screen energy. She'd teach them to tailor their writing to a television audience instead of a newspaper reader. She even proposed giving Gene and Roger a dog sidekick, who would help loosen up the hosts as part of a "Dog of the Month" segment, where Gene and Roger would expound on the worst movies playing in theaters.

This is where the disagreement begins.

Roger Ebert always claimed that he was skeptical about the show in those early days, particularly if it meant working with Gene Siskel. "When we were asked to work together on a TV show," Ebert wrote in 1999, "we both said we'd rather do it with someone else. Anyone else."

Flaum remembers it differently. As she recalls that fateful lunch in 1976, only one of the two critics was unsure about her offer—and it wasn't Ebert.

"Right away," Flaum says, "Roger wanted to do it."

That there exists some dispute about this conversation makes it an even more appropriate launching point for Flaum, Siskel, and Ebert's show. Because more than any other television series of its era, *Opening Soon . . . at a Theater Near You*—which later became known as *Sneak Previews, At the Movies with Gene Siskel and Roger Ebert*, and, finally and most famously, *Siskel & Ebert*—was founded on the notion of opposing viewpoints.

All television programs are rooted in drama and conflict: good versus evil, cops versus robbers, doctors versus devastating illnesses, space explorers versus evil alien invaders. *Siskel & Ebert* was the first and perhaps greatest TV show in history where the struggle between the two antagonists was entirely intellectual. Tensions were never resolved with fistfights or shoot-outs, but with conversation and analysis. Hell, for the entirety of their twenty years on television, Roger and Gene clashed and quarreled without ever getting out of their seats—comfy chairs in a Chicago studio designed to look like a cozy movie theater balcony. And yet their verbal sparring matches often contained more suspense than the movies they reviewed.

For more than two decades after that lunch at the Oxford Pub, Gene Siskel and Roger Ebert carried on a nonstop battle for critical supremacy. As they developed their on-air skills, their sometimes heated but always heartfelt conversations helped *Siskel & Ebert* grow from a cult series on one public television station to one of the biggest syndicated series in history, broadcast to hundreds of markets around the country. Millions of Americans, including many who had very little interest in movies, tuned in to *Siskel & Ebert* every week to see what they would fight about next.

And Gene Siskel and Roger Ebert could argue about anything. Even when they agreed about whether a film was good, they sometimes vehemently disagreed about *why* it was good.

In 1987 they both recommended Oliver Stone's *Wall Street* while simultaneously diverging in their opinions about every single facet of the film. Gene thought Michael Douglas overacted as the scheming stock trader Gordon Gekko; Roger felt Gekko was the strongest element of the picture and countered that Charlie Sheen was the weak point of the film. Gene believed *Wall Street* only really worked as a pulp drama; Roger argued it was on par with classics like *The Graduate* and *Sweet Smell of Success.* Gene argued that *Wall Street* paled in comparison to Stone's previous movie, *Platoon*; Roger rejected that juxtaposition entirely because the movies were so totally different in subject matter and tone.

But Roger and Gene's squabbles were about more than just the movies. When an argument concluded, they would quarrel over who started the altercation in the first place. They even bickered over something as simple as what to order for lunch. For a period in the 1990s, the exhausted *Siskel & Ebert* staff resolved this endless battle the only way they knew how: by forcing both men to get the *same* lunch every day. That way, there could be no complaints from one or the other over who "won" the lunch order. (The identical lunch order, if you're curious: tuna salad in a pita with lettuce and tomato from the famous Chicago deli D.B. Kaplan's.)

The differences of opinion even extend into the origin of the show and some of its most famous aspects. Throughout the years, many variations of Gene and Roger's famous squabbles have been printed in newspapers, magazines, oral histories, and books. In some tellings, Siskel and Ebert's literal trademark—their thumbs up and down ratings system—was first introduced in the mid-1980s. In fact, it came much earlier, after their first move from PBS to syndication. Where Siskel and Ebert are involved, almost everything is up for debate.

Certainly *Siskel & Ebert* was one of the more surprising hits in television history. Gene and Roger got much more comfortable on camera, and eventually mastered the art of televised debate, but they never really became more telegenic. In a strange way, their lack of TV-ready-ness became an asset. They were never mistaken for actors playing roles, although later, others *would* try to play *their* roles as disagreeable TV film critics. Siskel and Ebert became TV stars specifically because they didn't look like TV stars.

(Later in life, Roger loved to relate a story that Jack Nicholson once told Gene Siskel: the first time *Sneak Previews* aired in Los Angeles, Nicholson received a frantic phone call from his friend and fellow actor Harry Dean Stanton. "Jack! Turn on your TV!" he instructed. "There are two guys talking about the movies, and they don't look like *anyone* on television.")

As their fame grew, Siskel and Ebert became household names, or at least *one* household name, spoken as if it were one word: "Siskelandebert." Some articles about the show referred to them collectively by the nickname "Siskbert," as if they were a single, conjoined entity—although one longtime producer recalls being instructed on his first day on the job never to refer to them that way in their presence because they both hated it so much. (They disliked traveling together because it greatly increased the chances of them being recognized. Separately, they were two Midwestern-ers in V-neck sweaters. Together, they were a celebrity.)

To casual fans, they were "the Bald One" and "the Fat One," which not only placed them in the tradition of classic mismatched Hollywood duos like Laurel and Hardy, it also subtly enhanced their combative brand—although it never stopped them from being mistaken for one another, a source of endless irritation for both.

Siskel would later claim that one of the things he was most proud of about the show was the fact that they were sometimes described "as having the most authentic relationship on television." But Siskel and Ebert were authentic about *everything*. There was nothing fake about their reviews, their viewpoints, or their inexhaustible need to compete and beat the other. They were as legitimate in their passion for their movies as they were in their desire to win every debate about them. With Gene and Roger there were conflicts and drama constantly, whether the cameras were rolling or not.

But *Siskel & Ebert* was much more than a couple of guys yelling at each other. For the two decades Siskel and Ebert's shows were on the air, they provided an oasis of intelligent (if frequently heated) debate in a desert of bland television talk. In the process, they turned film criticism from a solitary pursuit plied by a handful of journalists and scholars into a massively popular endeavor— and sometimes a spectator sport—practiced by thousands and watched by millions.

As the show grew, so did Roger and Gene's influence, which they wielded to support causes they believed in and films they felt deserved to be seen by wider audiences. When they loved a movie, they didn't just review it, they championed it over and over; sometimes upward of half a dozen times in a span of a few months. Some of the most famous filmmakers of the last half century owe their careers to Siskel and Ebert's support. Their fans and followers became the next generations of critics, filmmakers, and TV producers; their influence continues to reverberate through all those worlds.

All of that came later. At the Oxford Pub in 1976, all Gene Siskel knew was he'd shot a pilot for a TV show that turned out poorly. Most budding broadcasters would be delighted to have a TV producer pitch them their own regular series. But Gene Siskel was not like most budding broadcasters. Fearless, smart, and supremely confident in his own abilities, he was not easily swayed by Flaum's ideas. In fact, as their lunch began, his mood was downright hostile. It had been weeks since the *Opening Soon* pilot aired, and she was the first person from the station to get in touch with him. No one else from WTTW had reached out. And that pissed him off.

Put off by WTTW's poor communication, and never one to mince words, Gene threw down the gauntlet. "Tell me why I should do this," he ordered.

"Because," Flaum replied, "I can teach you how to be better."

Siskel considered her words.

"If we go ahead and do this right," Flaum continued, "we'll be the most watched half-hour series on public television. There will be a lot of success. It will be a big deal."

At least that's what Flaum remembers. This is another source of disagreement in the *Siskel & Ebert* origin story. In Ebert's account of this lunch, Flaum's predictions were even bolder.

"You boys have no idea how far this show is going to go," Ebert remembered Flaum telling them. "One day you'll be in national syndication. You'll be making real money. You wait and see."

Siskel mulled over the situation. He may have been skeptical about the show's prospects after its initial misfire, but he was also ambitious. If Flaum was good to her word, the reconfigured *Opening Soon* could be a major opportunity . . . even if it was a big break he would have to share with his archnemesis.

"Okay," he finally said. "Let's do it."

Whatever Flaum specifically promised Gene and Roger on that wintry Chicago day in 1976, Siskel and Ebert's partnership exceeded even her loftiest predictions. In a few years, *Opening Soon . . . at a Theater Near You* became the highest-rated half-hour show on all of PBS. But that was just the tip of the iceberg for Gene Siskel and Roger Ebert, who took the format they pioneered with Flaum into national syndication, first at Tribune Entertainment and later at the Walt Disney Company's Buena Vista Television. They turned the idea of two guys talking about movies into a veritable multimedia empire.

In less than a decade, film criticism became big business on television, with *Siskel & Ebert*'s format the model for all of it. While their competitors came and went, Gene and Roger had front-row balcony seats through a quarter century of upheaval in Hollywood.

They witnessed the rise and fall of a golden age of American film-making, followed by a revolution in the movie industry brought about by three little letters: VHS.

And Gene and Roger's on-screen dynamic and lively debate inspired copycats beyond the world of film criticism on TV. Flip through your television's cable channels any night of the week, and you're guaranteed to find journalists and commentators locking horns over politics or sports in a way that looks exactly like *Siskel & Ebert*.

No wonder, then, that the names Siskel and Ebert remain synonymous with criticism on and off television, and their influence on the world of popular culture remains as strong as ever, even though both men have been dead for over a decade. This is the story of how it all happened, according to the people who were there.

(Just don't expect them to always agree.)

CHAPTER ONE

EBERT BEFORE SISKEL

When you went on an interview, you took eight sheets of copy paper, folded them once, and ripped them in half using a pica stick. Then you folded them again. Now you had a notebook of thirty-two pages to slip in your pocket with your ball-point. You had a press card. You were a reporter from the *Chicago Sun-Times*.

—ROGER EBERT

R oger Ebert didn't set out to be a film critic.

He never went to film school. He never even took a single film course; none were offered at his college. He didn't spend his formative years studying the art of motion pictures. He went to the movies as a boy, but not any more than an average American kid growing up in the 1940s and '50s. When the *Chicago Sun-Times* made him its film critic in March of 1967 it wasn't because he had written extensively about movies, or because he ferociously lobbied his bosses for the promotion (although he happily accepted a $25-a-week raise as a result). At the time, Ebert was working as a reporter at the *Sun-Times* primarily to support himself while he earned his PhD in English at the University of Chicago. When the film critic position opened up, he was given the job. He was twenty-four years old.

Ebert thought he might someday make a good newspaper columnist, like legendary *Chicago Daily News* writer Mike Royko. He later said he also would have been very happy taking that doctorate in English and becoming a professor—reading books, traveling, and perhaps attempting to write the Great American Novel. Those were his plans as a young man, as much as he had plans at all.

He never did finish that doctorate—but he remained the *Sun-Times*' film critic for the rest of his life, eventually becoming one of the twentieth century's foremost writers, thinkers, and speakers about movies. None of that was by design. In his memoir, *Life Itself*, Ebert wrote that most of the turning points of his career "were brought about by others" and his life had largely unfolded "without any conscious plan." He also says that the writing style that won him a Pulitzer Prize and a devoted audience of millions of viewers and readers throughout more than forty years as a critic emerged "without great pondering" when he first began writing reviews at the *Sun-Times* and never changed very much through all his years of work. Later in the same book, he said that, at least as he experienced it, "so much of what happens by chance forms what becomes your life."

That was what he privately told the people closest to him as well. His wife, Chaz Ebert, says the word he used to describe many of the biggest moments in his life was "serendipity." One opportunity after another presented itself to him, through no intent or careful calculation of his own. And every time Ebert seized one of those opportunities, it seemed to work out well.

"Each move," she says, "was a good move, but not a planned move."

Roger Ebert's preternatural skills as a critic grew out of his roots as a journalist, which he began honing at an age when most children are still mastering basic writing skills. While in grade school, he received a toy version of a hectograph, a crude printing press that used gelatin to transfer ink to paper. With it, he produced his own newspaper, the *Washington Street News*, which he then gave to neighbors.

His interest in publishing could be traced back to his interest in reading, which developed even earlier, and which he attributed in turn to one of the central facts of his life: that he was an only child who spent much of his early years feeling pitifully lonely. Born on June 18, 1942, to Annabel, a bookkeeper and business manager, and Walter Ebert, an electrician at the University of Illinois, young Roger grew up with few playmates. To occupy his time and sate his curiosity about the world, he found himself drawn to the books in his childhood home at 410 East Washington Street in Urbana, Illinois.

"I always felt left out," Ebert recalled in a 1989 interview. "I was the only kid in my neighborhood who went to Catholic school. And everybody else of my age for six blocks around went to the public school and got to belong to the public Boy Scout troop. And so they were all off winning their merit badges and I was at home reading. And I was able to go on and be much more successful in life as a result."

Those feelings of isolation did not entirely dissipate as an adult. The Roger Ebert described by family and friends is a complicated and in some ways contradictory person. On the one hand, he was an incredible storyteller and showman; the consummate life of the party. Director Ramin Bahrani, a fan of *Siskel & Ebert* since childhood, struck up a friendship with Ebert after the critic accepted Bahrani's personal invitation to attend a Sundance Film

Festival screening of his debut feature, *Man Push Cart*. Bahrani says he was shocked by the Roger Ebert he spent time with at Ebert's Overlooked Film Festival (nicknamed "Ebertfest"). When the day's screenings were done, Ebert would take festival guests, including Bahrani, to his favorite restaurant—Steak 'n Shake—where he would hold court telling dirty jokes.

"It was a whole side I didn't know," Bahrani says. "Seeing him unleashed, he was a force of nature. He was so funny and charming, and he knew how to run an event and keep everybody entertained."

Ebert's longtime colleague at the *Chicago Sun-Times*, media columnist Robert Feder, describes him as a similar presence in the paper's newsroom. "It was always a treat when he came in," Feder recalls. "He would hold court—literally. He would stand in the middle of the features department and start telling these incredible stories and just carrying on. In the beginning, it would be to no one in particular and then a crowd would form. That was a common occurrence. It was incredible. He would imitate other people at the paper—he'd have their voices down, he'd tell these stories. And he would always laugh the loudest at his own jokes."

That was one side. But there was another, quieter side that his more gregarious public persona was in some ways a cover for. Ebert later blamed his feelings of isolation on his poor eyesight as a child, which went undiagnosed for years because his parents never got his vision checked by a doctor. "I was an earnest little boy," he said. "I was very nearsighted, so I read all the time. I was an only child, introspective. Real loud and demonstrative in class, but that was just a cover-up." Living with his parents on Washington Street, he would ride his bike around Urbana and the campus of the University of Illinois as, in his words, "a solemn kid, ignored and invisible, studying the students."

"Roger saw himself as kind of alone against whatever was out there," explains Chaz Ebert. "Not in an angry way; in an almost existential way. He identified a lot with people, individuals who took a stand and it wasn't a group decision. It was an individual decision to do something, to change something, to challenge some standard. That's how he saw himself in the world. . . . One of his favorite things to do is sit at a café alone by himself and have a cup of coffee."

Indeed, in Ebert's book about the Cannes Film Festival, *Two Weeks in the Midday Sun*, he describes a moment of "enormous happiness" of a kind he only felt once or twice a year while sitting "at a table in a square where no one I knew was likely to come, in a land where I did not speak the language, in a place where, for the moment, I could not be found. I was like a spirit returned from another world." In this passage, which Ebert later reprinted in *Life Itself* in a chapter titled "All by Myself Alone" (in which he also describes a beloved pastime he calls "Being by Myself in a City Where No One Knows Who I Am and No One Knows Where to Find Me"), he said these brief interludes filled him with the belief that "the thing that is really me sits somewhere quietly at a table, watching it all go by."

In other words, Roger Ebert possessed a gift crucial to all great journalists as well as film critics: razor-sharp observation skills. He once paraphrased Irish poet Brendan Behan in describing critics as "eunuchs in a harem: they see it done nightly, but are unable to do it themselves." Ebert came of age in the turbulent 1960s, and while he never made a secret of his own liberal politics, he later wrote that he "used journalism to stay at one remove" from his convictions. "My life," he wrote, "has followed that pattern. I observe and describe at a prudent reserve."

But where a reporter may be able to get by simply observing

and describing at a prudent reserve, Ebert possessed a secondary skill essential to great criticism: the ability to express the way a movie worked on his heart and his mind even as it happened in real time. He was just as good at explaining what a film meant as describing what it felt like to watch it. Reading a Roger Ebert review, you could imagine you were right there in the theater with him. And his language was so clear and so evocative that he made all kinds of supposedly esoteric movies—foreign films, silent movies, art house fare—seem completely accessible, and even exciting.

"When he wrote it was just like a guy who was talking to you: 'Here's a movie I saw. Here's what I think about it,'" says Ignatiy Vishnevetsky, a film critic who worked with Ebert on the final version of his movie review program. "There's something conversational about his writing. It just reads like a person talking. He was very good at that."

The first movie that really made an impression on Ebert was *A Day at the Races.* Walter Ebert was an enormous Marx Brothers fan who had seen their vaudeville act at Champaign's Virginia Theatre. For three days leading up to the movie's premiere in Urbana, all Roger heard about were Groucho, Chico, and Harpo. When the big day finally arrived, he wasn't wildly impressed with the comedy; most of it went over his head. Instead he was transfixed by the sequence where Harpo Marx played the harp. He'd never seen a harp before. As Harpo's fingers raced across its strings, he turned and looked into the lens of the camera. Young Roger Ebert swore he was smiling at him.

"What struck me during that movie," Ebert said, "was that there could be communication between myself and the screen. Movies were not simply something to look at up there. Sometimes the people in them would have things to say directly to me." As an adult, Ebert would say that sometimes he still felt like movies were speaking directly to him.

Growing up in Urbana, Ebert's primary home for movies was the Princess Theater on Main Street, an art deco movie house that held almost seven hundred filmgoers—or, on Saturday afternoons, seven hundred wild, screaming kids, who would pack the place to enjoy double-feature matinees. Nine cents bought you admission to cartoons, newsreels, trailers, a serial, and two movies. Later in life, Ebert would bemoan the way modern movies often failed to challenge and surprise the viewer, as if the screen were "a mirror and the people on the screen and the people in the audience have the same values, and the same background, and the same knowledge." As a child, he went to the Princess to learn about faraway cultures, to fantasize about what it might be like to live in places beyond the confines of his small Midwestern town.

The first movie Ebert ever really loved was one that spoke directly to his hunger for knowledge and his interest in different places and people: 1952's *Hans Christian Andersen*, a Danny Kaye musical loosely based on the life of the famous Danish author. The fact that it was about a writer no doubt appealed to young Roger, but what really excited him was the fact that it took place in a foreign country—and that such an exotic place really existed. After the movie was over, Ebert vowed to his father he would visit Copenhagen the following year. (Ebert was ten at the time.)

Instead, Ebert's crucial experience the following year came when *Houdini*, the 1953 biopic of the famous magician starring Tony Curtis and Janet Leigh, arrived in town. By the time *Houdini* opened in theaters, the bookish Ebert had read and reread Houdini's biography over and over. When the movie came out, he was furious—the movie was *nothing* like the book.

"That isn't what really happened! That's not what it was really like!" the eleven-year-old Ebert yelled in frustration. When he recalled the incident decades later on an episode of *Siskel & Ebert,* he credited it as an important milestone in his life: "It might have been the first moment I became a movie critic."

Ebert's earliest writings, however, had nothing to do with film. A few years earlier, Ebert had another one of his serendipitous experiences, when a stop on his newspaper delivery route included a pair of college students who loved science fiction. When they left school at the end of the year, they gifted him a box full of old issues of *Astounding Science Fiction*, a periodical that published influential sci-fi authors like Robert A. Heinlein and Isaac Asimov. Around the time of the incident with *Houdini*, Ebert began exploring the collection he'd acquired. One magazine listed a variety of sci-fi fanzines, so Roger sent away for a copy of the most highly regarded of the bunch, *Yandro* by Buck and Juanita Coulson.

That, he said, "was one of the most important formative acts" of his entire life.

Before long, Ebert was fully immersed in the world of science fiction fandom. He read professional magazines and fanzines, and he wrote letters to all of them—some of which reveal a budding interest in criticism and critical impulses. His letter to the sci-fi pulp magazine *Amazing Stories* in August 1957 implored the editor to "by all means keep the book reviews! I don't read them for advice on which books to buy—I have them before they are reviewed, but I just simply get a kick out of finding someone else's opinion on a book I've read."

Years later, Ebert would credit his time as a hard-core sci-fi fan as essential to his development as a writer. Fandom, he said, was the place where he "became critical," writing "smart-ass locs [letters of comment] about other people's reading" with a "kind of kibitzing outsider world view." (Yet again, Ebert adopted the mindset of an observer set apart from everyone else around him.)

For a while, Ebert even published his own fanzine, titled *Stymie*. Credited to "Rog Ebert, who should know better," the debut issue opens with a piece titled "A Biased View" about the Democratic National Convention of 1960 and promised "a fairly regular section of comment and criticism on Thomas Wolfe." *Stymie* no. 1 also included a short story called "Oh, How They Watched," and even a couple poems. (One, titled "Room," credited to "re," included the verse "Old hats jumbled on boxes. / Debauched girls from the country.")

More important than any literary breakthroughs in *Stymie's* pages was the confidence the zine gave Ebert to keep writing and commenting, and to keep publishing his own work. Ebert next created a weekly newspaper called the *Spectator* while he was still a freshman at the University of Illinois. Without the money to sustain the paper long-term, he sold it for $200 and went to work during his sophomore year at the school's paper, the *Daily Illini*.

That was hardly Ebert's first experience as a journalist. Ebert began covering high school football for the local daily, the *News-Gazette*, while he was still in high school himself. He was so young, in fact, he needed to get a special pass from the police in order to stay out late enough to write his stories about the Friday night games. Ebert was never much of a football fan, but he loved the freedom that sportswriting afforded. A great sportswriter could transform a humble ball game into an epic clash of mythic proportions—as Ebert did when he led his piece on his own high school team's surprising loss to spoil a potential perfect season: "The glass slipper was shattered and broken, the royal coach turned into a pumpkin, and the Cinderella Urbana Tigers stumbled and fumbled and fell."

The Urbana coach wasn't too happy to be compared to a pumpkin and briefly banned Ebert from the team's games. But the editors at the *News-Gazette* were delighted by the evocative prose, and they entered the piece in an Associated Press writing competition. This was a contest for professional journalists in Illinois, not students; Ebert took the top prize in the sportswriting category anyway. He proudly presented his award to his father, weeks before he died of lung cancer. Ebert later said that nothing he ever won—including the Pulitzer Prize—ever meant more to him than that.

At the *Daily Illini*, he went from columnist to news editor to editor of the entire paper by his senior year. Ebert was in charge on November 22, 1963—the day that President John F. Kennedy was assassinated. He became an *Illini* legend that day by standing up to the pressman after he discovered—while printing was already underway—that an ad featuring a pilgrim holding a musket looked like it was pointing right at a photograph of Kennedy. He raced to the pressman and told him a change needed to be made; they would *not* print the paper with a picture of a gun pointing at Kennedy's head.

"You hear that sound, Roger?" the pressman responded. "That's the sound of newspapers being printed."

Ebert repeated: "We're not going to print that tomorrow. We've got to stop the presses."

"Ebert became famous to us for that," said Roger Simon, an award-winning political columnist and writer who trailed Ebert at the *Daily Illini* and the University of Illinois by a few years. "Here was a kid, taking control of an adult situation, and making a news judgment. An important one."

Ebert's own writings about the Kennedy assassination in the *Illini* read like the work of a far more mature columnist than a kid

25

who had recently celebrated his twenty-first birthday. Four days after Kennedy's death, Ebert published an op-ed of his own full of horror, frustration, and indignation. It began with "The shame is ours. Out of the numbed confusion of the last four days, the sense of that shame is slowly taking hold. We walked in silence in the rain Friday afternoon, each enclosed by the knowledge of death's finality, but now this knowledge is no longer enough to shield us." Clearly, he did not need the occasion of a major football game to write a dramatic lede.

After graduating from Illinois, Ebert spent a year of post-graduate study abroad—not in Copenhagen like he'd wanted after watching *Hans Christian Andersen*, but in Cape Town, South Africa—and then another couple semesters studying back home in Champaign. He got accepted to the PhD program at the University of Chicago, but he needed a job as well. During Ebert's tenure at the *Daily Illini*, he'd written some freelance articles for several Chicago papers, so he wrote to a few of them asking for a job. One editor passed his info along to Jim Hoge, the *Chicago Sun-Times'* city editor (and future editor in chief), who invited him to come in for an interview. Ebert arrived in Chicago, and Hoge and a few other members of the staff took him to lunch. By the end of the meeting, Ebert had a job working on the Sunday magazine section. His foot was in the door, and it stayed there for the next forty-seven years.

His ascension to the *Sun-Times'* film critic desk a short time later was another of Ebert's happy career accidents. He was simply in the right place—and the right age—at the right time.

In March of 1967, the paper's film critic, Eleanor Keen, retired. She wasn't fired, she wasn't forced out; she took an early retirement package. In his first months at the *Sun-Times*, Ebert had filed a handful of pieces about the movies, including one from the press

junket for Warner Bros.' adaptation of the musical *Camelot*. Warners' publicist in Chicago, Frank Casey, liked what Ebert wrote,
and when Keen retired, Casey suggested Ebert to *Sun-Times* editors
as her replacement. That was that.

Today, if a major metropolitan newspaper needed a film critic,
it would surely look for one with more experience. In 1967, though,
Ebert's youth—he turned twenty-five that June—was an enormous asset. All over Hollywood in the late 1960s, a movement was
underway as traditional genres and filmmakers began to lose favor
with the younger audience that made up an increasingly large segment of the moviegoing public. The top-grossing films of 1967
weren't musicals like *Camelot*; they were edgy dramas about dis-
affected kids, like *The Graduate* and *Bonnie and Clyde*, the latter a
thrilling crime story about a pair of lovers turned bank robbers
(Warren Beatty and Faye Dunaway) whose Depression-era criminal exploits captivated the nation. The film, directed by Arthur
Penn, contained shockingly graphic violence that was unheard
of for a Hollywood movie of its day. *Bonnie and Clyde* alarmed
audiences—and many critics.

In fact, when *Bonnie and Clyde* first opened in theaters in the
late summer of 1967, it so scandalized the critical establishment
that they panned it across the board. Bosley Crowther, who'd been
writing film reviews in the *New York Times* since before Roger Ebert was born, called it "a blending of farce with brutal killings" that
was "as pointless as it is lacking in taste." *Newsweek*'s Joe Morgenstern said *Bonnie and Clyde* was a "squalid shoot-'em-up for the
moron trade." Practically the only critic who disagreed was Roger
Ebert, who immediately recognized it as the first masterpiece of
his tenure as the *Sun-Times*' film critic. He gave *Bonnie and Clyde*
four stars and called it "a milestone in the history of American
movies, a work of truth and brilliance." He correctly predicted that

in the future it would be seen as the "definitive film of the 1960s, showing with sadness, humor, and unforgiving detail what one society had come to. The fact that the story is set 35 years ago doesn't mean a thing. It had to be set sometime. But it was made now and it's about us."

Despite the largely negative reviews, audiences connected with *Bonnie and Clyde*, turning it into an unlikely smash hit. Women started dressing like Dunaway's Bonnie Parker; the film was ultimately nominated for nine Academy Awards, including Best Picture. Its success was so overwhelming that those who had previously reviewed it negatively faced a backlash. Joe Morgenstern saw the movie a second time and wrote a new review, conceding he had been wrong about the film. Bosley Crowther held firm in his assessment, even after a second viewing; by early 1968, the *New York Times* replaced him as their critic after twenty-seven years on the job.

Ebert may have lacked a formal education in film, but he went to film school on the job. His syllabus consisted of the old movies he would watch between press screenings at Chicago revival houses like the Clark Theater, an old movie palace in the Loop where $2.95 got you a ticket, free parking, and a three-course meal at the Chinese restaurant next door. His professors were the directors he interviewed for the *Sun-Times*, who he peppered with questions about technique and form. His textbooks were *Esquire* critic Dwight Macdonald's *On Movies*, Andrew Sarris's *Interviews with Film Directors*, and Robert Warshow's book *The Immediate Experience*, which contained a line that leaped off the page at him: "A man watches a movie, and the critic must acknowledge that he is that man." Putting himself into his reviews—sharing his immediate experience of the cinema—enabled him to write honestly and emotionally about everything. It became his signature style.

In those days, Ebert did not want to stay a film critic forever. In a 1969 letter to a former professor from the University of Illinois, he wrote that "a lifetime of such work would make [one] a moron." But his approachable approach to criticism quickly caught on. His reviews were syndicated in dozens of newspapers around the country. By 1970, *Time* magazine noted his popularity in an article that hailed him as Chicago's "community critic." He began writing profiles of Hollywood stars like Robert Mitchum, Lee Marvin, and Groucho Marx for the *New York Times* and *Esquire*.

Some of these publications tried to recruit Ebert to leave the *Sun-Times* and join them full-time. "He talked to the *Washington Post*, he talked to the *New York Times*," Chaz Ebert says. "They all wanted him, and he turned them all down. He would joke, 'I don't want to learn new streets.' He knew Chicago. He was comfortable. He liked his colleagues, his editors, and he was loyal to the *Sun-Times*. He didn't want to go anywhere else." That didn't change, even after Ebert won the Pulitzer Prize in 1975, making him the first film critic to earn the award.

In his free time away from criticism, Ebert pursued earthier interests. During his first years at the *Sun-Times*, he became interested in the work of an adventurous director whose films were crammed with taboo subject matter, unpredictable editing, adventurous cinematography, and—most important—loads of beautiful, busty women in various stages of undress. The director's name was Russ Meyer, and since the late 1950s, he had reigned as one of America's foremost purveyors of cinematic smut. Meyer, who learned cinematography working in the Signal Corps during World War II, had a commercial breakthrough in 1959 with *The Immoral Mr. Teas*, a nearly silent comedy about a man who suddenly gains the ability to see through women's clothing. The ever-practical Meyer shot the film for about $25,000. It grossed roughly sixty times that amount.

Meyer continued producing these sorts of so-called nudie-cuties—exploitation pictures with nearly as much humor as sex—through the 1960s until, at the end of the decade, he had another financial windfall with the softcore comedy *Vixen!*, about a lonely and sexually adventurous woman bedding everyone in sight, including men, women, even her own relatives. This time, Meyer spent about $75,000 on the film. It grossed roughly $8 million; about $68 million in 2023 dollars.

The film was so successful it attracted attention from Hollywood and the mainstream press. It also impressed Roger Ebert, who had seen *The Immoral Mr. Teas* back in his college days. In the *Sun-Times*, Ebert gave *Vixen!* three stars, calling it "the best film to date in that uniquely American genre, the skin-flick" and crediting Meyer as the only craftsman in a genre "filled with cheap, dreary productions."

Ebert respected Meyer's willingness to test the boundaries of good taste, his unique camera angles, and the way he undercut his movies' selling points—the sex scenes—with winking humor. It also didn't hurt that he shared Meyer's ceaseless fascination with women's breasts. ("Ever since I became aware of them, I've considered full and pendulous breasts the most appealing visual of the human anatomy," Ebert wrote in his memoir.)

After *Vixen!* began breaking box office records, the *Wall Street Journal* covered it on its front page, which prompted Ebert to revert back to his old ways as a fan and write an encouraging letter to the editor. The *Journal* printed it and Meyer read it. He sent Ebert an appreciative letter of his own, and a fast friendship was formed.

Yet again, Ebert was the beneficiary of a serendipitous series of events. Shortly after Ebert and Meyer began corresponding, movie studio 20th Century Fox took notice of Meyer's groundbreaking success with *Vixen!* as well. Fox had been slow to adjust to the youth movement sweeping through Hollywood, and the studio was reeling from a series of big-budget flops like *Doctor Dolittle*, movies that seemed completely out of touch with modern audiences. Fox needed hits, and fast. Given Meyer's knack for turning a little money and a lot of skin into big box office, they decided to take a chance on him.

One of Fox's few big hits of the late 1960s was *Valley of the Dolls*, a melodrama based on the best-selling novel by Jacqueline Susann that followed a trio of women as they pursued showbiz success and succumbed to assorted vices. Fox suggested Meyer make a sequel; Meyer, in turn, invited Ebert to come write it with him. Roger took a leave of absence from the *Sun-Times*, flew out to California, and spent six weeks cranking out a script.

There was just one problem: neither Meyer nor Ebert had ever read *Valley of the Dolls*.

They screened the film adaptation on the Fox lot and made the bold decision not to write a straightforward sequel to the wildly successful movie. Instead, their plan was to repeat its basic formula—beautiful women who succumb to various Hollywood temptations—with a fresh group of faces, filtered through Meyer's unique visual (not to mention sensual) sensibilities.

The resultant film, titled *Beyond the Valley of the Dolls*, combined surreal imagery, dark humor, violence, Hollywood satire, and plenty of sex. It culminated with a sequence where a hotshot record producer, Ronnie "Z-Man" Barzell, goes on a killing spree. Ebert and Meyer had based many of the characters in the film on real-life pop culture figures of the time; Z-Man was an obvious riff on the famous songwriter and producer Phil Spector. (It was a curious coincidence when, thirty years later, the real Spector was convicted of the murder of actress Lana Clarkson.)

Through the years on *Siskel & Ebert*, Ebert would occasionally quote the famous French director Jean-Luc Godard, who once said that the way to criticize a movie was to make another movie. Godard's line was essentially a more practical variation of Ebert's own philosophy, which he espoused many times in print and on television throughout his career: "It's not *what* a movie is about, it's *how* it's about." In other words, you can make a masterpiece or a disaster on any subject; there's nothing that precludes any concept from yielding a good or bad film. All that matters is how the filmmakers execute the material through the choices they make in terms of casting, acting, editing, cinematography, music, and so on.

Viewed through that lens, Ebert and Meyer's *Beyond the Valley of the Dolls* was itself a great work of film criticism. *Valley of the Dolls*, for all its sex and drugs, was almost impossibly stiff, tedious, and turgid. *Beyond the Valley of the Dolls*, drawn from the same basic story outline, was frenetic, goofy, funny, and sexy. If *what* these two movies were about was all that mattered, then *Valley of the Dolls* and *Beyond the Valley of the Dolls* would be equally good (or bad) movies, because their *whats* are identical—three young, attractive women sinking in show business quicksand. It's the *hows* that make them different—and make *Beyond the Valley of the Dolls* superior.

Ebert loved the experience of working with Meyer and was proud of the film—a *Beyond the Valley of the Dolls* poster Meyer signed to Roger still hangs in the Eberts' townhouse in Chicago—and he collaborated several more times with Meyer on screenplays for his movies. In 1977, Meyer called Ebert with another offer. The Sex Pistols were making a movie. The band's manager, Malcolm

McLaren, loved *Beyond the Valley of the Dolls* and wanted Meyer to direct the Pistols' film. Meyer, in turn, wanted Ebert to write it.

"What sort of picture will it be?" Ebert asked Meyer.

"McLaren says he wants to do the flip side of *Beyond the Valley of the Dolls*," Meyer replied.

"But *Beyond* itself was the flip side of *Valley of the Dolls*," Ebert said.

"You figure it out," Meyer said, shrugging.

Ebert, who knew almost nothing about the Sex Pistols before Meyer's call, penned a punk rock riff on *A Hard Day's Night* initially titled *Anarchy in the UK*. The script opened with a millionaire rock star, loosely based on Mick Jagger, as he exits his Rolls-Royce and murders a deer with a bow and arrow. The act is witnessed by a girl who, at the end of Ebert's script, returns to kill the star and shout the line "That's for Bambi!"—inspiring the screenplay's final title, *Who Killed Bambi?* Meyer shot the killing of the deer—but shortly after that sequence was filmed, the production collapsed. *Who Killed Bambi?* was never finished.

Beyond the Valley of the Dolls, on the other hand, was immediately profitable, recouping its $900,000 budget many times over. Within a few years, *Beyond the Valley of the Dolls* grew into a cult film; Mike Myers referenced it in his own spoof of 1960s pop culture, *Austin Powers: International Man of Mystery*, when he had its title character borrow Z-Man's immortal line, "It's my happening, and it freaks me out!" In 2016, *Beyond the Valley of the Dolls* got a Blu-ray release from the Criterion Collection, the company whose home video releases of canonical cinematic masterpieces have become the gold standard of the industry.

But in 1970, reviews of the movie were not kind. Most critics neither understood Meyer and Ebert's scattershot humor nor found it particularly funny if they did. While the vast majority of *Beyond the Valley of the Dolls'* notices were unkind, one was especially cruel. It awarded the film zero stars and dismissed it as "a cesspool on film."

It didn't come from an out-of-touch Bosley Crowther–type about to be put out to pasture. In fact, the critic who wrote this review was even younger than Ebert, and he was a fan of some of Meyer's prior work. Those movies had been funny and sexy, this critic argued, while *Beyond the Valley of the Dolls* was a disaster that unfolded "with all of the humor and excitement of a padded bra." The review complained about the lack of nudity and sexual tension, and said the photography of star Edy Williams, who had recently become Meyer's third wife, "could be grounds for divorce."

Meyer had written many of his past hits himself, so the critic laid much of the blame for *Beyond the Valley of the Dolls'* creative failures at Ebert's feet. "Boredom aplenty is provided by a screenplay which for some reason had been turned over to a screenwriting neophyte," the pan read.

The scathing review never mentioned Ebert by name, but its author knew him well. That's because since 1969 he had been Ebert's counterpart at the *Chicago Tribune*. His name was Gene Siskel.

CHAPTER TWO

SISKEL BEFORE EBERT

Seeing a great movie is still the great pleasure of my job. But then it's an added pleasure to be able to interact with the movie: to think about it, to talk about it, to write about it. That, too, is a lot of fun.

—GENE SISKEL

On June 27, 1995, a three-piece suit from the Leading Male on Kings Highway in Brooklyn, New York, sold at auction at Christie's for $145,500. Ordinarily, a polyester suit from a neighborhood store in New York City might set you back a couple hundred dollars. But this was not an ordinary polyester suit.

The three-piece ensemble sported a single-breasted white jacket with a wide lapel, a matching white vest, and white bell-bottom pants with a size 28 waist. The suit also came with a black Pascal of Spain shirt of a unique design; it contained a fastener to attach it to a clasp beneath the pants' waistband. Once buttoned, the shirt would never slip out of place, no matter how hard you danced.

On a rack, it may not have looked like much. But when John Travolta wore that suit as he strutted across the rainbow-colored dance floor of the 2001 Odyssey disco in 1977's *Saturday Night*

Fever, it instantly became a legendary piece of film fashion; perhaps the single most famous suit in the history of cinema. Travolta actually had two identical suits made for the famous scene where he performed his disco duet to the Bee Gees' "More Than a Woman," so that when one became slick with sweat he could change into the other one and filming could continue without interruption.

There was certainly no disputing the suit's authenticity; the inside lining bore an inscription from Travolta himself. It read:

> To Gene,
> So here's to a classic,
> your friend, John Travolta

The Gene was Gene Siskel. In his original 1977 review of *Saturday Night Fever* in the *Chicago Tribune*, Siskel called it a "very good new movie" with "flashes of reality and tons of energy." He also dinged the movie for its "derivative mix of *Rocky* and *Mean Streets*" and gave it 3.5 stars out of 4. When he made his list of the best films of 1977 a few weeks later, Siskel ranked *Saturday Night Fever* fifth, ahead of the original *Star Wars* (#7) and behind Woody Allen's *Annie Hall* (#1) and Steven Spielberg's *Close Encounters of the Third Kind* (#4).

But something about *Saturday Night Fever* spoke to Gene Siskel. If the movie had flaws, they began to feel insignificant as he went back to see the movie a second, third, and fourth time. The endless rewatches weren't done out of professional obligation; he simply loved the film. By the time Siskel bumped into the film's director, John Badham, at a dinner in Washington, DC, he had seen *Saturday Night Fever* seventeen times and possibly knew it better than Badham himself. The director later recalled that when they crossed paths at the dinner, Siskel immediately launched into a lecture about every minor gaffe and continuity error in the film, even pointing out mistakes Badham hadn't realized were visible on-screen.

So when one of Travolta's white suits wound up being auctioned off for charity in 1978, Siskel decided he needed to have it. Actress Jane Fonda bid $1,900—but Siskel bid $2,000 and won. He held on to the *Saturday Night Fever* suit all through the 1980s and into the '90s. But then John Travolta had a major career resurgence with *Pulp Fiction* and *Get Shorty* back-to-back, and Siskel sensed an opportunity to capitalize on Travolta's renewed cache by auctioning the suit off to the highest bidder.

It was a gamble—but Gene Siskel loved to gamble, on anything and everything. He'd pitch pennies at a wall with a buddy for hours. He'd play dice games with TV cameramen that some suspected he'd found a way to rig. He was especially fond of betting on horses. The Chicago screening room where critics saw most movies in the 1990s was around the corner from an off-track betting parlor. If there were even a couple minutes between a morning and afternoon screening, Gene could be counted on to sneak away to place a few bets. Or more than a few; one time, Roger Ebert got so sick of waiting for him to return that he ran down to the OTB and dragged him back upstairs so they could finally start the movie.

Lateness was a perpetual state of existence for Siskel. Coworkers say he was always pushing things off, always racing to get something done at the last minute. As Roger Ebert once put it, Gene's life was "a running battle with the realities of time." *Siskel & Ebert* executive producer Stuart Cleland describes Gene as a "constant procrastinator" who kept all of his editors on edge waiting for his copy. (Siskel once told Cleland that the advantage of procrastinating was that "every now and then you'll be told that the thing you've put off is no longer required.") Associate producer Carie Lovstad says lateness was part of Siskel's creative process; even if he had something finished early "he would be revising it, looking at it again, always down to the wire. He wasn't manic, but he was hyper, high energy—that was part of the fun for him. He was always trying to see how much he could get away with."

Christie's estimated that, with Travolta's renewed popularity, the *Saturday Night Fever* suit might sell in 1995 for $30,000 to $50,000. Instead, an anonymous bidder nearly tripled that. At the time, it was the highest price ever paid for a costume from a movie, a record that stood for several years, until someone paid $250,000 for the Cowardly Lion costume from *The Wizard of Oz*.

What about *Saturday Night Fever* resonated with Siskel? He wrote once that the film appealed to him in a "visceral way" because it "portrayed a wild adolescence I hadn't experienced but that I could enjoy vicariously on film."

But *Saturday Night Fever* is not simply a vicarious escape into a wild adolescence. The fleeting moments of joy Travolta's Tony Manero experiences while dancing stand in stark contrast to the rest of his bleak existence. Tony's father doesn't respect him or his love of the disco. Tony makes so little money as a clerk at a hardware store that he can barely afford his Saturday night trips to the 2001 Odyssey. And, as Tony slowly begins to realize over the course of the movie, his only friends are a gang of violent misogynists. These are not necessarily the kinds of story lines that one enjoys purely for their visceral escapist pleasures.

When asked about his job, Siskel would sometimes say he covered "the national dream beat." His reviews in print and on television reflected his belief that movies were much more than two hours of mindless entertainment. Buried beneath their beautiful surfaces were what he described as "the coalesced vapors of the consciousness of a society," and therefore if you look carefully at movies a lot of people love, you'll learn what they fear and desire.

For example, Siskel argued that the enormous popularity of disaster movies like *Airport* and *The Towering Inferno* in the 1970s tapped into Americans' paranoia of an impending apocalypse in a decade roiled by gas crises and political turmoil. And he regarded most movies as attempts to locate the source of evil in the world, an extension of an even more fundamental issue that preoccupied people: the meaning of life itself.

"I think a lot of people do wonder," Siskel once mused, "Why do people die? Why do I have this unhappiness? Why? Why do I suffer? Was I put on this planet to suffer? What is this? Is this somebody's cruel joke? You know—I gotta work all day. I mean, what happened? I didn't ask to be born. Now, why do I have all this junk going on? I think it's a basic question."

For Siskel, movies were always about the macro; the national dream beat. But if it's true that you can understand a country by looking at the movies it loves, then it also stands to reason that you can understand an individual by looking at the movies they love. And Gene Siskel loved *Saturday Night Fever*—a movie that happens to be about all of the existential issues Siskel described. Tony, Travolta's lost teenager, feels with every fiber of his being that there must be something more to his life than working a crummy minimum-wage job. The only time he finds a respite from Siskel's "basic question" is when he's dancing at the disco—when he's wearing that $145,500 white suit.

Siskel did not harbor secret dreams of becoming a dancer, but after the tragedies he endured in childhood, he earned the right to question why life contained so much pain and suffering. Eugene Kal

Siskel was born in Chicago on January 26, 1946, to Nathan and Ida Siskel. Both his parents died before Gene was ten years old; his father when he was four, and his mother five years later, both of illnesses. Siskel and his two older siblings, William and Arlene, were raised by their aunt and uncle, Joseph and Mae Gray, in the nearby suburb of Glencoe, alongside the couple's own children.

Gene was so young when his father died that he had no memories of the event, but he later told the story of finding out that his mother had passed away. He was watching a baseball game when the news was relayed to him.

"It didn't register," he said. "I thought she was alive for a significant time after she was dead. I couldn't handle it, obviously. I used to pray for her to get better after she was dead."

In those days, Siskel would escape to the movies, where a lot of his childhood favorites, like *Saturday Night Fever* years later, chronicled the lives of heroes who used innate talents to escape from life's tragedies. The earliest movie he recalled seeing, the Walt Disney animated classic *Dumbo*, told the story of a little elephant who is separated from his mother and then learns to soar through the air by flapping his enormous ears. Siskel admitted to *Playboy* interviewer Lawrence Grobel that *Dumbo*'s appeal related directly to his "psychological history" and that the character's "separation from the mother was terrifying to me." In a 1988 *Siskel & Ebert* episode, Siskel said an additional element of the film moved him: he felt uplifted by the sequence in which the circus train chugs along the track while huffing, "I think I can! I think I can!"

Siskel's local theater in those days was the Nortown on North Western Avenue, in Chicago's West Ridge neighborhood on the North Side. Before he moved to Glencoe, Siskel lived eight blocks from the theater and its two-thousand-seat auditorium, complete with a balcony designed to resemble a sunny Mediterranean sea-port. Visiting the Nortown became a Saturday afternoon ritual for the young Siskel; if the movie was bad, he and his buddies would hang out in the upstairs lobby, throwing around a rubber football until an usher would shoo them back into their seats. (He was also a fan of Friedman's delicatessen next door, especially their sour pickles.) When Disney's *Peter Pan*—a film about an orphaned boy who finds joy and a surrogate family in a magical escape from the real world—played the Nortown for ten weeks in 1953, Siskel went to see it ten times.

Like Roger Ebert, Siskel also had an intense reaction to the 1953 movie *Houdini* starring Tony Curtis. While Ebert was mostly frustrated by the film's infidelity to its source material, Siskel was mesmerized by the magicians' power to control their audience, and fascinated by the way, like Tony Manero and Dumbo, Houdini's remarkable gift masked "the unhappiness underneath." The following year, he also enjoyed *The Glenn Miller Story*, a biopic of the popular band leader, which he treasured for what he called "the adoring marriage between Jimmy Stewart and June Allyson. It was comforting to an eight-year-old to see a home life like that on the big screen."

Siskel didn't talk a lot about his childhood, but colleagues believed his rocky early years left an enormous impression on his personality. Stuart Cleland says the trauma of losing his parents probably resulted in the way he could sometimes be "guarded and wary." Jamie Bennett, who worked with Siskel at Chicago's local CBS affiliate in the 1970s, said that as long as he knew Gene he was "very apprehensive" about money matters, adding, "He was always worried about making sure that things would be taken care of if he got sick or if he passed away—and this is even before he got married. He was just concerned about those issues."

While Ebert found his calling as a reporter by the time he was in high school, Siskel took much longer to discover his passion for journalism. At fourteen, he saw *Inherit the Wind*, Stanley Kramer's adaptation of the play based on the Scopes "Monkey" Trial, with Spencer Tracy as crusading attorney Henry Drummond. ("Who could see this movie," Siskel asked in 1991, "and not view the courtroom as one of mankind's greatest achievements?") With that goal in mind, Siskel attended Culver Military Academy; there, his membership in the Philosophy Club inspired him to major in philosophy at Yale University. His freshman year, he saw and was dazzled by his very first art film: Hiroshi Teshigahara's *Woman in the Dunes*. Recalling the experience, Siskel said, "It told me that the cinema could be more than standard stories."

Raised in a household with two siblings and three cousins, Gene also cultivated a competitive streak that only grew more intense over time. Friends say Siskel was a man consumed with a need to win everything and anything, no matter how seemingly trivial. George Pataki, the former governor of New York and a classmate of Siskel's at school, noted that Gene would cheat if he had to in order to win, even at something as insignificant as a game of ping-pong. ("Not in a mean way," he added, "but by getting you laughing so hard you couldn't hit the ball back.")

With Gene, almost anything could be turned into a competition. He could be a particularly tough negotiator when his contracts in print or television came due. While Jamie Bennett was still at CBS in Chicago, he had to iron out one of Siskel's deals with the station, a process that stretched on and on because Siskel would not budge on his demands.

"I was negotiating with him, and he wanted a color TV," Bennett explains. "Believe it or not, not everybody had a color TV yet, and he wanted one thrown into the deal. I tried to explain to him we didn't have any deals that had color TVs in them. And his agent represented a number of people at the station, and if I gave Gene a color TV, then Bill Kurtis, who was a colleague of his, the anchorperson, the agent was gonna want a color TV set for Bill Kurtis. So I just said, 'I can't do it.' And we got done with absolutely everything except this color TV issue. And I said, 'Let me see what I can do, I'll see if I can get you a color TV.' And then he left on a vacation."

While Siskel was away on his trip, Bennett decided to play a prank on him. He called the prop department at the station and told them to dig out an old television set, paint the screen with color bars, and sneak it into Gene's apartment so that it was waiting for him when he got back.

"Gene was not amused by that. *I* was very amused by it, but *he* was not amused by it," Bennett says, laughing. "I'd gotten him, and he loved to be the winner. Everything was competition. But he never got the color TV—and he wanted me to remove the prop one from his apartment. I had to get someone to go over and pick it up."

Gene's love of competition found its way into his writing as well. At the *Tribune* he founded an annual "Beat Siskel" contest around guessing the winners at the Academy Awards; it started as a lark in 1971, with a first prize of dinner for two and tickets to a movie, and grew steadily until, by the late '90s, the contest drew almost thirty-five thousand entrants competing for $10,000 in prizes. And Gene loved to pit movies against each other to see which was the best; to see how a new favorite compared with the established classics in its genre. He often measured movies' success in tests of his own devising, which essentially turned filmmaking into a personal sort of competition, with him as the ultimate authority.

His most famous film test eventually became known as "The

Gene Siskel Test": "Is this film more interesting than a documentary of the same actors having lunch?" But through the years, Siskel suggested many other rubrics for judging motion pictures,
including:

The Great Movie Test: If you rewatch a classic over and over,
do you get new things out of it each time? If yes, then it is a
truly great film.

The Author Test: Does this movie about a famous author
make you want to read their books? If yes, then the movie
succeeds.

The Scratch Test: How often do you scratch yourself during
a horror film out of nervousness—or as a practical joke, how
often do you scratch the person you went to the movie with
just to frighten them? The more scratching, the better.

The Road Movie Test: Does a movie about a road trip make
you want to travel along the same route? Do you recognize
any of the places they visit? If it's memorable, it's a good
movie.

Marlene Iglitzen, Siskel's wife, says the tests all came from
Gene's love of competition. "Tests are facts and analysis under
pressure," she says, "which made the win that much sweeter."

After graduating from Yale, Siskel spent a year in Los Angeles
on a fellowship from the Coro Foundation, a group that provides
training for future leaders in public affairs. Shortly after complet-
ing the program, though, Siskel received a 1-A classification, and
enlisted in the Army Reserve. He wound up at Fort Benjamin Har-

rison in Indiana, where he finally discovered his gift for reporting—although not necessarily by choice.

"They asked me if I wanted to be a truck driver or a cook or a journalist. I didn't take too long to pick a journalist," Siskel later explained.

At Fort Benjamin Harrison he spent ten weeks in the Department of Defense's Information School, learning the basics of newswriting and dipping his toe in the world of pasteups—the laborious process by which newspaper layouts were created at the time. When he returned to Chicago in early January 1969, he'd caught the same bug for journalism that had so consumed Ebert a few years earlier. But at twenty-two years old, Siskel didn't have Ebert's years of experience honing his craft in local and college newspapers.

Siskel didn't care. On January 20, 1969—the same day, he liked to joke, that Richard Nixon was sworn in as the president of the United States—he walked into the *Chicago Tribune*. He was armed with recommendations from his Fort Benjamin Harrison journalism instructor and John Hersey, a teacher at Yale and a reporter for *Time* whose writing about the survivors of the Hiroshima nuclear attacks became a hallmark of twentieth-century journalism. He filled out an application and, despite his inexperience, was given a job on the spot as a reporter in the neighborhood news section. His starting salary: $150 a week.

The move stunned his family, loyal (and liberal) *Sun-Times* readers who couldn't understand why he would take a job at the *Tribune*, a bastion of conservative news coverage since the days of Abraham Lincoln. (Siskel never had a great answer for that question; asked once why he chose the *Tribune* over the *Sun-Times* or anywhere else, he claimed he happened to be the closest to their offices and went there first.)

Siskel quickly became a fixture in the newsroom of Tribune Tower, the grand neo-Gothic skyscraper built in the 1920s that loomed over the Chicago River just north of the Michigan Avenue Bridge. The tower's facade, dotted with pieces of other iconic world locations like the Alamo and the Great Wall of China, befitted a periodical that called itself the "World's Greatest Newspaper." It was the sort of building that demanded attention—just like Gene Siskel, who, it became clear, would not be contained by the sleepy neighborhood news section for long.

Within months, Siskel landed a regular column. One day, the neighborhood news section editor asked Siskel what his ambitions were at the paper.

"Your job," Siskel replied without hesitation.

When a stunned colleague asked why he would say something like that to his boss, Siskel replied, "Candor. It is powerful. It knocks people off their feet. They are not used to it. Try it some day. If you've got the guts."

Siskel's column soon led to extra assignments interviewing people from the world of business and entertainment. He had always loved movies, but prepping to talk about the craft of filmmaking with artists particularly excited him. So when the *Chicago Tribune*'s film critic, Clifford Terry, left the paper to take a Nieman Fellowship at Harvard University in the late summer of 1969, Siskel decided to make his move.

The *Tribune* initially planned to make Terry its film critic again when he returned from Harvard in a year. In the meantime, a handful of reporters would cover the movies that came to town. Siskel thought that was a terrible idea—especially since he believed he could do the job all by himself.

"Late one night, just a day or two before Cliff left, I put some paper in my typewriter and wrote a memo to the Sunday editor,"

Siskel later said. "I told him how much the *Tribune* had to lose if there wasn't a single voice reviewing movies, like all the other papers in town. And I told him it should be me." Siskel stuck the memo in an envelope, left it on the editor's chair, and went home. He assumed that would be the last he would hear about it, but the next day, the editing staff summoned Siskel to a conference room and gave him the job. Siskel's trademark candor had worked. When Clifford Terry returned from his Harvard fellowship the next year, Siskel remained the *Tribune*'s film critic.

(The story sounds fanciful, but years later an executive at the *Tribune* took a peek in Siskel's personnel file. There, amid assorted applications and salary forms, was the original letter. Presented with it, Siskel remarked, "You know, by now, sometimes I almost wondered if I really did this, or if I made it up. I guess this proves it.")

One of Siskel's earliest fans was Hugh Hefner, whom he'd met through a mutual friend, actor Anthony Newley. Around the same time Ebert ventured to California to make *Beyond the Valley of the Dolls*, Siskel became a regular at the Playboy Mansion with the Bunnies, where he'd play Hefner in Monopoly and show up for the Sunday parties. Marlene Iglitzen says Hefner was struck "with the way this young Yale philosophy major carried himself with such poise and self-assurance."

Siskel himself once told an interviewer that Hefner was a "movie nut" who got to preview new films "earlier than the critics' screenings. So it was a natural attraction for me," which sounds suspiciously like a defensive *Playboy* reader claiming he read the magazine strictly for the articles. (A *Playboy* publicist said in 1987 that the young critic was well-behaved during his tenure at the mansion, claiming, "Siskel was there in his jeans and running shoes. He was shy and nice and a yuppie before his time.") Whatever Siskel's interests in the *Playboy* world, his affiliation was short-lived; Iglitzen says Gene "soon realized that as a journalist and a critic the relationship was inappropriate. He amicably distanced himself soon after."

Back at the *Tribune* film critic's desk, Siskel began to develop a process of writing film reviews he stuck to for the rest of his life: "The movie begins, and I try to decide how well it's accomplishing what it's trying to accomplish." He found he had to think along two parallel tracks simultaneously: one watching the movie, the other watching himself as he watched the movie, trying to understand his own reactions. Going to the movies, he said, "alters you, for better or for worse. And you respond to it on that basis."

A good film critic, in Siskel's view, demanded "a certain rigor . . . having principles, holding to them, measuring what you're saying, trying to be accurate." Although he claimed he had no pre-conceived notions or rules about what defined a good or bad movie, when asked what made for an enjoyable night at the theater, he frequently quoted filmmaker Howard Hawks, the auteur who di-rected such classics as *His Girl Friday*, *Gentlemen Prefer Blondes*, and *Rio Bravo*. During an interview, Hawks told Siskel that a good movie "has three good scenes and no bad scenes." ("I'm more interested in the no-bad-scenes concept," Siskel would later add.)

Siskel was a good critic, but he was an outstanding inter-viewer, both in print and later on camera. He felt his philosophy toward that side of the job was perfectly expressed by *All the Pres-ident's Men*, the 1976 dramatization of *Washington Post* reporters Bob Woodward and Carl Bernstein's investigation into the Water-gate cover-up. He particularly loved the scene near the opening of the film where Robert Redford's Woodward notices a well-dressed man at a court hearing for the burglars who broke into the Water-gate Hotel.

"He can't figure out why this guy is there. So his journalistic instinct is to keep poking him, and, in about two or three scenes, we see him not take 'no' for an answer. . . . And that is a nice image of a journalist. That's what we get paid to do, which is to bug people, to find out what's really going on."

Bugging people, finding out what was really going on, and not taking no for an answer were all specialties of Siskel's, who stood out in the world of movie press junkets. The film community was largely a chummy environment, where most journalists were terrified to express any kind of negative opinion lest they offend someone important and lose their access to future interviews. Siskel, on the other hand, delighted in asking tough questions. He could be relied on to ask anyone he interviewed to tell him "the truest thing" they knew about any subject, good manners be damned.

And he had no issue expressing his sincere opinion to anyone he interviewed, no matter how big a star they might be.

He asked Madonna, "Why haven't you had more success in movies?" He told Eddie Murphy he needed to "submit to great directors" and reminded him that instead Murphy directed himself—"not to great success"—prompting a shocked reaction from the comedian. Speaking with Denzel Washington about *Malcolm X*, he warned the actor that "white people are gonna be afraid of this movie" and asked him if playing the role of the civil rights leader made him like white people more or less. When Oprah Winfrey, a friend and fellow celebrity in the Chicago media scene, was nominated for an Academy Award for her work in *The Color Purple*, Siskel told her flat out: "You are *not* going to win." He advised her to instead bronze the biscuit she was served at the annual Academy nominee luncheon—which she did.

In perhaps his greatest act of journalistic chutzpah, Gene slammed former Beatle Paul McCartney's directorial debut, *Give*

My Regards to Broad Street, to McCartney's face during an interview for Chicago's Channel 2 news. After a few questions about the Beatles' legacy, Siskel got around to discussing the movie, which he dismissed as "mindless music video madness." A flabbergasted McCartney looked directly into the camera and responded, "You know he's rubbished this film? And I'm sitting here doing this bloody interview for him! I mean, isn't that terrific?"

After the interview package concluded, Siskel remarked, "It was a kick to talk to him, of course, any Beatle fan would be thrilled to do so. I just hope he makes a better movie next time."

Just as he had when he told his boss he was aiming for his job at the neighborhood news desk, Siskel's criticism could always be counted on for honesty above all; he never let his personal feelings about whoever made a movie affect his judgment about the final work of art. *Sneak Previews* producer Ray Solley calls Gene "the original Simon Cowell," the guy with the balls to look someone dead in the eyes and tell them, "You were wrong. And that is a terrible idea." Roger Ebert once said that Gene "doesn't care if you like him or not. And I'm not always sure that's a good thing."

But it was for his audience, who could trust that if Gene said it, he meant it. They never had to question whether his review was being softened to spare someone's feelings or because he felt he was "supposed" to like or dislike a film based on the broader critical consensus. As Al Berman, Gene's producer at *CBS This Morning*, puts it, "I believed every word that Gene Siskel said when he was reviewing. Didn't mean I agreed with everything he said, but I believed him."

Occasionally, Siskel's total commitment to critical honesty landed him in awkward situations. On a trip to Hawaii in 1985, Siskel watched his daughter Kate strike up a conversation with another little girl at the pool, only to discover that the other child's father was Robby Benson, a rising star in Hollywood whom Siskel had publicly called one of his least favorite actors. (On *At the Movies*, he had even imitated and mocked Benson's "soft little sweet voice.") Writing about the incident later in the *Tribune*, Siskel said he was "mortified"—while hastening to note, "I knew I was right about what I had written, but maybe I was a little too rough." The Siskels and the Bensons repeatedly bumped into each other throughout their stay in Hawaii, which Siskel compared to "running into someone to whom you have owed a lot of money for a very long time." Still, even after all the tension, Siskel said he doubted he would review Benson any differently in the future, although he did concede, "I probably won't mock his voice on TV. I owe that much to his daughter."

But if Gene Siskel was the sort of critic who could barely allow himself to go easy on an actor after their daughters had played together, the private Siskel was a different person. Yes, when his competitive side kicked in he'd stop at nothing to win, and he could be absolutely ruthless with rivals in the entertainment business. Yet despite his competitive streak, and despite his love of brutal honesty, friends and coworkers of Siskel's say he could also be incredibly selfless and kind. He happened to be in New York City when Al Berman's first son was born, and he wound up being the first person to visit him and his wife in the hospital.

"He came with a huge bouquet of flowers," Berman recalls. "I wasn't running [*CBS This Morning*], I was like the number two on the show. And he just hung with us. And for my wife and myself, that was so meaningful and such a wonderful gesture, and that was indicative of the kind of guy he actually was—true to the bone, honest, gracious, and giving."

Some of Siskel's acts of kindness were totally anonymous. After working as an assistant producer on *Sneak Previews* in the early

1980s, John Davies wound up producing and directing a variety of documentaries, shorts, and series around Chicago. Eventually, the local Fox affiliate, WFLD, gave Davies his own show, *The New 9:30*, a spoof of the nightly news. It was only after Siskel had passed away that John learned the reason Fox took a chance on him: Gene Siskel had vouched for him.

"When Gene died, the former general manager of the Fox station in Chicago who had hired me called me and said, 'Hey, John, I hope you know the whole reason we hired you was because of Gene Siskel.' I said, 'Really?' 'Yeah, he told us that we wouldn't lose with you. That you were a good investment.'"

These were not isolated incidents. Siskel once overheard *Siskel & Ebert* assistant producer Janet LaMonica having lunch with the television studio's phone operator, who was complaining that she couldn't afford to buy the new pair of glasses she needed. A week later, the operator returned for another lunch with LaMonica, sporting new glasses.

"You're not going to believe this," she told LaMonica. "After I left, Gene caught up with me in the hall and gave me the money for the glasses."

In the 1990s, Carie Lovstad became close with Siskel while working on *Siskel & Ebert*, first as a production assistant and then as an assistant and associate producer. While Roger Ebert had a personal assistant to help keep his schedule organized, Gene did not until Lovstad unofficially assumed that role.

Lovstad says Gene wasn't perfect, but he would sometimes stun her with his generosity. In the early 1990s, the first Starbucks in Chicago opened up right across from *Siskel & Ebert*'s offices. Siskel was immediately hooked, and he would come in to work with a cup of coffee, telling anyone who would listen, "Buy Starbucks stock! Buy Starbucks stock!" While that might have been good advice for someone in Siskel's financial position, Lovstad was making around $20,000 a year and in no position to purchase stock in anything. Still, Siskel wouldn't let it go, and eventually Lovstad got fed up.

"Stop it with the Starbucks stock! It's crazy talk! I have a shitty apartment, a shitty car, once in a while I go to a shitty restaurant for dinner! I have no money to buy stock in anything! Please stop saying that!"

Siskel realized what he'd done and dropped it. Then, a year later, Lovstad got married. Siskel's wedding present: $1,000 in Starbucks stock.

"Just let it go and see what happens," Siskel told her. "If you need to spend it, spend it. But if you don't, just let it ride."

"So far," says Lovstad, "I've seen more than $160,000 from it. I still have some to this day."

Lovstad remembers Siskel as someone who could drive her "totally crazy" with his demands one second and be deeply apologetic about them the next. During one tense situation, Siskel had her so stressed-out—she no longer remembers why—that she started having chest pains. When Siskel realized what was happening he yelled, "Don't let me do that to you!" and forced her to leave the office with him and take a walk around the neighborhood. "You can't let me do that to you," he told her.

He also surprised her by soliciting her feedback on projects, even though she was still a relative newcomer to the show. The first time he did it, she replied, "It doesn't matter what I think," assuming that it really didn't; who cared what a lowly PA thought about the inner workings of a hugely successful syndicated television show? But Siskel did, and he instructed her: "I *never* want you to *not* tell me."

Siskel's desire for candor didn't necessarily extend to everyone, though. At times, Lovstad says, Siskel would get a "cat that ate the canary look on his face" when something would go wrong at the show, and he would jokingly instruct her that when she someday wrote a tell-all about *Siskel & Ebert*, "Don't put this in the fucking book!"

Indeed, despite Siskel's dogged approach to interviewing others, he was fiercely and paradoxically private about his own life. He agreed to interviews about film criticism, *Siskel & Ebert*, and his Jewish faith, which he credited with teaching him right from wrong, but few about his personal life or his family. (He married Marlene Iglitzen, a producer at WBBM, in 1980 and together they had two daughters, Kate and Callie, and a son, Will.)

Sometimes surprising autobiographical confessions would emerge from his reviews. While assessing the incredible popularity of the 1990 comedy *Home Alone*, Siskel said the film tapped into a common fear of children about being left home alone—confessing that he remembered, and remained haunted by, the first time he was left home alone. ("I stood by the window most of the night just waiting for my family to come home.") During the *Siskel & Ebert* review of the coming-of-age drama *School Ties*, about a Jewish teenager who encounters anti-Semitism at his prep school, he revealed that while he attended Culver a classmate had handed him a piece of toast with a swastika smeared on in jelly.

Siskel's star rose quickly at the *Tribune,* all through the early 1970s. He wrote reviews, filed interviews, and wrote inventive features. He wrote frequently about his biggest movie pet peeve, people who talked in the theater, and repeatedly used his columns to offer a twenty-five-cent tip to any usher who removed a loud talker from an auditorium. (If they removed a crying baby, he'd bump the tip up to fifty cents.)

Then he actually decided to try out being an usher himself—
putting on a uniform and spending the movie policing the patrons
at the State-Lake Theater. He got a kick out of shining a flashlight
on troublemakers, but he took something else away from the experience. "When I walked back up the center aisle," he said, "I saw
something then that I had never seen before—the light from the
screen illuminating the faces of the audience . . . white, black,
Latinos—all kinds of people brought together under the glare of
that reflected light." Even as Siskel's profile in Chicago grew, he
insisted that his greatest professional high came from getting a
great piece into the *Tribune*.

But no matter how adventurous his coverage, no matter how
exclusive his interviews, Siskel had a problem: he was perpetually
measured against the guy with his job at the *Chicago Sun-Times*.
Roger Ebert had a two-year head start on Siskel's criticism career,
and in that time he'd amassed a loyal readership. And that was before Ebert won the Pulitzer Prize in 1975.

Although Siskel never disputed his rival's writing skills, watching him win an award he didn't have drove him crazy. One *Tribune*
editor recalls Siskel's obsessive focus on beating Ebert to stories.
Whenever he did, he would revel in his perceived victory, announcing, "Take that, Tubby, I got him again."

Siskel had no idea that within six months of Ebert's Pulitzer
victory the two would be working together on the show that would
change both of their lives—and the worlds of film and film
criticism—forever.

CHAPTER THREE

OPENING SOON AT A THEATER NEAR YOU

If they're going to claim to be truthful and try
and impress me, I'm going to challenge them
on being truthful.

—GENE SISKEL

The genius of *Rashomon* is that all of the flashbacks
are both true and false. True, in that they present
an accurate portrait of what each witness thinks
happened. False, because as Kurosawa observes
in his autobiography, "Human beings are unable to
be honest with themselves about themselves. They
cannot talk about themselves without embellishing."

—ROGER EBERT

t would be an exaggeration to say that from the first moment
there were films there were also film critics. But it would not be
that much of an exaggeration.

The earliest motion pictures, screened as novelties in devices
like the kinetoscope—a large box that played a loop of film for a
single customer peering through a small viewing window—came
to prominence in the early 1890s. Narrative filmmaking followed

a few years later. The first film review in the *New York Times* came right on its heels, on April 23, 1896.

Most historians credit a man named Frank E. Woods as the world's first true film critic. He started working at the theatrical trade paper the *New York Dramatic Mirror* around the turn of the twentieth century, first in ad sales and copywriting. In 1908, the *Dramatic Mirror* expanded its beat to also cover movies. By the end of the decade, Woods contributed a regular column to the *Dramatic Mirror*'s film section titled "Review of Late Films."

Woods wrote about the potential of film as an artistic medium at a time when most people—including a fair number of filmmakers—believed it had none. He tirelessly championed directors who pushed the boundaries of cinema as a storytelling medium, and he was especially supportive of D. W. Griffith, the filmmaking pioneer who went on to direct *The Birth of a Nation*. Still regarded as one of the most important and influential (not to mention shockingly racist) movies in the history of the medium, the film's co-screenwriter was none other than . . . Frank E. Woods, who left his gig as the film critic for the *Dramatic Mirror* in 1912 to work for D. W. Griffith.

"Review of Late Films" was part of a concerted effort on the *Dramatic Mirror*'s part to attract advertisers from the world of motion pictures to the newspaper, and for much of the first half of the century, that held true of the movie reviews in most newspaper arts sections. While serious film criticism could be found in film journals, specialized publications, and some magazines, the reviews in most newspapers were almost all utilitarian in nature. For readers, they provided details on opening and closing dates, cast members, run times, and some general remarks about the picture's quality. For the publications, they provided content to run around— and a draw to bring in—advertisements about movies.

Film reviews were considered such an unimportant part of most newspapers that few dailies employed a full-time critic. The woman that Roger Ebert credited with changing all of that was Judith Crist, who became a national celebrity in the early 1960s thanks to a series of lacerating reviews of big-budget movies in the *New York Herald Tribune*. A lifelong movie lover, Crist worked at the *Herald Tribune* as an editor and reporter for almost two decades before she finally got her dream gig as the paper's movie critic. Once she did, she wasted little time making her mark. Six weeks after she officially inherited the title of *Herald Tribune* critic, she wrote a merciless pan of 1963's *Spencer's Mountain*, a drama based on the same novel that later formed the basis for the hit TV series *The Waltons*.

Directed by Hollywood lifer Delmer Daves, *Spencer's Mountain* boasted an A-list cast, including Henry Fonda, Maureen O'Hara, and James MacArthur. Crist wasn't impressed and claimed that "for sheer prurience and perverted morality disguised as piety [it] makes the nudie shows at the Rialto look like Walt Disney productions." The film's distributor, Warner Bros., banned Crist from its screenings, while Radio City Music Hall, which was exhibiting *Spencer's Mountain* in New York City, pulled all its advertising from the paper. This was not the chummy boosterism sort of film criticism found in a Frank E. Woods column.

While papers typically fired or reassigned film critics who ran afoul of the studios (and thus endangered those precious advertising dollars that kept their arts sections afloat), the *Herald Tribune* backed Crist and wrote an editorial defending her right to free speech. Warners and Radio City Music Hall soon both relented. Emboldened, Crist then bashed an even bigger target: Joseph L. Mankiewicz's *Cleopatra*.

The historical epic to end all historical epics was the most expensive American movie ever made to that time. (It cost $31 million in 1963 dollars, the equivalent of $600 million today. That's about $200 million more than *Avengers: Endgame*.) Crist called *Cleopatra* "a monumental mouse," ticked off another studio (Fox this time), and earned another massive wave of attention for her efforts. Otto Preminger dubbed her "Judas Crist," and Billy Wilder said inviting her to review your movie was like asking the Boston Strangler for a neck massage.

After eighteen years at the *Herald Tribune*, Crist was an overnight sensation—and the first nationally famous film critic. All the attention, Ebert said, "led to every paper in the country saying, 'Hey, we ought to get a real movie critic.' When I got my job in '67, that was still part of the fallout from Crist."

Crist also paved the way for Gene Siskel and Roger Ebert in another medium. The year before Crist became the *Herald Tribune*'s film critic, the entire New York newspaper industry temporarily shut down as part of a citywide strike. Hungry for work, she went to the local ABC TV affiliate, where she delivered movie reviews during nightly newscasts. Her work brought her to the attention of NBC producer Al Morgan, who made her the *Today* show's first drama and movie critic—not to mention the first drama and movie critic anywhere on network television. She remained at *Today* for a decade.

In a speech, Crist once described this period as "the Age of the Critic, when cities across the nation were busily building more stately mansions known as cultural centers and Americans were responding with 'You've given me my culture, now tell me what to think of it.'" But a critic is only as interesting as the movies they have to write about—and in the late 1960s there were an awful lot of good movies to discuss.

By the time Roger Ebert became the *Sun-Times'* critic in 1967 and Gene Siskel took over the critic position at the *Tribune* in 1969, American movies were in the midst of a renaissance period that came to be known as "the New Hollywood." This was an era marked by widespread experimentation in mainstream motion pictures and the rise of young directors like Francis Ford Coppola (*The Godfather*), Martin Scorsese (*Taxi Driver*), and Peter Bogdanovich (*The Last Picture Show*). It was also a great time for international movies, with masters like Ingmar Bergman, Akira Kurosawa, Federico Fellini, and Jean-Luc Godard all still working at or near the peak of their artistic powers.

Today, movies are one of a near-limitless array of viewing options including television shows, YouTube clips, and TikTok videos. But in the late 1960s and early '70s, movies weren't just popular, they were *important*. They dominated the cultural conversation. They were the most influential and widely consumed art form on the planet.

They were also big news. No wonder, then, that newspapers like the *Sun-Times* and the *Tribune*, and TV programs like the *Today* show, wanted in on the film criticism business. When Crist departed *Today*, her role was filled by another writer-turned-broadcaster: a *Ladies' Home Journal* columnist named Gene Shalit.

Shalit started at *Today* in 1969 and was promoted to a member of the morning show's core cast in 1973. He remained a *Today* show fixture until he retired in 2010, reviewing hundreds of movies and interviewing nearly as many stars and filmmakers in his "Critic's Corner" segment. The enormously coiffed, extravagantly mustachioed Shalit once joked that he was "the forerunner of everybody ugly on television." He quickly became synonymous with TV film criticism, best known for his endless supply of witty puns and quick quips. (Perhaps his single greatest pan: he dismissed the notorious 1987 bomb *Ishtar* in three words: "*Ishtar* isht horrible.")

In other words, Gene Siskel and Roger Ebert were far from the first film critics on television, and the debate format had long flourished in other media. In fact, even before there was television, there were numerous debate shows on radio, where forums of experts discussing social and political issues flooded the early airwaves. The first of these shows, *University of Chicago Roundtable*, began in 1931. It featured members of the college's faculty and other intellectuals, politicians, and journalists sitting around a specially designed triangular table, where they faced one another as they discussed topics ranging from the role of women in society to the state of cancer research.

But while some of these early public-affairs discussion shows did make the jump from radio to television—like *Meet the Press*, which still airs weekly on Sunday mornings on NBC—most televised debates of the era were so comparatively civil and polite they barely resembled a debate at all. In 1971, CBS's *60 Minutes* launched a popular recurring segment called "Point/Counterpoint," which pitted a conservative thinker (James J. Kilpatrick) against a liberal one (first Nicholas von Hoffman, then later Shana Alexander). Though the topics were often urgent and timely, the conversations were respectful and genteel—*so* respectful and genteel, in fact, that they weren't recorded in the same studio at the same time. (Kilpatrick and Alexander "debated" each other on *60 Minutes* for about five years, but only met face-to-face once in their entire lives.)

This was the world into which the very first iteration of *Siskel & Ebert* was born. Most everyone agrees on the key players in the story of its creation. As to which of the key players deserves the most credit for giving birth to the show, that's a subject of debate far more complicated than anything on "Point/Counterpoint."

It all happened at Chicago's public television station, WTTW. Founded in 1955, WTTW—the call letters stood for "Window to the World," a reflection of the original executives' lofty ambitions for the channel—quickly grew into one of the most-watched public television stations in the country. One of its early chairmen of the board was Newton Minow, the attorney and Federal Communications Commission chair who gave one of the most famous speeches in the history of television when, in a 1961 presentation to the National Association of Broadcasters, he called commercial television a "vast wasteland."

It was Minow who recruited William J. McCarter to become WTTW's president and CEO in 1971. McCarter, who had served in the 45th Infantry Division during the Korean War, got his start in television working on Dick Clark's *American Bandstand*. (Later, at WTTW, he played a hand in launching *Soundstage*, the station's long-running concert series.) After stints at other public television stations like WHYY in Philadelphia, WNET in New York, and WETA-TV in Washington, DC, McCarter was tapped by Minow to lead WTTW, where he would remain until his retirement in 1998.

McCarter is widely credited with turning WTTW into a powerhouse of public television. When McCarter joined the station in 1971, there were just three commercial broadcast networks, a handful of local independent stations, and PBS. Cable packages with dozens or even hundreds of stations were still years away; the internet and its near-infinite entertainment options were further off than that. As the president of a large local public television station like WTTW in Chicago, he wielded an enormous amount of influence.

"He was on a separate level of television executives—not just in Chicago, but in America," says former *Chicago Sun-Times* media columnist Robert Feder. "You cannot overstate his importance [to the creation of *Siskel & Ebert*]. He was one of the founding fathers of public television in America, and he put WTTW on the map as a major production center, and really the crown jewel of local PBS stations in America during the time he ran it. And one of his things was creating an environment where things like *Sneak Previews* could be incubated."

"WTTW when we were doing *Sneak Previews* was a very active producing station," says Michael Loewenstein, who spent decades designing sets for Channel 11's various projects. "We did a lot of music, we did *Soundstage*; Ken Ehrlich, who went on to produce the Grammys, produced a lot of music shows. We did a lot of specials with Steppenwolf Theatre, New York City Ballet. That is no longer the case, and it's sad for all of us, because we loved working there then. Not that it was a perfect place to work, but the opportunities were really wonderful."

"It was a place filled with young, creative people," says longtime *Sneak Previews* producer Thea Flaum. "Bill McCarter was open really to anything. If you had an idea, you could bring it to them and they would say, 'Okay, let's try it. What do you need to try it?'"

So was McCarter the person who came up with the idea for *Siskel & Ebert*? Flaum says emphatically yes.

"The president of a television station is something like Napoleon—not that he was Napoleonic in any way. But it was a good idea, and it was kind of lying there at the time because Gene Shalit was doing movie reviews on the *Today* show with film clips," Flaum explains. "And if you think about it—the way Bill McCarter thought about television—if ever there was a form of criticism that was designed for television, it would be the movies, because you can show people what you're talking about. Not music, not books, but *movies*."

"I was anxious to light a fire under public broadcasting," McCarter said in a 2011 interview shortly before his passing after a battle with cancer. "I didn't want Channel 11 to be a classroom; I wanted it to be entertaining. Creating a vibrant movie review show fit that vision. Asking Gene and Roger to host the show was a no-brainer. There weren't too many people in the country that had their credentials."

Roger Ebert and Gene Siskel always gave Thea Flaum credit for their TV success. She was the one who coaxed them to give the show a second try at that fateful lunch at the Oxford Pub, and she was the one they said figured out how to turn their ramshackle on-screen rapport into a winning television formula. But Flaum didn't work on the original pilot, or pitch WTTW the original concept of two critics talking about the latest movies in Chicago. And through the years, when Gene and Roger were asked about how they first got involved in what became *Siskel & Ebert*, they gave somewhat different accounts of how it happened.

Several months before that lunch between Flaum, Siskel, and Ebert at the Oxford Pub, another lunch took place that was arguably just as important to the show's inception, although it's often gone unmentioned in accounts of *Siskel & Ebert*'s origin.

Ebert himself discussed it in an extensive 1987 history of *Siskel & Ebert* in *Chicago* magazine, where he claimed that the very first concept for the show "emerged" from a lunch at the French restaurant Le Perroquet between McCarter and Nick Aronson, the director of the Office of Radio and Television at the University of Chicago.

Nick Aronson himself says that description is accurate—but, at least from his perspective, it's not the *entire* story. Aronson knew

Roger from their time together as students at the University of Illinois. Although Ebert had first arrived in Chicago in 1966 to attend graduate school at the University of Chicago, within a few years his work as the *Sun-Times'* film critic had earned him a side job as a lecturer at the university's extension program, where he taught film classes until 2006.

"We were always looking for shows to do with professors and people who were affiliated with the University of Chicago," Aronson says. "And I was doing a show on WBBM radio—which was the CBS-owned, all-news station in Chicago—called the *University of Chicago Review of the Arts*. We would have professors do ninety-second reviews of all kinds of cultural things that were going on: books, nightclub acts, movies, plays. And I would have Roger do things for us which were *not* movies. So he would review a play, he would do a nightclub, and it was fun for him. And obviously, the people enjoyed it as well. So one day he and I were having lunch, and I suggested to him that we could extend the *University of Chicago Review of the Arts* into a television program."

Ebert was interested, so Aronson called WTTW's William McCarter and set up the lunch at Le Perroquet with the three of them and Aronson's boss, Don Bruckner, the University of Chicago's vice president of public affairs. There, Aronson says, he laid out his vision for the show: a weekly review of the arts he planned to call *Opening Night*. Ebert would be the regular host, joined each week by a rotating roster of cohosts based on whatever topic the show was covering on that episode. A week on jazz might include an appearance from a local music writer; a show about new literature could feature interviews with notable Chicago authors. If the subject was movies, Aronson says, he thought the perfect cohost would be Ebert's counterpart at the *Chicago Tribune*, Gene Siskel.

According to Aronson's account of the lunch, McCarter seemed "sort of cool to the idea," and in several subsequent phone calls he would offer Aronson no more about *Opening Night*'s prospects than to repeat variations of the phrase "We're talking about it." Not long afterward, Aronson recalls opening a newspaper and reading all about WTTW's new program: a movie review show called *Opening Soon . . . at a Theater Near You,* starring Roger Ebert and Gene Siskel.

So what did Aronson think when he saw his idea—or at least a very similar idea—on WTTW a few months later? "It was a little bit disappointing to read that and not to hear about it from Mc-Carter or anybody else involved in the project," he admits. "I do remember my boss saying, 'Isn't that our idea?' And I said, 'Well, it's pretty close.'" (Presented with McCarter's quote about how "creating a vibrant movie review show" was part of his vision for WTTW, Aronson replies, "Probably all of that is true, but the idea came from the lunch we had. He finished the drawing, but the picture was started at that lunch.")

But Aronson wasn't the first person to put Roger Ebert on WTTW's radar. Back in 1973, the WTTW programming department had licensed a batch of films by the great Swedish director Ingmar Bergman and went looking for an expert to host the series and put them in context for viewers. That's where Ebert came in, doing the very first work on camera of his professional career.

It's not hard to see why WTTW wanted him. As the *Sun-Times* film critic, Ebert had proven himself particularly adept at explaining the appeal of obtuse movies to a readership that didn't know Ingmar Bergman from Ingrid Bergman. In person, Ebert was a marvelous storyteller who delighted in regaling crowds with an Irish drinking song or excerpts from his most recent movie reviews. Ebert had never experienced a moment of stage fright in his life—until he stepped on set to host *The World of Ingmar Bergman* at WTTW. When he showed up for the shoot, he was paired with producer/director Dave Wilson, who laid out what he insisted would be an easy plan for the series:

"We'll figure out how long each movie is. Then the difference between that and two hours is how long your part is."

If the movie was 110 minutes, that was relatively simple. But if the movie was an hour and a half long, well, Ebert had a tall task, especially as a total novice to the world of broadcasting.

"It would seem to be fairly easy to speak six or seven sentences into a television camera (especially for someone like myself, who has rarely shut up for more than three minutes at a stretch)," Ebert recounted in 1989. "I found that the lights, the cameras, and the patient faces of the studio crew were like giant sponges that soaked up every thought I had, or would ever have, on the subject of Ingmar Bergman." Then Wilson made it even harder.

"Well, Roger, now you've done three shows and you're coming along really well," he said when Ebert arrived for another taping. "I can see that you're a natural television personality. Now, today, we're going to have you walk and talk at the same time. You'll start at the film strip and as you're walking over here to this chair, you'll be speaking."

"It only took us about eight hours to get that shot," Ebert joked.

Despite Ebert's rocky start, *The World of Ingmar Bergman* proved successful enough to earn a Chicago Emmy nomination and to get Ebert's foot in the door at WTTW when the station decided to try pairing two film critics together in a single show.

Meanwhile, Siskel had also expanded his film criticism activities from beyond the *Tribune* to television, when he became the critic for WBBM Channel 2. Throughout the 1970s, the station grew into a local news powerhouse, thanks to popular anchors Bill Kurtis and Walter Jacobson, and a format that emphasized hard-hitting journalism over telegenic stars. In 1974, Siskel got a call from the station's news director, Van Gordon Sauter.

"We're starting a new afternoon newscast, and we'd like you to come over and cover the beat the way you cover it for the newspaper," he said.

Siskel was immediately drawn to Sauter's use of language— describing the world of movies as a beat, just like any other that might be covered at a newspaper. He agreed to a meeting at Sauter's office at Channel 2. Once Siskel got there, Sauter pitched him on why he wanted Siskel for the job.

"In the past, news directors have looked around their newsroom and tried to find the person with the longest hair—either really or psychologically—and said, 'You're our film critic.' I want to do things differently. I want to find someone who knows the movie beat and see if I can train them to talk in front of a camera."

Siskel was one of several respected newspaper reporters who joined the station during that period. Instead of a glamorous TV studio, Kurtis and Jacobson hosted their newscasts from the WBBM newsroom, where contributors like Siskel would sit in for their segments. The channel's unofficial slogan at the time: "It isn't pretty, but it's real." With his receding hairline and pull-no-punches approach to criticism, Siskel fit right in.

Many years after the *Opening Soon* pilot, when asked how *Siskel & Ebert* came about during an interview on the WTTW news program *Chicago Tonight*, Siskel said he was at his desk at the *Tribune* and received a call from WTTW. The initial pitch he heard sounds an awful lot like Nick Aronson's idea for *Opening Night*.

"We're thinking of doing a weekly review of the arts here at Channel 11," said the voice on the other end of the line. "One week it'll be movies, one week it'll be plays, another week books, et cetera. And we'd like to start with the movies." But the person who called Siskel wasn't Nick Aronson or Bill McCarter. It was WTTW producer Eliot Wald.

Wald told friends it had been *his* idea to partner Ebert and Siskel together on a movie review show. And during a speech at a 1998 benefit dinner for the Chicago's Museum of Broadcast Communications, Ebert largely agreed, saying that Wald "had the original idea at WTTW in the first place." (In the same speech, Ebert gave McCarter credit for being the one "who first put our show on the air.") Wald called his role in creating the first version of *Siskel & Ebert* "probably the best thing I ever did professionally."

"Eliot Wald was the guy that got to [Gene and Roger] and said, 'We're gonna put you in a studio together,' and got WTTW to pay for a pilot," says *Sneak Previews* producer Ray Solley.

Following his years in public television, Wald worked for the groundbreaking Chicago improv comedy group the Second City before moving back to New York to become a writer on *Saturday Night Live*. There he met Andrew Kurtzman, who became his writing partner; together, the pair became successful Hollywood screenwriters—successful enough, in fact, that several of their scripts were produced and then reviewed on *Siskel & Ebert*, including the Richard Pryor and Gene Wilder comedy *See No Evil, Hear No Evil*, which they gave two thumbs down. Gene and Roger didn't play favorites with anyone—even people who helped launch them to television stardom.

"He was brilliant," says Jane Shay Wald of Eliot, who died of liver cancer in 2003. "I guess every widow says that about her late husband. One of his obituaries called him a visionary. And I know that has since become one of those words that everybody says about everybody. But at that time, it was not so widely applied— and he was. He had such a lively mind, and he had an opinion about everything. But he was really open to hearing other people's points of view."

That last part surely influenced *Opening Soon*'s format, which paired two critics of opposing viewpoints to review films together. During his travels in the Chicago newspaper world prior to his time at WTTW, Wald had met both Gene Siskel and Roger Ebert. When the concept of a movie review show began to percolate at Channel 11, Wald considered them the ideal hosts.

"He thought they were both very, very smart, and they loved film," Jane Shay Wald explains. "And he thought it could be a lot of fun to watch two very smart guys, who knew film, who had very different personalities, relate to each other on camera."

If Eliot Wald wanted to find two hosts with different personalities, he couldn't have done much better than Gene Siskel and Roger Ebert, who were about as different as two heterosexual white men born at roughly the same time in roughly the same place could possibly be. Ebert published his first newspaper while he was still in grade school; Siskel only discovered his passion for journalism after he had graduated from college and stumbled into doing newspaper work during his stint in the Army Reserve. One of Ebert's earliest journalism jobs was as a sports reporter covering high school football games, but he had no real interest or aptitude for sports, while Siskel zealously followed the Chicago Bulls with an intensity to rival the team's most fervent fans. (He eventually parlayed his film review work at WBBM and his passionate Bulls fandom into a side job covering the team's locker room for the station.)

The two men also had drastically different concepts of their shared profession. To Siskel, a film critic was like any other reporter. They had a beat, and they covered it. He compared a movie review to a report about a fire—"only, the fire," Siskel explained, "is my reaction to the movie. And I jump off into that approach."

Ebert, in contrast, said if he had to sum up what a critic did in a single word, he would pick *teacher*. "What we're trying to do," he explained, "is share everything we found out about the movies with people who are interested in that. And so that's a vocation in a way. If a movie is bad, I still have a job to do. If it's good, I'm very pleased."

The contrasts didn't end there. The two men had different tastes in art. (Siskel liked abstract expressionism; Ebert collected English watercolors.) They had different lifestyles for most of their relationship; while Siskel married Marlene Iglitzen in 1980 and became a father just a few years later, Ebert remained a bachelor until 1992, when he married Chaz Hammel Smith. Even after they grew closer and their working relationship made them wealthy and famous, the two men still rarely socialized.

"If Roger and Gene had met as two guys doing something else, they would *not* have gravitated toward each other," says Nancy De Los Santos, one of their longtime TV producers. "Gene didn't respect a lot of people. Roger loved everyone. Gene had a much more cynical view of the world than Roger. As much as he would go to the ends of the earth for his family, he did not really trust people outside of his circle."

"Gene also kind of kept people around him at arm's length, except the inner circle," agrees fellow producer Laura C. Hernández, who adds one more difference between the two: "Gene would always think before talking. Roger would just talk."

They even had different memories of meeting each other for the first time. When asked in 1987 to describe his earliest encounter with Siskel, Ebert told a variation of a story he often recounted to summarize the awkwardness of their relationship. One day, Ebert recounted, shortly after Gene had first got the job reviewing movies for the *Tribune*, the two of them arrived at a movie screening simultaneously. While they hadn't yet met, Siskel's reputation—and his status as Ebert's new competitor at the *Tribune*—preceded him. Rather than exchange pleasantries, the pair stood in tense silence while the elevator made its slow trek up to the seventh floor.

Siskel recalled an alternate initial meeting. He remembered bumping into his *Sun-Times* counterpart while he (Siskel) was kissing the manager at the 3 Penny Cinema in Lincoln Park. "Roger saw me and got a little perturbed," Gene claimed. "I had worked my way into the subculture of Chicago film. I was someone who couldn't be trifled with."

While their memories of that first introduction differed quite drastically, both versions had something very important in common: in each of their minds, hostility was baked into their relationship from the moment they laid eyes on each other. In Siskel and Ebert, Eliot Wald had found two opposites who did not so much attract as repel each other in unpredictable and potentially exciting ways, like the poles of two equally powerful magnets. If Wald could find a way to capture that friction on camera, he would have something truly unique in the landscape of 1970s television.

That, as it turned out, was a very big if.

Production on the *Opening Soon . . . at a Theater Near You* pilot—which, according to an internal WTTW schedule, was actually called *Opening Friday* until shortly before the cameras rolled—began on Monday, November 17, 1975. The talent had a two-hour dry run in the studio, while the postproduction staff at WTTW prepared the all-important film clips, which on that episode included scenes from the Al Pacino true crime thriller *Dog Day Afternoon*. On Wednesday the nineteenth, the set was built and lit, with the hosts seated in director's chairs in front of a mock-up of a movie theater screen. The production was such a ramshackle affair that Eliot Wald provided some of the set dressings himself.

Then, on Thursday, November 20, came the long shoot day. The schedule called for a preproduction meeting at 11:00 a.m., followed by a facilities check and rehearsal from 1:00 to 2:30. The plan called for shooting the show from 3:00 to 4:30 with four cameras, including one on a crane. But very little of the show went according to plan in those days. And while skilled TV veterans could easily record a thirty-minute television show in ninety minutes, Roger and Gene were not yet skilled TV veterans. Especially not when they had to work together.

Problems started before they even got to the studio. Both men nervously guzzled coffee in the WTTW offices as they waited for the shoot to begin. As they headed down to the set, a member of the station staff stopped them: no drinks were allowed in the studio, a rule handed down by Bill McCarter himself.

Suddenly, the coffee became more than a way to boost their energy level; it became the key to postponing the start of the terrifying production as long as humanly possible. The two men sipped their cups like death row inmates who know they're headed to the electric chair as soon as they finish their last meal.

"We were just petrified," Ebert said.

That became quite clear once the cameras began to roll. Within a few years, Siskel and Ebert would develop an uncanny ability to anticipate the rhythms of each other's speech, enabling their reviews to flow naturally and dramatically from one point to the next. That skill came later, though, through years of repetition and practice. On November 20, 1975, Gene and Roger still disliked each other—and they'd worked so hard to avoid talking to each other for the six years they'd competed for the title of Chicago's preeminent newspaper critic that when it came time to talk on camera they were totally unprepared. If the *Opening Soon* pilot looked like a recording of two men having the first conversation of their lives, that's because that wasn't far off from the reality of the situation.

"If you look at the early tapes from the PBS era, you cannot believe that this has any future," says A. O. Scott, who was a fan of *Siskel & Ebert* long before he became chief film critic at the *New York Times*—and even longer before he hosted the final incarnation of Siskel and Ebert's show at Buena Vista Television. "They're almost the worst caricatures of themselves. They speak in these monotone voices. They talk the way that film people are 'supposed' to talk. The liveliness that became part of Roger's TV personality later on is just not there. They're just sitting there, kind of droning."

WTTW aired the *Opening Soon* pilot, droning and all, on Wednesday, November 26, 1975, at 7:30 p.m. A TV listing in a local newspaper described the show as the "first of a series of half-hour specials designed to inform and entertain film goers" with "excerpts of new movies, commentary, and criticism." (The competition on TV in Chicago that Wednesday night in 1975: an episode of Mel Brooks's forgotten sitcom *When Things Were Rotten*, the soon-to-be-canceled detective series *Ironside*, and a film version of Herman Melville's *Moby-Dick*.)

Indeed, watching the *Opening Soon* pilot, it is somewhat astonishing there was ever a second episode. It does not look like the foundation of a TV empire; it barely looks like a TV show at all. Ebert mumbles. Siskel rambles. They may have chugged coffee on the walk to the studio, but they might as well have been taking muscle relaxers; their on-screen presence is downright somnambulant.

The opening credits, set to the tune of Billy Joel's "Root Beer

Rag," included stills of iconic movie stars like Al Jolson, Charlton Heston, and Lee Marvin—a stark and jarring contrast to the two schlubs who hosted the show. In the opening seconds, a shaggy Siskel announced the show's concept: "Two film critics talking about the movies." He also said they were hoping to "sort of be a newsmagazine about movies, and we want to show you what's playing in town, what's coming to town, and maybe also take you behind the scenes and show you a little bit about the movie business."

True to his word, Siskel and Ebert only spent a small portion of the pilot's twenty-eight minutes actually reviewing films—and there are certainly no thumbs up or down in sight. Instead, they both sat stiffly, draped in garish plaids, as they recapped the events of the recently concluded Chicago International Film Festival—because if there's one thing people love to watch on television, it's lifeless descriptions of past events they can no longer attend.

Ebert talked about some of the "exhilarating" animated shorts that played the festival in a tone of voice that suggests less exhilaration than total exhaustion. Siskel kvetched that the audience enjoyed the festival's big world premiere, Milos Forman's *One Flew Over the Cuckoo's Nest, too* much; they made so much noise, he was distracted by all the cheering. Given the total lack of energy he and Ebert displayed in their first episode, it made perfect sense that he would be annoyed by the sight and sound of people enthusiastically enjoying themselves.

Unlike the *One Flew Over the Cuckoo's Nest* premiere, the *Opening Soon* pilot was met with zero fanfare. No one declared it a momentous turning point in film, television, and criticism history. No one said much of anything about it at all. Without Thea Flaum, who would soon be handed the reins of the show, the first in a series of half-hour specials would have likely also been the last.

After the University of Chicago, Nick Aronson moved on to the local NBC station, WMAQ, where he worked as director of communications until 1992. By that point, Roger had begun contributing movie reviews to the ABC affiliate in town, WLS-TV. Aronson met with him several times to try to convince him to leave WLS to come to WMAQ without success. In those conversations, Aronson says, Ebert "always mentioned that meeting at Le Perroquet and how it all started.

"Other people can take credit; it's fine with me," Aronson adds. "It doesn't matter. There's nothing in it anymore, obviously. And they're all gone. I'm the only one that really is left from that meeting."

That fact alone makes it impossible to ascertain who, if anyone, deserves recognition as the singular "creator" of *Siskel & Ebert*. Even if Nick Aronson had the earliest seed of the idea that became *Opening Soon*, his concept involved covering many different art forms—and it was William McCarter who recognized that movies more than any other art form deserved a debate show on television. And even if McCarter sensed the opportunity, it was Eliot Wald who executed the plan and found a way to bring together Siskel and Ebert at a time when they desperately wanted to stay as far away from each other as humanly possible.

The show these men collectively developed was ultimately about the magic of differing viewpoints, so it's almost poetic that there are so many opposing opinions about *Siskel & Ebert*'s inception. And the fact that the *Opening Soon* pilot was anything but an instant success shows that it's not always the idea that is of principal importance in television. Certainly, the idea at *Siskel & Ebert*'s core—two passionate and opinionated critics debate the latest movies—is a good one. But an idea so simple required flawless execution, particularly on the part of the show's hosts and writers.

Their charisma and chemistry were key . . . and in the pilot, Gene and Roger had none.

The only people who could truly create *Siskel & Ebert* were Siskel and Ebert themselves, along with their next producer, who inherited the job of figuring out how to turn their furious rivalry into an unbreakable alliance.

CHAPTER FOUR

THE FIRST-TAKE SHOW

Our job was and continues to be to beat each
other in print every single day of the week.
And one day a week we get together, sort of a
truce is called. We try to beat each other on TV.

—GENE SISKEL

I agree with what you observe;
I disagree with your interpretation.

—ROGER EBERT

The most famous movie theater in television history wasn't a
real place—but it was *based* on a real place.

From 1925 to 2012, 445 Central Avenue in Highland Park, Illinois, was home to an unassuming two-story movie house. It
opened as the Alcyon; in 1965, it was renamed the Highland Park.
Through the years, the Alcyon and the Highland Park screened
films like *The Lady of Scandal* starring Ruth Chatterton and *The
World of Henry Orient* with Peter Sellers. The Highland Park also
appeared *in* movies; in Tom Cruise's breakthrough hit, *Risky Business*, his character drives past the theater's unmistakable Tudor
Revival facade and color-blocked marquee.

In its final years before its demolition in the late 2010s, the theater housed four screens. But in its glory years, before it was subdivided in an attempt to compete with larger suburban multiplexes, it held just one cavernous auditorium. It even had a balcony.

As a kid growing up in Highland Park, Michael Loewenstein knew that balcony well. Loewenstein had worked at WTTW as a scenic designer for fifteen years when he was approached to work on the set for *Opening Soon . . . at a Theater Near You*. Instructed to design a movie theater, he immediately thought of the Alcyon.

"It had a Spanish look to it, with rough plaster walls," Loewenstein says. "It was sort of a moderate version of some of the big movie palaces downtown. And that was good. From a television point of view, it had some detail to it, and also this certain look, this Spanish look."

But copying the look of even a moderately sized movie theater was difficult in WTTW's cramped studio space. Loewenstein says he initially wanted to put Gene and Roger into the theater's orchestra section, but he quickly realized that in order to "get the feeling of the volume" of a big auditorium he would have to cheat using a technique called forced perspective, a trick of photography and architecture that fools the human eye into believing something is bigger than it actually is.

"To make it real size would have made weekly setup impossible," explains Loewenstein. "So I started thinking about using the balcony."

That balcony—"*the* Balcony," as it was affectionately known through the years—featured full-sized seats acquired from old movie theaters and furniture companies. (Loewenstein's files include an ad for Chicago Used Chair Mart on West Grand Avenue, which boasts, "We can make them like new . . . cheaper than you think!") Everything beyond the Balcony's brass rail was a miniature, built about one-third of the size it would really be in an actual theater. Loewenstein's architectural drawings for the original *Opening Soon* set reveal just how meticulously the forced perspective had to be planned. The edges of the set's side walls were different heights; closer to the camera they stood fifteen feet high, but the side farther from the camera measured just thirteen feet, seven inches. Even the lighted exit signs hanging over the theater's doors had to be specially made at a slight slant away from the cameras; standard rectangular signs would have spoiled the illusion.

From exactly the right vantage point in the rear of the studio, forced perspective made the *Opening Soon* set look like a homey neighborhood movie house à la the Alcyon. Later versions of the Balcony would enhance the simulation even further with tiny versions of orchestra seats. (Crew members nicknamed them "the tombstones.") The set was so convincing that the show regularly received letters from fans who claimed to recognize the theater where they shot the show.

Loewenstein's balcony had two rows of chairs, with four seats on either side of the center aisle. Siskel sat in the first chair on the right side of the aisle, Ebert in the first seat on the left. For two decades, those seats were their TV home. But even *that* became a source of competition between the men, according to Mary Margaret Bartley, who worked with Loewenstein on designing later versions of the *Siskel & Ebert* Balcony.

The nature of TV production required Gene and Roger to appear to be the same height on camera, which they were not; Siskel was several inches taller than Ebert. "So Roger had a cushion to raise him up so that his head height would be similar to Gene's," recalls Bartley. This created a second problem: now Roger had a cushion and Gene did not. In Siskel's mind, this was not fair.

"Well, then Gene had to have a cushion, too," Bartley laughs.

The solution the crew eventually reached: Gene received a tiny cushion, while Roger sat on a much larger one. When both sat on their respective cushions, they looked about the same height on camera. (When *Siskel & Ebert* traveled to Florida to record shows at the Disney–MGM Studios theme park, the two pillows had to be shipped down to Orlando to ensure continued cushion parity.)

Roger and Gene would spend a lot of time in Loewenstein's Balcony over the next several decades, but never more so than in the show's early years. When Thea Flaum took over the producing duties on *Opening Soon . . . at a Theater Near You*, she was responsible for producing one twenty-eight-minute episode a month— and generating that much content every four weeks proved to be a struggle.

"It would take eight hours to get one show in the can, with breaks for lunch, dinner, and fights," Ebert once said of the show's early days.

The hosts' issues as they tried to turn their unsuccessful pilot into a successful series were twofold: they didn't know how to work on television, and they didn't know how to work with each other. Often, one issue would exacerbate the other. From the pilot episode of *Opening Soon . . . at a Theater Near You*, the show opened with the hosts introducing each other rather than themselves.

"The name of the show is *Opening Soon . . . at a Theater Near You*, two critics talking about—and sometimes arguing about— the new movies in town. This is Roger Ebert, film critic of the *Chicago Sun-Times*," Siskel would say.

"And across the aisle from me is Gene Siskel, film critic for the *Chicago Tribune*," Ebert would respond.

But Ebert had won a Pulitzer Prize for film criticism shortly before *Opening Soon* began airing on PBS, and it was decided that detail would get included in his introduction. After all, few shows on television in 1976 could boast a Pulitzer Prize winner as cohost.

Which meant that, episode after episode, Siskel had to not only introduce his rival, he had to remind the audience that his rival was a Pulitzer Prize winner, too. And he had to do it all with a cheerful smile on his face. That didn't sit well with Siskel.

"I think Gene was insecure about his writing," says assistant producer John Davies. "So whenever Gene would give me his copy to type up, he would never write 'Pulitzer Prize–winning film critic.' He would write things like 'And to my right is Roger Ebert, film critic for the *Las Vegas Shopper News*.' That's what would go in the teleprompter. And of course Roger would see it, but he knew Gene was going to say it right. And Gene did—but during rehearsal he would say, 'And to my right is Roger Ebert, film critic for the *Las Vegas Shopper News!*' He just had a hard time saying it right. It was a joke, and yet it *wasn't* a joke."

Ironically, given Siskel's insecurities, Ebert had just as much trouble as Siskel—or maybe even *more* trouble—learning to write film criticism for television. By all accounts, Ebert was the more naturally gifted writer of the two men—in print. Television, however, was a different story.

"When he typed a review on an old typewriter," says producer Ray Solley, "he typed faster than you could possibly imagine. And he would never make mistakes. He could knock out a several-hundred-word review in a matter of minutes and zip it out of the typewriter and hand it to the editor."

But writing a review for print was not the same as writing a review for television. On Sunday mornings, Gene and Roger would schlep over to Thea Flaum's house, where they would all sit around her dining room table, going over their typewritten scripts—line by line, and in some cases word by word—to make them work for a TV audience.

"Roger, you're such a wonderful writer, but you know the show is only half an hour long. That review won't fit in half an hour. And Gene has to do something, too," she once advised during one of these intensive training sessions.

"But I worked on all of this! It's all great," he said in frustration.

"That," she replied, "is what the newspaper is for."

Ebert wasn't the only one who struggled with that learning process. On one episode, John Davies was typing up Roger's teleprompter script and happened to see Roger's review for the same movie that was intended to run in the *Chicago Sun-Times*.

"I thought the review for the paper was better than the one for the TV show," Davies remembers. So he decided to change the TV script and add back some of the material from Roger's print review. Big mistake.

"I had not yet understood," Davies admits, "that the TV script needed to be more conversational. It wasn't meant to be the print review that would go in the newspaper. I hadn't made that leap yet. So I changed it."

When the revised script appeared in the teleprompter, Roger recognized it immediately—and he was not happy.

"Who did this? *Who changed this?*" Ebert yelled.

The rest of the staff slowly backed away from Davies. (At least that's how he remembers the moment.) Eventually, he admitted he switched the TV script to mimic Ebert's print review.

"Don't ever do that. Don't *ever* change something I give you to type up. You type it up the way I gave it to you. I'll make the changes down here. You don't make them for me! Going forward, my new name for you is going to be 'the Functional Illiterate.'" Davies says Ebert did call him the Functional Illiterate for "a while," until Gene finally told him he needed to stop.

"They were never going to be malleable by TV standards," adds producer Ray Solley, who describes Gene and Roger as two artists who were difficult, iconoclastic, and perhaps even dysfunctional. "They would be willing to change their outfits, or Roger's glasses—what the best size would be, making them nonreflective. That was not an issue. But if you took a look at their copy and said, 'What you wrote about that movie doesn't make sense, I've not seen the movie nor have I read the book that movie was based on so therefore I have no idea what you're saying' . . . then there would be huge arguments. Things like 'How dare you tell me I don't know what I'm doing!' And 'How dare you edit my copy!' And 'I won a Pulitzer Prize, what have *you* won lately?' So there was a great deal of learning on *our* part of how do you deal with people that know what they're doing and have a process and have a system, and how do you take *your* process and *your* knowledge and meld that?"

Solley continues: "You have to remember: We're talking about two guys who not only didn't work with each other, they were competitors."

Gene and Roger even addressed the tension between them in a 1979 episode of the show, during a segment where they answered viewer mail. Responding to a letter from a fan who asked, "Why don't you guys have a few drinks together? You don't seem like you like each other very much!" Ebert replied, "We are competitors. We have been competitors for ten years. You work for the *Tribune*, I work for the *Sun-Times* in Chicago, the two morning newspapers. So professionally we are competitors."

Siskel replied, "Yes, I like to beat your brains out in print any time I can."

"Okay, well, I always enjoy doing that, too. But I suppose I have a grudging respect for you as a film critic," Ebert said.

"I suppose I do, too," said Siskel.

"Right. And when we leave the studio, we drive in separate directions in separate cars," Ebert quipped.

To try to get everyone on the same page—and to bring a little more cohesion between the two stars—Thea Flaum instituted a rule: every week as production began on a new episode, the cast and crew would assemble at Conference Room A at WTTW and watch the previous week's show.

"She would have a watch-and-comment-and-learn session with the two of them," producer Ray Solley explains. "They learned from watching and from being tutored by her before they went into the studio for the next show. So anything that had slipped backwards from the past couple of tapings would be addressed quickly before you went into the next tape. She was responsible for keeping a pretty tight rein on the process, and on them. And they ended up loving that about her."

"It would be the director, the producers, me, and Gene and Roger. That's a very good way to get better," Flaum adds. "Because you've seen it, and then you go down and you do it again, and you do it better; you don't make the same mistakes. We did that for years."

Among the mistakes that were observed and corrected in those early review sessions, one of the biggest was simply the way both men carried themselves on camera. For all of the off-screen tension and intensity between the hosts and the crew in the first months of *Opening Soon . . . at a Theater Near You*, none of it translated to the screen. On camera, Roger and Gene continued to appear lethargic, uncomfortable, and sometimes downright bored. Ebert would lean back with his right arm draped across the back of his chair. Siskel crossed his legs and slouched. They looked like they were recording the show after sitting through an all-night movie marathon.

With Flaum's help, they started working on their energy level and their posture. She also worked with Roger and Gene to lay out ground rules for the show in order to make it as useful and interesting to potential viewers as possible.

The first rule, Flaum says, was ensuring that they were only going to "talk about the things that people could see."

"People watching television aren't stupid," Flaum explains. "So you can talk about anything, but if you're going to talk about lighting, point out what there is in the clip—let's find a clip that shows what you want to talk about."

Another rule: sharper on-screen outfits. Gene and Roger would never be mistaken for movie stars, but in early episodes their clothes were downright ugly: loud patterns, cream-colored turtlenecks, and massive lapels. Flaum instructed them to purchase new wardrobes.

"Thea Flaum came up with the idea," Siskel said in 1996. "On the show we just wore blazers and sweaters, the same kind of clothes people really wear to go to the movies on a Saturday night. We've always wanted viewers to feel as if they were just eavesdropping on a couple of guys who loved movies and were having a spontaneous discussion." The show emphasized that idea by having Gene and Roger continue to talk even as the lights dimmed in the Balcony and the closing credits began to roll. That single choice made an enormous, if subliminal, impact on the viewer. It suggested these guys would be talking whether there were cameras present or not, and it offered a subconscious invitation to the viewer: come back next week, and you'll see them in the same seats, having the same great conversation. (Or not; during one talk show appearance, Siskel confessed that when they couldn't think of anything to say during the final fade-out, he and Roger would just say, "Blah and blah and blah" over and over until the director called cut.)

Flaum says that it was clear to her from her first show "that this was something that really worked." It took audiences a little longer to catch on—but little by little, Gene and Roger got more comfortable with each other and with the cameras. Their on-screen demeanor improved, and so did their ratings. By the second episode, the Central Educational Network, a subdivision of PBS, wanted to air *Opening Soon.* By episode 3, they were on eighty different public television stations around the country.

As the show got bigger, its title became a problem. *Opening Soon . . . at a Theater Near You* was a mouthful. It was also so long it couldn't fit into the most essential promotional tool any television show in the mid-1970s had: the TV listings in *TV Guide* and the newspaper arts and entertainment sections. In the days before streaming and on-demand entertainment, those listings determined how people planned their evenings in front of the television set. And because *Opening Soon . . . at a Theater Near You* was so long, most listings condensed it, typically to just *Opening Soon*—which wasn't very descriptive at all.

"The internal joke," says Ray Solley, "was that *Opening Soon* could be a mall. It could be a shoe store. So that didn't help us. We needed a movie-related title. Thea's husband at the time came up with the title. He said, 'Let's call it *Sneak Preview*,' to which Thea said, 'Well, but it's more than one movie in a show.' Then he said, '*Sneak Previews!*'"

("Actually, about half a dozen people suggested the name *Sneak Previews*," Flaum said in a 2011 interview. "But I had a problem with it because a sneak preview in the movie business is a very specific thing—namely, a film that hadn't been released yet that the studios would show to an audience to get their feedback. But everyone else thought it was a good idea, so that was that.")

Thanks to its gradually increasing popularity on PBS stations around the Midwest, the newly christened *Sneak Previews* expanded to a weekly show in the fall of 1978. When it did, it also got a new opening-credits sequence scored to a licensed song called "Summer Vacation" that was originally written for an episode of the 1950s sitcom *The Adventures of Ozzie and Harriet.*

Set in a bustling movie theater, the *Sneak Previews* credits opened with the title on a glittering theater marquee. An unseen patron buys two tickets—which also have the *Sneak Previews* title on them. The hosts' names appear on a popcorn bucket and a box of candy, respectively. (Unlike later iterations of the series, Ebert was credited first, followed by Siskel.) Then the soda machine malfunctions, leading to a series of shots—designed by the show's first director, Patterson Denny—where hands frantically pound on the various soda buttons and the coin return lever, before a *Sneak Previews*–branded fountain cup drops into a dispenser upside down, sending soda flying everywhere.

Intentionally or not, the credits captured the mood of the occasionally volatile *Sneak Previews* set, where things could descend into chaos at a moment's notice. "There were a lot of arguments about scripting and movie choices," says assistant director Laura C. Hernández. "It just seemed like the discussions were big and tense about a lot of those things. Movie clip choices—that was *always* a bone of contention."

Movie clips became one of *Sneak Previews*' secret weapons, and the source of endless tension and behind-the-scenes headaches. This was the late 1970s, a time when the internet—much less an Internet Movie Database—was still almost twenty years away. There was no YouTube filled with movie trailers and film clips. Honest, unbiased information about movies—especially the latest movies opening in theaters—was rare and difficult to come by.

It was *so* difficult to come by, in fact, that in most cases the movie studios themselves did not make clips from their films available for journalistic purposes. Today, every major movie that gets national distribution comes with an "electronic press kit" filled with scenes that reporters or critics can use in their news reports or reviews. When *Sneak Previews* premiered on PBS, that simply wasn't done. It was, in *Sneak Previews* producer Nancy De Los Santos's words, "back in cave people days. It was so crazy."

The process of making clips for the show was arguably even crazier. Because the film clips weren't provided by the studios—or if they were provided, they weren't relevant to the topics Gene and Roger wanted to discuss on the air—the staff of *Sneak Previews* made their own clips, at the show's own expense.

"Someone from the staff always went to the screenings with Gene and Roger," explains Thea Flaum. "Gene and Roger would call out particular scenes where maybe there was a point they wanted to make, that we would use."

It was the staffer's job to keep detailed notes on the clips Roger and Gene wanted. But it wasn't as simple as running a stopwatch and jotting down the exact time when a particular scene they wanted appeared in the movie—because this was the late '70s, when movies were projected on enormous reels of 35mm film. Each reel contained about twenty minutes of the movie and the changeovers between reels were indicated by cue marks—little white circles in the upper right-hand corner of the frame. So it was up to the staff member to keep constant watch on those reel changes, because when the screening was over, they would take those specific reels with the clips the hosts demanded (and *only* those specific reels; they weren't allowed to take the entire movie) and haul them in enormous, twenty-pound cans to a local film-transfer facility, where they would copy the specific scenes to videotape, which would then be inserted into *Sneak Previews*' reviews.

It's hard to believe that Hollywood studios gave a television show they had no control or oversight over the authority to freely edit clips of movies into their show, but that's how things were done for years and years. ("I can't imagine the legalities of that, but we got permission. We never had it in writing," Ray Solley marvels.) The only director in those days who pushed back against the practice was Woody Allen, then at the absolute zenith of his fame and power in the movie business, following his Academy Award–winning comedy *Annie Hall*.

When Allen released *Manhattan* in 1979, Roger and Gene each told Ray Solley they wanted two specific scenes to use during their review. Allen provided just one clip from the film for any and all television coverage and, of course, it wasn't the scene Gene or Roger wanted to talk about.

"Thea Flaum's mantra was 'Somewhere, someplace, there's a person sitting at a desk that can say yes,'" says Solley. It was his job to find that person.

Solley called the film's Chicago publicist and got nowhere. Then he talked to the publicist's boss; no luck there, either. Then he called Allen's powerful agents and producers, Jack Rollins and Charles Joffe, and left a message explaining the situation.

Two days later, Woody Allen called the *Sneak Previews* office at WTTW.

"I hear that these two guys—I know Roger, I know Gene, I love them both," Allen said (according to Solley). "I don't have much time to talk, but I am happy to help you get a clip. What is it that they want and why?" Allen wasn't just helping out of the goodness of his heart; he was subtly trying to pry loose some information about what the critics were planning to say about his movie. (If he was planning on refusing the clips if Siskel and Ebert wanted to pan the movie, that didn't matter; they both loved *Manhattan*.)

This wasn't the last time Roger and Gene tussled with Woody Allen over clips. In 1983, they couldn't convince him to sign off on some scenes from his faux documentary, *Zelig*. When they wouldn't relent, Allen personally wrote them a long letter explaining "the difficulty in excerpting something that I consider representative and meaningful" from his highly unusual film. He insisted that it was not a decision designed to "create an aura of specialness, suggest that it is an untouchable masterpiece or something that we are ashamed of," and hoped "it will not be too disruptive" of the show's typical format. He closed with a "final suggestion": "Perhaps you might try reviewing my film showing clips of *Mommie Dearest* or *Conan the Barbarian*, both of which could help me enormously at the box office."

Though selecting, lugging, transferring, and then returning the heavy canisters of films—because they had to return them to whatever theater or screening room let them borrow the reels they needed—was, in Nancy De Los Santos's words, "a huge process," it was also one that made *Sneak Previews* unique in its heyday. Because the show made its own clips, nobody else on television had them, giving movie lovers an extra incentive to tune in each week.

"It just seemed to me that we needed to do things that would distinguish us from the stuff that they would now be seeing every day on the *Today* show," explains Thea Flaum. "You needed to show clips that they hadn't seen before."

Choosing their own clips—and tailoring them to precisely the arguments Gene and Roger wanted to make, either for or against a film—also integrated the movies far more cohesively into the show. *Sneak Previews* wasn't just a place to see a scene or two from a new movie. Instead of trying to make their comments match up with whatever promotional materials the studios provided—and thus showing their viewers only what the studios wanted them to see—Gene and Roger worked the other way, finding scenes that suited *their* arguments. As a result, *Sneak Previews* offered much more honest and accurate criticism. In some ways, Siskel and Ebert gave a clearer view of movies on television than they ever could in their newspapers.

"On television, pictures carry more weight than words," explains Ray Solley. They also add weight to words. If Gene was blown away by the cinematography in a movie—enough to say that it made you forget you were in a movie seat and took you away to a totally different world, that in its own way a particular film was "as strange and as foreign with its photography and sounds as *Star Wars*," he could back it up with images from that movie to show just how truly beautiful it was. (That film he was describing was the classic *Days of Heaven*, which Ebert immediately hailed as a "masterpiece" from "a brilliant young filmmaker named Terrence Malick," making just his second feature.)

"Their clips totally supported their reviews," agrees John Davies. "As soon as the movie companies got sick of that, they started sending out electronic press kits. But then Gene would say things like, 'Listen, although this clip is good, the movie stinks!' And then we'd show maybe ten seconds of the clip."

Although *Siskel & Ebert* became synonymous with its thumbs up or down ratings system, that came later. In the days of *Sneak Previews*, the show concluded with a roundup of the episode's reviews and a "yes" or "no" vote for each film, a choice that was only settled on after what Thea Flaum calls a series of "long arguments" about the best way to rate movies on the show.

Initially, both Gene and Roger insisted that *Sneak Previews* should use the star ratings they assigned to movies they reviewed in the *Tribune* and the *Sun-Times*. Flaum and the rest of the staff were equally adamant that stars were a bad idea, mostly because they were confusing. Some film critics used a scale from zero to four stars; others used zero to five. Some only used whole stars, while others also gave half stars, which made things even more complicated.

With the stars vetoed, the discussion then turned to the possibility of assigning letter grades like in school: As, Bs, and so on, down to Fs for the real stinkers. But that presented similar issues, in that some grades would leave the critics' final judgments somewhat ambiguous. (Was a B– a recommendation? Was a C+ a warning to stay away?) Plus, Solley claims, there was some concern that public television assigning movies letter grades would play into the stereotype that PBS shows were "educational TV." That evolved into the simpler system of "pass" or "fail," but calling every movie Gene and Roger didn't like a "failure" felt too harsh and extreme; just because a movie didn't entirely work didn't make it a complete failure.

"So then it went to 'Okay, what else can we do that's clean and clear and is very binary?'" recalls Ray Solley. That eventually became "yes" or "no" because, Solley says, the *Sneak Previews* team realized it answered one of the questions at the root of every movie review: Should I spend my time and money and go see it?

Each *Sneak Previews* also included one segment where the answer to that question was always a resounding no: "Dog of the Week," where Roger and Gene shared the worst movie they'd watched since the previous taping. A series staple from the *Opening*

Soon pilot, it was quickly upgraded with an actual mutt, a tiny pooch named Spot the Wonder Dog, who would leap into a seat next to Gene or Roger, bark a couple of times, and then sit with a slightly confused look on his face as they would take turns bashing some dreadful picture they'd seen at a local grindhouse.

Fans who are only familiar with later seasons of *Siskel & Ebert* might be surprised to see Gene and Roger, television's staunchest defenders of foreign and art house cinema, yukking it up with a canine sidekick. Some "Dog of the Week" segments look like an early prototype for future movie-riffing shows like *Mystery Science Theater 3000*; Gene or Roger would introduce a clip from a terrible bomb and then rapid-fire one joke after another about the cast, the director, the awful dialogue, or the ludicrous premise.

The act caught on, and it helped broaden the show's appeal in unexpected ways. One day, a letter showed up at WTTW. "My four-year-old son watches you every week," it read. "When I asked why, he said, 'Mommy, it's because those boys get to take their dog to the movies.'"

The scruffy Spot remained a fixture on *Sneak Previews* until the fall of 1981, when he was suddenly replaced by a new pooch: Sparky the Wonder Dog. "Welcome to one of the roughest jobs in television," Siskel said to Sparky during his introductory segment, to which Ebert replied, "Listen, kid, you're really going to earn your dog biscuits on this one."

The on-air reason for Spot's absence, according to Siskel: "Spot the Wonder Dog got a little tired of seeing all those lousy pictures." But a few years later, in an interview with the *Washington Post*, Roger and Gene revealed the truth: Spot was fired for asking for too much money. He was getting about $65 a show.

"There was a fee negotiated, apparently, for extra time. If we had a retake or a lunch break or a camera screwed up, the time sequence might change, and the dog would have to stay longer. And I think what happened was they wouldn't pay Bob Hoffmann, his owner, the overtime for his dog," Siskel explained, adding, "That was a totally arrogant little dog. He was a star. His trainer called him 'The Farrah Fawcett of Dogs.'"

"That was when they were negotiating," Ebert added. "The trainer said, 'You don't understand; this is the Farrah Fawcett of dogs.' The producer said, 'In that case we're looking for the Marjorie Main of dogs.'"

Spot's replacement had it even worse. By the summer of 1982, Sparky was out, and a third pup named Zeke was in. In the same *Post* interview, Ebert revealed that Sparky died of kidney failure, and even before that he had been very difficult to control on set. During one "Dog of the Week" segment, he'd ignored his cue and jumped out of the Balcony. Although Michael Loewenstein's set was only raised a handful of feet off the studio floor, on camera it looked like Sparky had deliberately flung himself to his demise. Talk about a dog-eat-dog business.

While Siskel and Ebert might have gradually built a reputation as champions of independent, high-brow cinema, on "Dog of the Week" they also discussed such cinematic disasters as *Caligula*, *Count Dracula and His Vampire Bride*, *The Kinky Coaches and the Pom Pom Pussycats*, *The Seven Brothers Meet Dracula*, *Dracula's Last Rites*, and *In Search of Dracula*. (Dracula had a pretty rough go of it on *Sneak Previews*.) Gene and Roger typically selected their own "Dog of the Week," but on one 1982 episode, they were both so disgusted by something called *The Beast Within* that they bestowed it with the special title "Very, Very Bad Dog of the Week." According to Siskel, it was "so bad and so heavily advertised" they needed to provide an extra warning to viewers.

Ebert called the special designation a "*Sneak Previews* Public

Service" and while "Dog of the Week" eventually became less of a film review and more of a weekly stand-up routine centered on a terrible movie, Ebert was also right. Most of the "Dogs of the Week" were cheap exploitation pictures that might not get reviewed in many newspapers. These sorts of "dogs" made their money by flooding a market with advertising, selling as many tickets as possible in a week or two before the word got out that, say, *The Gong Show Movie* wasn't exactly *Citizen Kane*, and then making a hasty getaway to the next unsuspecting city. "Dog of the Week" put a lot of movies on viewers' radars—along with a warning to stay far, far away.

Some of the early *Opening Soon* episodes qualified for "Dog of the Week" status, but little by little, the show came together. If Gene and Roger still didn't like each other, they at least could appreciate that their work together drastically increased their profiles in the film world, and even their paychecks. Gene Siskel once boasted to John Davies, "I write it once and I sell it four times"—because he could review the same movie for the *Chicago Tribune*, WBBM, *Sneak Previews*, and his syndicated *Tribune* column.

Still, despite *Sneak Previews'* gradual expansion into PBS markets all over the country, Gene and Roger were still not happy with the show, and especially with its prolonged production schedule. Due to their struggles with teleprompters, endless rehearsals, and each other, half-hour episodes still took all day to record. It didn't help that WTTW prided itself on its incredibly high-caliber technical productions.

"Now the environment is, take an iPhone video and show it on network TV, and it looks like crap and it doesn't even fill the screen, but it's cool," says Ray Solley. "In our day, [we thought,] 'We're showing professional Hollywood films with multimillion-dollar budgets as our meat and potatoes. And then we come back to the studio of a station in the Midwest and it's sloppy and you can't really hear them? None of our crew would allow that. We had a standard. And if it doesn't work, we're gonna do it until we get it right."

Getting it right could take a long time. Shooting would begin around eleven o'clock in the morning, then break for lunch, then record more, then break again, then finally finish up by seven or eight o'clock at night. It was an arduous process, with Gene and Roger at each other's throats—and sometimes both at the crew's throats as well. Something had to give.

Like everything else with Roger and Gene, the big breakthrough came because of a fight.

In a 2005 interview, Roger Ebert detailed the day that changed the show. It was a Thursday, which was the day all of *Sneak Previews*' episodes were taped. Many shoot days on *Sneak Previews* went slowly, but this one went *really* slowly. Gene and Roger did take after take, broiling under the hot studio lights at WTTW.

At last, Gene and Roger nailed a review that they were both satisfied with. Ray Solley, who had replaced Thea Flaum as producer of *Sneak Previews* after she received a promotion to executive producer, was not. Those hot studio lights had caught a reflection of Gene Siskel's wristwatch, producing a distracting flash in the camera. Despite the late hour, despite the frustration, they would have to try the review again.

"I just want to tell you," Siskel said to Solley, "that if we have to do this again, I'm going to get up out of this chair and I'm going to walk out of the studio and out of the station and never come back."

With that, Solley had enough. He threw his clipboard down and marched out of the studio.

"The next week," Ebert recalled, "our intern produced the show. Her name was Nancy De Los Santos. And she said, 'I'm gonna just let you guys talk. Because you can't really remember all of your three-by-five cards anyway. But you're better at just talking to each other.' And we did a show and said, 'This is the way it's supposed to be.' And so we went into Thea and said, 'Thea, we want Nancy to produce the show,' and that was fine with Thea. So Nancy became our producer. And that was the beginning of things getting easier."

At least that was how Roger Ebert told the story. Nancy De Los Santos tells it a little differently.

For one thing, she wasn't an intern on *Sneak Previews* one day and a producer the next. Though De Los Santos started at WTTW as an intern, by 1981 she had worked her way up to the position of assistant producer. There were no 3x5 cards involved with the show by that time, either—index cards and on-set notes hadn't been used since the days that Eliot Wald produced *Opening Soon . . . at a Theater Near You*. But she does remember there was a fight over a review that got marred by a flash of light off Gene's watch in the middle of a take. In her retelling, she picked up the reins (and the clipboard) after Ray Solley left the set and finished the episode.

Ray Solley says he has no memory of this incident—though he says if De Los Santos says it happened, then he believes her. "But," he adds, "there was never a moment of I walk off the set on the Wednesday or the Thursday and she takes over the next Wednesday or Thursday. It was much more evolutionary than a story of a weird problem and a blowup and a change of leadership in the space of an hour."

He *does* remember other times when frustration about long shoot days boiled over into arguments, when he occasionally left notes on Thea Flaum's desk that read things like "I can't believe what they put me through!" And he recalls a separate incident when Gene did threaten to quit. "You basically say, 'Okay, what's the best thing for the show right now?' And the best thing for the show is making sure that the talent is happy," Solley says.

"Ray would butt heads with them, as any producer would," confirms De Los Santos. "*I* butted heads with them when I was producer. We all did. Producers do that because they're the adults in the room. They're the ones saying, 'Well, hang on here, we can't do *that*. We have to do *this*.'"

Ray Solley actually returned to finish the remainder of the 1981 season of *Sneak Previews*, although De Los Santos was eventually promoted to the role of producer after she went to Thea Flaum and told her she wanted the job. And whether it was the matter of one big fight or a slow accumulation of weekly exasperation, the *Sneak Previews* formula did gradually change. "Instead of doing it over and over again to get it right, we would allow it to be a little sloppy," Ebert said in 2005. "Gene and I agreed: it's better for the people at home to feel that we are having the conversation for the first time. And that led within a very short time to the concept of 'the First Take Show,' where basically the show is done in real time."

"That's one of the things Ray Solley did too much of—he over-rehearsed them," echoes assistant producer John Davies. "And they really did not like that. I'm not saying Ray was a bad producer, but he was a bad producer for *them*. . . . They wanted that crosstalk where they took each other on and argued. They wanted that to be natural. And Ray would break it all the time. 'No, guys, you didn't make your points cogently enough. It wasn't smart enough. I don't get why you disliked the movie. I don't understand.' And it would really piss them off."

From that point forward, *Sneak Previews* and every subsequent iteration of Siskel and Ebert's shows prioritized authenticity of interactions over technical perfection. If there was a minor flub or a slightly awkward shot but the debate between the two hosts was particularly heated, it stayed in the show. Gone were the hours of rehearsal and the countless retakes. Rather than trying to perform the roles of the smartest and cleverest TV pundits, Roger and Gene would simply be themselves and react to each other accordingly— which, because they still regarded each other suspiciously and often disagreed violently with each other's opinions about movies, resulted in some thought-provoking and surprisingly dramatic television.

These lively, unrehearsed "crosstalks" became the key to the show's popularity. In first-take shows, Gene and Roger deliberately avoided hearing each other's opinions until they showed up at WTTW for a taping. With no rehearsals beforehand, what you saw on-screen were their genuine reactions to each other.

"It was a surprise to both of them," says *Sneak Previews* staffer Laura C. Hernández. "They didn't read each other's scripts, so they didn't know ahead of time. The spontaneity offered in that crosstalk was very valuable and very real to the success of who they became. And they were smart enough, and the people around them were smart enough, to know what that magic was."

Roger Ebert once said that when the show began to work, "it was because we started to argue and disagree. And our personalities were in evidence. And our personality conflicts were there. And we had chemistry because whatever we felt for each other was real. If it looked like we were mad at each other, it was because we were mad at each other." In another instance, Ebert described himself and Siskel as "tuning forks. Strike one, and the other would pick up the same frequency." To put it another way, while they were both outstanding soloists who could be appreciated on their own, they sounded best when they worked together in harmony (or, in their case, disharmony).

"So much of television is polished, refined, laugh-tracked, done so cleanly that it's incredibly boring," Gene Siskel said in 1985. "Sports and news are popular because they're live. We want the same feeling."

Siskel said he believed that quality unlocked what he called "the brainstorm" of their show and what made it appealing to viewers. "Frequently," he said, "when you see someone talking into the camera you think, 'What does *he* know?' Well, you have that surrogate on the set with us." When Gene or Roger reacted with shock and disgust to each other, they gave a voice to the audience. If, as the old adage says, everyone is a critic, then everyone could imagine themselves in Gene's or Roger's seat in the Balcony, pushing back against their latest rave or pan. That gave *Sneak Previews* a participatory and almost interactive quality decades before such concepts were common on television.

The more honest and raw Gene and Roger got, the better the show got, and the better the show did. By the early 1980s, *Sneak Previews* aired on hundreds of PBS stations around the country, including in New York and Los Angeles—markets that initially refused to carry the show because they believed two critics from Chicago had nothing to offer their high-brow audiences. Eventually, though, Gene's and Roger's gift for natural conversation and debate (and *Sneak Previews*' ratings) became undeniable. And once the show was playing in New York and LA, it began to catch the attention of other television shows, including the host of one late-night talk show who was bringing a similar level of innovation and no-nonsense Midwestern talk to the world of late night.

And he was in desperate need of good guests.

CHAPTER FIVE

ROMPIN' STOMPIN' FILM CRITICISM

I think the main difference [between himself and Siskel] is when we go into the theater, I am looking forward to having a good time and you are fearing having a bad time.

—ROGER EBERT

Given the way most movies are made, I think it's quite reasonable to fear having a bad time.

—GENE SISKEL

W hen *Late Night with David Letterman* premiered on NBC in early 1982, its 12:30 a.m. time slot came with rules set down by its lead-in, *The Tonight Show Starring Johnny Carson*. In order to ensure the two shows would complement and not compete with each other (or perhaps to ensure that the upstart Letterman would never eclipse the established but aging Carson), no *Tonight Show* regulars were permitted on *Late Night*. Letterman's staff had to send Carson's staff the names of potential guests to confirm compliance.

By matter of necessity, then, the early years of *Late Night* were filled with oddballs like comedian Andy Kaufman and German monologist Brother Theodore. *Late Night*'s interview segments looked nothing like the ones on the *Tonight Show*, or almost any other talk show, for that matter.

Which made it the perfect spot for Siskel and Ebert, who didn't look like anyone else on television.

They debuted on the show on March 1, 1982, a month to the day after *Late Night*'s first episode. (The other guests that night: Christopher Reeve and a New York dentist named Dr. Norman Hoffman.) As soon as Roger and Gene sat down, Letterman—never one to offer insincere praise—called *Sneak Previews* "terrific" and then complimented them on providing a break from the stuffy traditions of old-fashioned print film criticism.

"Most people, when a motion picture critic's image comes to mind, most people think of somebody who is kind of goofy, too esoteric, too intellectual, or on the other hand kind of bitchy and goofy," Letterman told Gene and Roger. "You guys are just nice, reasonable fellows reviewing films."

"I think we're film lovers," Ebert replied. "We're fans. We like films. We like to see good films. We're disappointed when we see bad ones. And we talk about them to each other, I think, the way a lot of people talk about movies to each other."

Letterman certainly thought so. He invited Roger and Gene back to *Late Night* (and then to the *Late Show* on CBS) at least once a year for the rest of Siskel and Ebert's partnership. For a while, they actually held the record for the most guest appearances on Letterman's show. In 1994 alone, they came on the *Late Show* six different times.

Watching their interviews, it's easy to understand why. Roger and Gene were great talk show guests: funny, quick, and game to discuss just about anything. The annual crop of summer blockbusters or Oscar nominations offered an endless supply of timely topics, but they were just as comfortable talking about themselves—their viewing habits, their personal histories, and, of course, the reasons for their biggest fights.

"They had this preternatural understanding of how to be on television," explains former *Late Show* executive producer Rob Burnett. "And what made them entertaining, at least in our world, was that they seemed to really dislike each other. I don't know how much of that was for the camera, although I saw little moments off camera that I don't think it was a full act. Maybe they also loved each other; that happens to married couples, I suppose. But there was just this undercurrent of disdain between the two of them that I always found so entertaining."

"They had competition with each other about that as well, in sort of the field of who could be the best guest," says Jamie Bennett, a Disney executive during *Siskel & Ebert's* first years with the company. "They thought through everything they would say and what they wouldn't say. They didn't rehearse, but they did think it through. They looked very spontaneous. They were very good on live TV. But most people wouldn't have known how much they cared about how they would come off. They saw one of their occupations as being guests on the talk shows. That was part of who they were and what they did."

"In our world," Burnett continues, "we very often divided people up into 'You Know How to Be on a Talk Show' and 'You Don't Know How to Be on a Talk Show.' And Siskel and Ebert, maybe because they hosted a show themselves, they just had this natural understanding of 'Well, we need to bring it.' And their form of bringing it wasn't Bill Murray or Tom Hanks or Howard Stern or one of these people who are gonna come out and kill. It was more 'We're gonna provide our brand, and Dave can play off that brand.' And it worked beautifully every time."

"There used to be a sign backstage that Letterman put up," says another former *Late Show* executive producer, Robert Morton. "As you walked out from the wings there was a sign on the mirror that said 'Hit the chair and go.' It was Letterman lingo. *They* were the ultimate hit-the-chair-and-go guests. They would sit down and get right to the point. Letterman loved the way they interacted with each other."

That interaction gave them an advantage over almost every other talk show guest in television history. Most TV interviews are one-on-one, and if a guest's anecdote bombs, it's up to the host to pick up the pieces and muddle through. With Roger and Gene, a flub by one was an excuse for the other to sling a few fresh insults, which would spark more of the bickering that they were famous for. Robert Morton says the *Late Night* team called Siskel and Ebert "autopilot guests."

Arguing, Morton says, laughing, "was part of their DNA."

The act never failed to bring down the house. Within a few years of *Sneak Previews* entering national distribution, Siskel and Ebert didn't even need to say something funny to get a reaction from the *Late Night* crowd; simply disagreeing with each other was enough to send the audience into hysterics. They were like rock stars playing their greatest hits. It was just that, in their case, their "greatest hits" were calling each other fat and bald.

On the September 10, 1993, edition of the *Late Show*, for instance, they got into a heated exchange about *Free Willy*, a harmless children's film about a boy who helps a killer whale escape from captivity. Before Letterman could even get the title of the movie out, Siskel was already groaning about the picture, which he clearly loathed. The title character, he explained, wasn't good-looking enough to care about.

"I once asked Spielberg why you like creatures in his films," Siskel continued, his arms flailing and his voice rising with excitement. "Because of the eyes! The whale's eyes are set so far apart you can't even see them."

Sensing an opportunity, Ebert pounced. "*This* is Gene's criticism of *Free Willy*: that you can't see both of the whale's eyes at the same time."

The crowd erupted.

"Now *that*," Ebert added, "is rompin' stompin' criticism!" After the cheers died down, Ebert continued. "I cared about Willy and I cared about the kid."

Siskel's eyes widened. This time, Ebert had given Siskel an opening. "You *identified* with Willy. I wonder why!"

A huge *"WHOA!"* echoed through the Ed Sullivan Theater. Ebert, never sensitive about his weight, hammed it up for the crowd, adjusting his glasses and looking off forlornly into the distance. When the audience finally settled down, Letterman said, chuckling, "Oh, you kids! I love it when you spat!"

It wasn't just Letterman who loved them. By the mid-1980s, Gene and Roger were talk-show-circuit staples. Every few months, when they had a season premiere or special episode to promote, they'd make the rounds. They weren't picky or elitist about where. They gabbed with Oprah Winfrey and they also appeared on Milwaukee's *Dialing for Dollars*. They defended the artistic merits of *Return of the Jedi* on *Nightline* and debated viewers over the phone on *Donahue*. Gene played himself on an episode of *The Larry Sanders Show*, while Roger hawked books on the Better Shopping Channel.

(Gene's solo appearance on *Larry Sanders* was unusual—and

the source of one of Roger and Gene's biggest fights. As *Ebert & Roeper* and *At the Movies* producer David Plummer tells it, "Gene did *Larry Sanders*, but the *offer* was for *both* Gene and Roger. But then Roger couldn't be there, so they agreed, 'Okay, we're going to cancel it. We're not going to do it.' Well, Roger went on vacation and Gene called the producers back alone and said, 'No, I'll do it.' Roger didn't even find out that he did it until shortly before the episode aired. And Roger was just livid.")

Alone or together, Roger's and Gene's TV guest spots did more than promote their show or expose their personas to potential viewers outside the world of cinephilia. It began to shift that public image of film critics that Letterman talked about in their first *Late Night* visit.

"They were number one on PBS, but PBS didn't have the reach of ABC, CBS, or NBC," says longtime *Siskel & Ebert* director Don DuPree. "In the early days, and even today, PBS had a little bit of a stuffy reputation. And I think that was the image of film critics before *Siskel & Ebert*. But then you have two guys who weren't stuffy, who looked like us, not like people you usually saw on TV, and they could hold their own with Dave." Within a few years, the audience's concept of a film critic morphed from a goofy, esoteric intellectual into . . . Siskel and Ebert.

Even Johnny Carson started booking them, a crossover between *Tonight Show* and *Late Night* guests be damned. Ebert later claimed that their first *Tonight Show* with Carson was the moment both he and Siskel realized they had made it in television. That doesn't mean the appearance went off without a hitch. Gene and Roger were so nervous about their debut on the most iconic talk show in history that they abandoned their separate dressing rooms to provide each other with moral support. Carson came by to introduce himself before the show, and two men who were never at a loss for words were struck speechless.

"Roger," Gene sputtered after Carson left, "you and I do not belong here. We belong at home in Chicago, watching this on TV." In a 1996 interview, Roger claimed this moment was the only time in Gene and Roger's entire relationship that they ever hugged. "They started playing the *Tonight Show* theme," he said, "and we were scared shitless."

A *Tonight Show* writer arrived with a warning: Johnny might want to discuss the best films of 1985, so they better have some titles ready. It was a typical talk show request that Gene and Roger had fielded many times before. There was just one problem: Roger and Gene were both so awed by meeting Carson that their minds went completely blank. Desperate for material, they frantically called producer Nancy De Los Santos and had *her* tell them *their* favorite films of the year.

Nervous or not, they did well enough to get invited back on the *Tonight Show* over and over. In time, they got comfortable with Johnny—maybe *too* comfortable. In their December 12, 1986, appearance on the *Tonight Show*, they followed Chevy Chase, who was there to promote his new Christmas comedy, *Three Amigos*. For the first few minutes, everything went smoothly. Siskel, Ebert, and Carson all named their favorite Chevy Chase movies, while Chevy, seated next to Roger on the famous *Tonight Show* couch, smiled warmly. With some coaxing from Johnny, Chevy even trotted out his old *Saturday Night Live* bit where he'd sarcastically lip-synch a stuffy person's speech behind their back—with Roger cheerfully playing the role of Chevy's patsy.

Then Carson steered the show directly into an iceberg. "I hate to ask you to pick a dog," he said, "because it's not fair sometimes to the people who make the movies. But is there something out there that is really so bad?"

Faced with the choice of risking his credibility as a critic by lying or potentially hurting Chevy Chase's feelings, Ebert didn't hesitate. "I can't really recommend *Three Amigos*," he replied, bashing the very film Chase was there to promote. After a chorus of boos from the studio audience, Ebert added, "It's the Christmas picture I like the least. This is kind of hard to say because Chevy Chase has made a lot of good movies and God willing he will make a lot more good movies in the future."

"With your help!" Chase shot back sarcastically.

After the show, Chevy found Roger and Gene's dressing room and confessed: he didn't like *Three Amigos* very much, either. Still, he would never say that on the air, and no one else would, either—except Siskel and Ebert. That was another key reason for their talk show success: they were fearless. The power of candor that Siskel had talked about back in his early days at the *Chicago Tribune* was even truer on the talk show circuit—because it was even more uncommon there. Over and over, Gene and Roger took a wrecking ball to the unwritten rules of talk shows that required guests to be polite and supportive at all times.

The following year, Ebert told an interviewer that this spontaneous and somewhat awkward exchange with Chevy Chase on the *Tonight Show* provided an epiphany about the appeal of *Siskel & Ebert*. "I got a lot of letters from that—and generally when we're on the Carson show, I don't get any letters," he said. "'How could you be so mean, how could you be so cruel, how could you be so rude?'—that type of thing. But other people sent in letters saying, 'It was refreshing to hear someone telling the truth on television for once.'

"Siskel and I talked about this afterward and we thought that maybe the reaction to that helps explain why people are interested in the format of our show. They sense that we are actually telling the truth about what we think about the movies." Gene's and Roger's unflinching honesty was upending their audience's expectations left and right.

"What works on television is authenticity," agrees Ben Mankiewicz, a longtime host at Turner Classic Movies who also hosted *At the Movies* in the late 2000s, after Roger Ebert finally left the series. "When it works, there is a strong presence with a defendable point of view, not a character. And Siskel and Ebert had points of view."

That wasn't the first time Siskel and Ebert criticized Chevy Chase to his face, either. In 1982, Roger and Gene guest-starred on the season premiere of *Saturday Night Live*; they appeared as themselves and reviewed three of the sketches from earlier in the night. (They also reunited with their first producer at *Opening Soon . . . at a Theater Near You*, Eliot Wald, who was on the *SNL* writing staff at the time.) Gene and Roger wrapped their segment up by awarding a "Dog of the Week" to the show's host—none other than Chevy Chase. (They also took some shots at Chase's performance in the appropriately titled *Oh! Heavenly Dog*.)

Reading their reviews from cue cards—something they had never done before—Gene and Roger weren't nearly as comfortable or relaxed as they were speaking spontaneously in their debut appearance on *Late Night with David Letterman*. The rehearsal for the sketch had gone poorly and the producers wanted to trim it down. Ebert grew concerned he had less lines than Siskel. Then Siskel got upset that *his* role was getting diminished. Ebert had to count every word of dialogue—not lines of dialogue, *words* of dialogue—to make sure they each had exactly the same-sized part.

"By the time we went on the air," Ebert later said, "we were both complete basket cases."

Nonetheless, they got enough laughs on *SNL* to earn a return appearance on the 1983 season premiere, and then a far more extensive role on a spring 1985 episode: as the special guests on the first and only "*Saturday Night Live* Film Festival." Essentially a glorified clip show of popular *SNL* short films interspersed with new material, the week's live segments included sketches featuring just three performers: Gene Siskel, Roger Ebert, and Billy Crystal. Roger and Gene traded quips with—and absorbed some tasteless fat jokes from—Crystal's pompous talk show host Fernando, and then got two entire segments to re-create the *Sneak Previews* format and critique the shorts that played throughout the night.

They applauded a couple of sketches, but where they deemed it appropriate, they didn't hold back. When Ebert offered mild praise to a film about convicts learning to write in prison, Siskel dismissed the entire premise as "kind of stupid." Of another short he hated, Siskel said, "Here is a film that went nowhere absolutely fast."

Even when the pair had good things to say about the shorts, they still found ways to be critical.

Ebert noted that they had given a positive review to a film called "Video Victims" in their 1982 *SNL* appearance, and suspected the producers only played it again during their 1985 episode because it was guaranteed to get praised. "They knew they would have one in the bag if they put it on the show. Real courageous, fellas!" Siskel huffed.

In their first *SNL* guest spot, Siskel joked that they were brought in to give the "first live review of a television show still in progress." It was a cute line, but Gene and Roger didn't just play along with the gag. The fact that they openly and honestly mocked *Saturday Night Live*'s uneven writing during an episode of *Saturday*

Night Live was totally unprecedented. Maybe it's not too surprising they never returned for another *SNL* Film Festival after that.

Their confrontations with Chevy Chase and the *SNL* cast were extreme examples, but by no means unusual for Gene and Roger. In their early appearances on *Late Night with David Letterman*, they regularly brought along clips from movies they hated, and then proceeded to make fun of them at length. They showed up on a *Tonight Show* episode in January of 1986 after actress Kate Capshaw, and within thirty seconds of sitting down opposite guest host Joan Rivers, Gene and Roger had both taken turns insulting Capshaw's film *Windy City*. (Roger called it one of the worst movies he'd ever seen.) When Rivers offered the critics an out, insisting that bad movies are the fault of their directors rather than their actors, Siskel interrupted and doubled down instead.

"Well, now wait a minute," he declared. "It *is* the actor's fault for picking the script!" Boos rained down from the *Tonight Show* audience. Then Siskel called Capshaw's voice "whiny" for good measure. Writing about the encounter in the *Chicago Tribune* the following month, Siskel called the TV confrontation "fun" and said he was "looking forward to seeing [Capshaw] again in the movies, hoping that her next film would be praiseworthy." (He also wrote that, backstage after the show, Capshaw agreed with him about many of his comments, particularly regarding her screechy performance in *Indiana Jones and the Temple of Doom*, "saying that the concept for the role was that of George Lucas and not herself.")

"They loved doing the shows," says Don DuPree, "but the secret sauce was the hosts really liked them, too. If you're Johnny Carson, Jay Leno, David Letterman, Conan [O'Brien], a lot of your segments are movie stars plugging movies that they know are not any good. It's all spin. And then you get these two guys out there, and they actually tell you what they think about it and they make it entertaining and fun."

David Letterman in particular seemed to relish—and maybe even envy—their frankness. While the cameras rolled, he would generally offer polite praise for whatever movie Roger and Gene talked about. If they hated something, he'd often claim he hadn't seen it. Once the director called cut, though, he would let the insults fly. During the commercial break after a segment where Siskel, Ebert, and Letterman all heaped praise on the Oscar contender *The Piano,* about a woman whose finger is chopped off by a jealous admirer, Letterman leaned in to Ebert and whispered, "I gotta be honest with you guys. I hated that movie so much I wish he cut off *all* her fingers."

Despite their frequent appearances on *Late Night* and the *Late Show,* that was as close as Gene and Roger ever got to David Letterman, who preferred to keep most of his guests at a remove in order to preserve their conversations' freshness and spontaneity for the show. They became far friendlier with Jay Leno after he took over Johnny Carson's role as host of the *Tonight Show.*

Leno loved movies and saw everything, and was known to spend every possible minute up until showtime hanging out in Gene and Roger's dressing room. (He also once measured Gene's and Roger's thumbs on camera; Roger's was slightly longer.)

"He would spend an hour, dressed in jeans, talking about movies," remembers DuPree. "Five minutes before the show, they start playing the music, and Jay's still in jeans. He runs out, and the next thing you know, he's onstage, doing his monologue. And as you're listening to his monologue, you'd realize all of his jokes he'd tried out on you during the course of your conversation about the movies."

For all their bluster, Gene and Roger occasionally offered

glimpses of their softer sides. During a 1994 *Tonight Show* episode hosted by Jay Leno, the conversation turned to the art of acting, and how difficult it can be for movie stars to convincingly tell someone how much they love them. With the audience tittering in the background, Leno prodded Gene and Roger to give it a try.

Siskel went first. "Roger," he said with surprising sincerity, "this isn't going to be easy for me to say. My wife's backstage. We've been happily married for almost fifteen years. But I love you."

The audience cheered. Then it was Roger's turn, and a big smile spread across his face.

"Gene, this is going to come as an enormous surprise to my wife, and to everyone else who knows us, but, big guy, I love you."

It might have been pitched as a comedy bit couched as an acting exercise, but Ebert and Siskel weren't actors. They couldn't fake the kind of emotions they showed to one another on that *Tonight Show* episode. Despite their legendary penchant for bickering, they really were starting to get along.

That's not to say that their on-screen squabbles were a put-on. If anything, their fights on the set of the *Tonight Show* and the *Late Show* paled in comparison to their behind-the-scenes arguments—many of which were exacerbated by their talk show appearances and their endless competitiveness. They kept meticulous track of who received what perks (like their respective lines of dialogue on *Saturday Night Live*) so that they could ensure they were being doled out equally and equitably.

The most important perk was who was going to sit directly next to the host in any appearance, because the host generally directed more questions to whoever was in that seat, and thus whoever was in that seat got more opportunities to talk. At first, a coin flip determined who sat where. For years, a flip of a coin was Gene and Roger's standard way to resolve any dispute that reached an impasse. If they couldn't decide who would introduce an episode, or take the lead on a prestigious review, they would toss a coin and let the fates decide.

But then if one or the other was unsatisfied with the results of the flip—and one was *always* unsatisfied with the results of the flip—they would fight over exactly what they had been flipping for in the first place. If one of the men won a few flips in a row, that caused more arguments, along with accusations of cheating. (Though he never proved it, Roger always suspected Gene had somehow acquired a weighted coin.)

The fights over who sat opposite Letterman or Carson got bad enough that they decided to alternate who got the first chair from one appearance to the next. "And then *that* would always be an argument," Robert Morton says, "because Roger would say one thing, and Gene would say another thing." They were both so inflexible that they would then demand Morton play them a videotape of their previous *Late Show* appearance to conclusively verify who had sat next to Letterman last. "They'd argue like children about it!" Morton adds.

The arguments started long before they arrived for a taping. When they were flown out to New York or Los Angeles for talk shows, they would travel first class, but they didn't like to sit together. Through years of trial and error, they decided there were two best seats on the plane: in the front row by the window on the right side, which they felt was the single best seat, and in the third row by the window on the left side. Then the eternal struggle became: Who gets the first row and who gets the third row?

One particular flight out to Los Angeles for the *Tonight Show* resulted in a battle that Ebert complained about for the rest of his life. He and Siskel were at the gate waiting to board the plane when a fight broke out over who would get the prized first-row seat. Gene insisted it was his turn.

"No! It's mine! They gave it to me! It's my turn!" Ebert shot back.

Gene refused to budge. Shouting ensued. Siskel got so angry, he stormed off. For fifteen minutes, he vanished. Siskel only returned when the flight began boarding. Suddenly, his whole demeanor had changed.

"Roger," Siskel said, "I've cooled off, and I want to apologize. This is silly that we're standing here in front of all these people fighting over who gets one seat in first class and who gets the other. And I just want you to know, Roger, I'm sorry. I'm not going to fight like this. You take the seat in the front row, and I'll gladly take the one in the third row, and let's put this behind us."

Ebert was stunned by the gesture. "Really?" he asked.

"Yes, absolutely, Roger."

"Gene, that's very nice of you. I feel kind of bad about it."

"Don't, Roger," Siskel insisted. "Please, just take it and let's move on. This is a new chapter."

With the matter finally settled, both got on the plane, with Roger happily in the first row and Gene in the third. Typically, Siskel would sleep on long plane flights. But once the plane was airborne, Ebert began to hear Gene's voice echoing through the first-class cabin, laughing, telling jokes, and holding court. Baffled, Roger turned around to see what was going on.

And there, in the "less desirable" third-row seat, was Gene Siskel sitting next to supermodel Cindy Crawford.

Whether it was the pressurized oxygen or the jet lag, planes were a source of numerous altercations between the two. In another infamous midair incident, the pair were once again traveling together to an engagement, when Roger complained about the lack of legroom on the plane. A short while later, he received a note from the flight attendant.

"Mr. Ebert," it read. "We in the cockpit heard about your complaints about the MD-80 aircraft and we agree with you. We know you're an important journalist in Chicago; if you will keep our opinions private, the navigator didn't come in today, we have an extra seat up here in the cockpit. Please knock on the door when the seat belt sign is removed and you can fly with us."

Delighted by the compliments and the offer, Ebert waited for the seat belt sign to turn off. As soon as it did, he was out of his cramped chair and headed toward the cockpit. From two rows behind, Siskel watched in horror. *He* had written the note, after getting fed up with his partner's repeated whines about the plane's legroom, then passed it to the flight attendant to pass to Roger. But his deception worked too well—Ebert was about to knock on the cockpit door, which was liable to get him arrested or maybe even shot. Siskel sprinted toward him and grabbed him by the shoulder just as he approached the door.

"Mr. Ebert," Siskel smirked, "we in the cockpit are standing right behind you."

Roger and Gene became such talk-show-circuit staples that they came within days of hosting their own talk show. On February 14, 1990, they appeared as guests on the short-lived *Pat Sajak Show* on CBS. The doomed series had debuted a year before, but was already on its last legs by the winter of 1990. Things had gotten so bad that the show began bringing in guest hosts on Friday nights to spice up the format (and, Sajak later claimed, to audition potential replacements for him).

As usual, Gene and Roger were a big hit on *The Pat Sajak Show*, and the producers wanted them back—not as guests, but as Friday night guest *hosts*. The pair were actually scheduled to host the show twice. Their original March 23 engagement was postponed when the show was preempted for CBS's coverage of the NCAA basketball tournament. They were rescheduled for April 27, and *Siskel & Ebert* even put out a press release announcing the gig, complete with giddy quotes from Gene and Roger. ("If the guests are at a loss for words, we can always talk to each other," quipped Ebert.) But *The Pat Sajak Show* was canceled completely on April 9, and aired its final episode on April 13, two weeks to the day Gene and Roger would have made their late-night hosting debut.

A few years earlier, it would have been absurd to think two film critics from Chicago could host a nationally broadcast talk show. But by the mid-1980s, Siskel and Ebert were stars in their own right—especially in Chicago, where, David Plummer says, "aside from Michael Jordan and Oprah, they were at the top of the celebrity totem pole."

That made for some strange, and even surreal, experiences around the set of *Siskel & Ebert*. One time, Marlon Brando called the production office and asked to speak to Ebert. A staff member thought it was an impersonator making a prank call so he hung up on him. "Marlon Brando actually thought that was pretty funny," says Don DuPree. "Eventually, Brando convinced them it really was him and they put him through. And afterwards, Roger said, 'What an idiot you are! That was Marlon Brando!'"

Siskel and Ebert were full of surprises on these shows. A few minutes after revealing their deepest jealousies of one another on *Later with Bob Costas,* they shifted to debating the relative merits of movie theater candies, with Siskel betting he could guess the flavors of Dots gumdrops in a blind taste test. And that's how that 1992 *Later* episode ended: with one of Bob Costas's ties draped over Siskel's eyes as he correctly named three Dots in a row. When

Costas tried to trick Siskel by sticking two Dots together, Siskel named them both. For his trouble, he got to keep Costas's tie.

In other words, Siskel and Ebert took the movies seriously, but they didn't take themselves seriously, which became another huge reason for their popularity beyond *Sneak Previews*. When *Sesame Street* added a recurring parody of their show, Gene and Roger showed up to teach Telly Monster and Oscar the Grouch their "critic exercises"—which consisted of chanting, "Thumbs up! Thumbs down!" over and over while gesturing accordingly. In typical Gene and Roger fashion, the sketch ended in an argument, after Oscar asked whether it was possible to give a movie thumbs in the middle and Roger claimed it was and Gene insisted it wasn't. (Apparently Oscar didn't get *Siskel & Ebert* in his garbage can; the show never gave out thumbs in the middle votes.)

No one exploited Roger's and Gene's willingness to poke fun at themselves more effectively than David Letterman. In between their more traditional interviews, Letterman employed Siskel and Ebert as sidekicks and all-purpose punch lines. He threw them into a cop show spoof called *Siskel & Ebert on the Edge*. He had them resolve split decisions over movies by shooting free throws. (Gene, the massive Chicago Bulls fan, won that one easily.) And while Siskel and Ebert never made real commercials—even turning down a very lucrative offer to hawk Apple computers, a favorite company of Roger's, because they worried it would ruin their credibility as objective critics—Letterman convinced them to appear in a fake ad for a product called "Big Ass Ham." (Gene really loved the taste.)

Robert Morton says he can't remember Roger or Gene turning down a single comedy bit the show pitched. In fact, he claims, the sillier the idea, the more they would fight over who got to deliver the sketch's best lines.

"If you were to cast a comedy duo for a show," Morton notes, "they would be the perfect guys, regardless of their knowledge of film. They were like Abbott and Costello. Gene had an aloofness about him that Bud Abbott always had. And Roger was Lou Costello. They had that dynamic. I always looked at Roger like the petulant little kid, and Gene was like the snobby adult. They were the perfect regular guests for us. And they were lovely guys. They were part of the family. They were always on our lists for our Christmas and anniversary parties."

As Siskel and Ebert grew closer to the Letterman family, they began getting called in for segments that had nothing to do with movies. In one memorable sketch from 1994, they drove around suburban New Jersey with Letterman and a camera crew knocking on doors, offering to do random household chores like cleaning gutters or reciting the twenty-three helping verbs from memory. (Should you have a test in grammar class coming up, they are: am, is, are, was, were, be, been, do, does, did, have, has, had, shall, should, will, would, can, could, may, might, must, and ought.)

"As odd as it is to have David Letterman show up at your door," Rob Burnett says, laughing, "it's *really* silly to have David with Siskel and Ebert. Like, these guys offer *no* value to you in your home. There wasn't even a thousand movies on TV back then. *Now* that sketch would kind of make sense! As a piece, they could go around and go, 'Hey, we know you all sit down in front of Netflix and you argue for forty-five minutes about what to watch, but we're going to settle this for you.' Now that actually seems like a great idea. At that time, it was just pure silliness."

Letterman, Siskel, and Ebert were something of kindred spirits. Like Roger and Gene, David Letterman was a plainspoken Midwesterner who grew up loving movies and watching Johnny Carson. During a commercial break at one of their *Late Show* appearances, Letterman slipped Siskel a note.

"You guys," it read, "have got the world by the ass."

In *Letterman: The Last Giant of Late Night*, author Jason Zinoman writes that the late-night host's interviews "elevated a segment typically used for promotion dressed up with show business stories into something unpredictable, dramatic, and potentially exciting." That's why Siskel and Ebert were among Letterman's favorite guests; that's exactly what they did every single time they popped in on *Late Night* and the *Late Show*.

"It is electric with him," Siskel said in 1998. "It's like being in that old video game Pong. We sit there, real close quarters, and try to one-up each other."

There's probably no better example of Roger's and Gene's flair for the dramatic than the February 10, 1994, episode of the *Late Show*. After some standard squabbles about their weight and hairlines, Letterman asked about a story he'd heard them previously tell involving their joint interview with actor Jack Lemmon. Gene started to speak, but Roger interrupted. *He* wanted to tell the story—as the butt of the story, Roger argued, he should be the one to tell it. Plus, he protested, Gene always told the story wrong, with too many digressions. Gene still refused to budge.

"Slap him, Roger!" Letterman yelled over the audience's screams of delight.

Roger wanted the audience to decide. Gene tried filibustering and kept repeating the first line of the story: "We're both interviewing Jack Lemmon—"

"You're *not* going to tell that story!" Ebert interjected, even more forcefully. "That's *my* story! I've been telling that story for fifteen years!"

Gene wouldn't quit. He started again: "Three people! Me, Jack Lemmon, and Roger—"

"I don't believe you're going to *do* this!" Roger cried, his voice cracking from the strain of yelling over Gene. "This is *my* story!"

Finally, Letterman had enough. "*I'll* tell the damn story!" he said.

And he did, explaining how Roger and Gene were interviewing Lemmon in a Chicago restaurant, when a woman came up to the table and immediately recognized Gene Siskel. When Siskel pointed out Jack Lemmon was at the table as well, the woman got even *more* excited. Then Gene pointed to Roger and said, "And look, ma'am, who is *also* here."

"Buddy Hackett!" the woman gasped.

The audience burst into applause. "I couldn't have told it better myself," Ebert deadpanned, before adding, "And Gene *certainly* couldn't have."

Ebert later wrote a column in the *Chicago Sun-Times* about the incident, revealing that they had been set up by Letterman's staff. During their respective preinterviews, *Late Show* producers told Gene to tell the Hackett story—and told Roger that Gene wanted to tell the Hackett story, but that he should interrupt him and then tell it instead. "Neither one of us had been prepared to cave in to the other," Ebert wrote. "Given our mutual stubbornness, it was inevitable that we would both insist on pressing ahead."

The result was a remarkable TV moment that only Siskel and Ebert could have produced. Anyone else would have eventually abandoned their position and let the other person talk. Not Roger and Gene. They were both so obstinate that they would rather derail an entire television show than let someone tell a story they believed they were better-equipped to deliver.

In his *Sun-Times* column, Ebert wrote that Siskel was initially embarrassed about their screaming match. But as they were leaving the theater that night, a *Late Show* producer flagged them down.

"That," the producer announced, "was *great* TV."

With Roger and Gene, it always was. Like *Sneak Previews* itself, their talk show interviews brought something that was otherwise missing from early '80s television: reality. Surrounded by phony chumminess, they cut through the bullshit with unflinching honesty. Sometimes they didn't like the movies they were there to talk about. Sometimes the host got on their nerves. Sometimes they couldn't stand each other. And when they couldn't, they said it. They spared no one's feelings. And in a world where everyone makes nice, that was refreshing—even thrilling.

On a September 1999 *Late Show* episode, Letterman told Ebert that's why he loved having Siskel and him on. "When you guys came out here," he explained, "there was always great energy. And I liked to think that I was the third Siskel and Ebert, like the fifth Beatle." Letterman said on multiple occasions on the air that Siskel and Ebert were the reason the set at the Ed Sullivan Theater had two chairs. ("We never had two guests out there together," Robert Morton confirms. "There was no reason to have two chairs on that set. No reason at all. It was Siskel and Ebert, it's that simple.")

Letterman also sensed Siskel and Ebert's mainstream potential before even they did. Way back on their very first appearance on *Late Night* in March of 1982, Letterman asked Roger and Gene whether they might take *Sneak Previews* from PBS to commercial television. Neither man seemed particularly enthused about the prospect. Roger argued that on commercial TV they wouldn't be allowed to review so many documentaries, independent movies, and foreign films. Gene speculated that their debates might not flow as well if they were interrupted by commercials. And he praised *Sneak Previews* for allowing room for what he called "qualified remarks."

"One of the things we try and do," Siskel noted, "is not just the normal film criticism that you get with one person sitting in front of a camera introducing the film clip and saying, 'It stunk!' We try to moderate our opinions.

"So much of criticism," he lamented, "is simply thumbs up and thumbs down."

Roger and Gene might have been outstanding TV personalities, but they were lousy fortune tellers. Six months later, they would leave *Sneak Previews* for syndication, where they would continue to cover just as many documentaries, independent movies, and foreign films as before. And when they did, they would take "thumbs up and thumbs down" criticism to a whole new level.

CHAPTER SIX

TWO THUMBS UP

Wouldn't you love it if Nastassja Kinski came down off the screen and said, "Hi, Gene! Nice to see you. I'm gonna go sit next to Roger over here."

—ROGER EBERT,
REVIEWING *THE PURPLE ROSE OF CAIRO*

She would never say that.

—GENE SISKEL

Siskel and Ebert were creatures of habit. Once they settled into the *Sneak Previews* format, they continued using it with zero major alterations for almost twenty years across three totally distinct productions and a variety of producers and directors. Show staffers say if you wanted to convince them to make even a minor change to their routines, you had to convince them it was their idea in the first place—at which point they *might* sign off on it.

"When a new producer would come on the show, they would say, 'I would like to do it this way. And I want to do a camera shot this way, and I want to do a clip this way,'" says *Sneak Previews'* Ray Solley. "And [Gene and Roger] would go, 'No, no, no, that's not how you do this show.' It became a very comfortable and successful pattern for them. That's what they learned, that's what they had been taught, and they didn't want to deviate from it. Eventually, they sort of got to where they became a professionally married couple."

Part of that professional marriage involved the development of quirky rituals that they repeated week after week. After struggling so mightily with their chemistry and energy levels in the *Opening Soon . . . at a Theater Near You* days, they began starting each taping with the clapping game "Pease Porridge Hot," slapping hands as they chanted:

> *Pease porridge hot!*
> *Pease porridge cold!*
> *Pease porridge in the pot, nine days old!*
> *Some like it hot!*
> *Some like it cold!*
> *Some like it in the pot, nine days old!*

Gene and Roger also shared a secret handshake they performed regularly—but only with each other. They would shake each other's hands with their index fingers extended onto the other person's wrist so they could feel their pulse and ensure the other half of their duo was alive and present.

"That handshake, to me, said a lot," says *Sneak Previews* producer Nancy De Los Santos. "It said, 'I respect you, because we are shaking hands,' but at the same time, Gene said that it meant 'I need you. I need you to be *here.*' And that was from the heart."

Although Gene and Roger's relationship remained prickly and hypercompetitive all through their tenure on *Sneak Previews*, as the 1970s gave way to the 1980s, that handshake took on a more symbolic meaning as they decided to set aside their differences and jump into the unknown together.

By 1981, Gene Siskel and Roger Ebert were "the highest-paid dispensers of film reviews in the world." At least that is how they were billed in a May 6, 1981, article in *Variety* titled "Ebert, Siskel Earning Big Bucks; Draw Trade-Wide Notice as Chicago's Improbable Celebs." While the article claims "down-to-the-dollar figures are difficult to come by," it quotes "knowledgeable sources," who estimate that Siskel's "annual earnings from his newspaper and TV stints alone are in the area of $200,000," while Ebert was making about $180,000. (That's roughly $655,000 and $590,000 in today's dollars, respectively.)

The piece goes on to call them "mini-media conglomerates" and notes growing jealously about their enormous success in the journalism community. An anonymous "respected New York film critic" complained that "neither Siskel nor Ebert seems to have a formidable intellect or a sensitive feeling for film." An unnamed executive at a film production company noted the power the two wielded over Chicago box office; after both hated the infamous 1980 bomb *Heaven's Gate*, the film "wound up doing worse in Chicago than in other big markets."

Ebert and Siskel may have been among the best-paid film critics in the world, but only because of their combination of jobs across print, television, and radio. As the hosts of *Sneak Previews* on WTTW, they weren't getting rich, although the exact specifics of their deals with public television are yet another aspect of the story of *Siskel & Ebert* that varies from telling to telling, and from teller to teller. An article from *Crain's Chicago Business* in 1981 pegged their *Sneak Previews* salaries at "$30,000 or so." Ray Solley never saw their checks, but heard they never made more than several hundred dollars an episode. A 2012 oral history of the show claims they earned $64,000 in 1982.

Whatever they were making, it wasn't much—and certainly not as much as Gene and Roger felt they deserved. "They were very happy there. They weren't looking to expand or to do anything else, as far as I knew," says Roger Ebert's wife, Chaz. "But they did begin to feel that WTTW was kind of taking them for granted. They felt they had started a cottage industry of film reviewing."

They may have had a point. By the early 1980s, *Sneak Previews* was the top-rated weekly half-hour show on PBS, broadcast in around two hundred markets across the country. Their reviews drove ratings on television and helped generate (or diminish) box office in theaters. They were bona fide stars—but at least at WTTW, they weren't being paid like them.

Enter Joe Antelo. In 1982, Antelo was a newly appointed executive at Tribune Entertainment, the syndication arm of the Tribune Company—the same media conglomerate that owned the *Chicago Tribune,* where Gene Siskel worked, as well as Chicago's WGN radio and TV stations. (The stations' call letters were taken from the *Tribune*'s masthead slogan, "The World's Greatest Newspaper.") Antelo worked his way up through the Tribune and WGN's sales divisions in New York, before moving to Chicago to take over the company's burgeoning syndication operation.

The early 1980s was a time of turmoil at Tribune Entertainment, with a lot of staff upheaval and a new president. The only successful syndicated hit the company had to speak of was the *U.S. Farm Report,* which was, well, a televised farm report.

Wanting to establish himself in his new position (and protect his job amid all the turnover), Antelo actively looked for new properties he could produce and syndicate. Antelo and his girlfriend

(and future wife), Liza, were voracious cinephiles, sometimes going to three movies in a single day. And both enjoyed watching
Sneak Previews on WTTW.

More important to Joe, his sister loved *Sneak Previews*—but
she *never* went to the movies. Still, she tuned in every week, and
then would discuss what she heard Roger and Gene discuss in her
phone calls with Joe. If people who didn't even care about movies
liked to watch *Sneak Previews*, Antelo figured, it was bound to be
an even bigger hit in syndication than it was on public television.

"I would watch it and say, 'What is this show doing on PBS?'"
Antelo recalled in 1998. "Movies are a mass-market item. This
show should be syndicated, and it should be on commercial television."

Not long after that epiphany, Joe and Liza traveled to Los Angeles. They were sitting in the airport waiting for a flight when
who should walk by but Roger Ebert.

"Hey, there's Roger!" Liza said to Joe. "You talked about doing
that show—did you ever get in touch with him?"

"No, I didn't," Joe replied. "I've got to do that as soon as we get
home."

Antelo didn't approach Ebert in the airport, but he *did* make a
call to Roger and Gene's agent, Don Ephraim. (Importantly—and
unusually for television stars on the same show—they shared the
same lawyer.)

A few days after their return to Chicago, Joe came home from
the office giddily excited.

"Their contract is up at PBS!" he said.

Antelo's timing was fortuitous, and not just because Roger and
Gene's deal with WTTW was set to expire. Part of the issue with
Channel 11, they later claimed, stemmed from the fact that WTTW
wanted to commercially syndicate *Sneak Previews*. The money the

show earned in syndication would then help fund the entire station.

"This is a very important point," Ebert said in 1996. "We didn't leave PBS to go on to syndication spontaneously. The PBS station in Chicago wanted to syndicate us." But—at least according to Gene and Roger—the station refused to cut them in on the syndication deal. Ebert described their attitude during negotiations—or the lack thereof—as "We're the arbiters of this thing, and you guys are just the hired hands."

"You know I *pledge* Channel 11, and I even got my *John Williams Conducts the Boston Pops* in the mail," Ebert said in another article from 1982. "But I don't want to donate my career for the next four years as a pledge to public television." Ebert and Siskel brought WTTW's offer to Ephraim, who told them that what they were being offered from PBS was 2 percent of what they should be paid.

WTTW's Bill McCarter, presented in 1983 with the claims of a *Sneak Previews* syndication deal that cut Roger and Gene out of any financial windfall, said, "I'm just kind of amazed at all of this. . . . I'm surprised at the hostility. I think this is an attempt to elicit an argument where there is none."

"I don't think Bill McCarter ever wanted to be in a situation where somebody beat him to the next big idea," says Ray Solley, who confirms that there were indeed people at WTTW who were "hired and tasked to figure out a way to monetize our programming"—not just *Sneak Previews*, but all kinds of WTTW shows. Solley says the attitude at WTTW at the time, rightly or wrongly, was "We know how to make TV shows and we know how to produce. That's what we do. We have a huge and wonderful creative team that is delivering on all levels. You are an incredible part of this—but you are a *part* of it. You are not it."

Having been handed a take-it-or-leave-it contract offer from WTTW, Gene and Roger decided to leave it. Ephraim began discussing a deal for a new show with Antelo, a process Liza Antelo says was "exhausting." Tribune's first offer to both hosts was $87,500 each, a fairly significant raise from even the most generous estimates of their *Sneak Previews* salaries.

Ephraim's reaction to the contract: "You're going to have to sharpen your pencil."

To sweeten the deal, Antelo offered the pair something they'd never get from WTTW: a percentage of the show's profits. That decision, says Liza Antelo, landed him in trouble with his boss, who stormed into his office upon learning of his plan and screamed, "You're paying them too much!" To which Antelo replied, "Oh, really? And how much money are *we* making?"

The answer was obvious: a lot more. While Gene and Roger would receive a significant portion of the new show's proceeds if it proved successful, the rest of the series' costs were minimal. Siskel and Ebert comprised the show's entire cast *and* the entire writing staff. Build a set, hire a few crew members, produce it out of WGN, where Tribune already had its own studios, and you had a ready-made and relatively inexpensive syndicated television series.

As negotiations continued, Ephraim put in a call to *Sneak Previews* producer Nancy De Los Santos.

"Roger and Gene want to have lunch with you. Are you available?" he asked.

De Los Santos assumed they just wanted to talk about some aspect of *Sneak Previews*. She said yes, and then showed up to a Chicago restaurant, where she found Gene and Roger—but no Ephraim. De Los Santos hadn't even ordered her food when the two men dropped a bombshell on her.

"We're leaving," Gene announced.

"What do you mean you're leaving?" De Los Santos replied.

"We're leaving. We're going into syndication."

"Really? With commercials? How are you going to do the show with commercials?"

"Well, we're going to work it out," Roger replied. "We have a good executive producer, and we want *you* to be the producer."

De Los Santos was so stunned she never got around to ordering lunch. But after going home and discussing it with her boyfriend, she called Roger that night with her answer: "Let's do this."

"It was that simple," says De Los Santos. "But it was a complete and total surprise. And then of course, the rumor mill started going at WTTW, because the very next day, they called Thea."

Actually, Flaum says, they asked *her* to produce their syndicated show first, adding, "They wanted me to come with them. Don Ephraim was a killer negotiator. And commercial television made them an offer that Channel 11 couldn't match. It was basically an offer they *couldn't* refuse. And they *shouldn't* have refused it. And for years, Gene would say to me, 'Aren't you sorry you didn't come?' And it would've meant a lot of money. But, man, I would have been tied to that show. Think of all the shows I later made that I never would have gotten to make. So, no, it definitely wouldn't have been worth it."

Roger and Gene had kept quiet all through their negotiations with Tribune. When the deal was finally done, they went to WTTW and announced their imminent departures. Suddenly, Ebert said, the station wanted to negotiate. But it was too late. Siskel and Ebert were leaving *Sneak Previews* to launch their own show.

When the news broke that Siskel and Ebert were ditching the respectable confines of public television for the Wild West of syndication, some—including at least a few colleagues from their old home at WTTW—felt they had sold out. While the move did ultimately make Gene and Roger wealthy men, they always maintained that the decision to leave *Sneak Previews* was an enormously risky one that could have backfired. At PBS, they were part of an established hit. In syndication, they would have to prove themselves all over again.

"At the time, we were both terrified about the move," Siskel said a few months after the launch of their Tribune series. "We thought we could run indefinitely on PBS, but we might be off the air in three months in syndication. Of course, we were burning our bridges when we went to Tribune. Channel 11 would be angry with us. We felt if we had to put our tails between our legs and go back to PBS, maybe we could get a station in Milwaukee or Madison to take us."

De Los Santos had her own concerns—primarily about how the show would work outside the protection of PBS. At WTTW, *Sneak Previews* had no sponsors to consider or please. At Tribune, the show would air with commercials—which would not only shorten the show by about six minutes every week, but also had the potential to impact the content of the series . . . if Gene and Roger let it.

"You always hear these horrible stories about how people change because sponsors say this or that, and you have to do it. We never had any of that," says De Los Santos. "Roger and Gene demanded the quality of the show to remain the same high standard. They wanted it to be true; they wanted it to be journalistically committed, and they also wanted it to be entertaining—and what is more entertaining than two people having a heated discussion about a movie?"

Despite De Los Santos's misgivings, the show might have actually worked *better* with commercials. In the *Sneak Previews* days, Gene and Roger would have to wrap up one conversation and then immediately dive into the next. Since their crosstalks were largely unscripted, they had to find those segues on the fly, a process that sometimes led to awkward and jarring juxtapositions. In syndication, when a discussion began to wind down they could just throw to a commercial. Freed from the pressure of having to gracefully move from one review to another, and settling into their roles as TV hosts after half a decade together, their Tribune show became a little looser, a little lighter, and a little more fun than *Sneak Previews*. It really did feel like you were hanging out with a couple of guys who loved to shoot the breeze during a trip to the movies.

Still, the revenue generated from those commercials didn't mean De Los Santos had an unlimited budget to spend on the series. In fact, the show's bottom line mattered more than ever before, and it showed on-screen. The high production standards (and endless retakes) at PBS that sometimes irked Gene and Roger ensured *Sneak Previews* always looked fantastic. There were no such safeguards in place at Tribune.

"You never saw anything on PBS that didn't look good. I was always looking for more money for the show at Tribune," recalls De Los Santos. "I was always struggling with the lighting people, because their idea, and the whole syndication world's idea, is: the less money spent on production, the more profit. And I would say, 'No! Put more money into production so your show looks good. You'll get more profit, because people can tell; the audience can tell.' When something looks shabby, you just go, 'Oh God, I don't want to watch that.'" Eventually, De Los Santos's request for a bigger budget earned her a visit from Tribune's head of sales. "Nancy, you just need to understand," he told her, "the commercial is the jewel, and the show is the setting."

When it premiered in the fall of 1982, the setting was officially named *At the Movies with Gene Siskel and Roger Ebert*. That title, as you can likely imagine, given Gene and Roger's competitive relationship, was the subject of intense debate.

Through the years, the most common story Gene and Roger gave about why it became *At the Movies with Gene Siskel and Roger Ebert* rather than the other way around involved their go-to resolver of all show disputes: the flip of the coin. But Nancy De Los Santos, who was in the room when the new show's title was chosen, says that, while most friction was hashed out with a coin flip, the new name became the topic of a "long discussion" between herself, Roger, and Gene, who was adamant that *Ebert and Siskel* did not work.

"But it's alphabetical!" Roger countered.

"It doesn't have the same zing. You've got to hear it, Roger. Believe me," Gene replied. "This is not me saying it because I want to be first. Just listen. *Ebert and Siskel*? It doesn't feel right. It doesn't sound right."

"And he was right," says De Los Santos. "*Siskel and Ebert* just sounds better. It sounds more like the dance team that they were. It was 'Fred and Ginger,' not 'Ginger and Fred.' 'Ginger and Fred' just doesn't have the same ring. And I don't think it's because it's now in our collective unconscious. *Siskel and Ebert* just sounds better."

Whether Gene managed to get top billing through persuasiveness or luck, Roger did agree to the order—on one condition that, to his chagrin, was never lived up to. Their contract at Tribune ran for four years. Ebert would play second fiddle in the title if, after two years, *At the Movies with Gene Siskel and Roger Ebert* became *At the Movies with Roger Ebert and Gene Siskel*. Gene signed off on that idea initially, but when the crew went out to the Pickwick Theatre in Park Ridge, Illinois, to shoot *At the Movies*' opening title sequence, they only filmed the marquee one way: *with Gene Siskel and Roger Ebert.* Two years later, it was determined it wasn't worth the expense of going back to the Pickwick to redo the titles. And that was that.

Ebert remained perturbed about the title for the rest of his days. In one 1998 interview, when Siskel insisted it wasn't his decision to keep the *with Gene Siskel and Roger Ebert* billing, Ebert accused him of purposefully refusing to fight for another opening-credits shoot because that meant he'd get to keep the billing order that kept him first. "Believe me," Ebert said, "if it had been *Ebert & Siskel* for the first two years; I promise you we would have reprinted the station airing to *Siskel & Ebert* for the next two years. I can guarantee you that!" (For once, Siskel did not disagree with his cohost.)

While Gene and Roger were at the movies, WTTW was at their lawyers. *At the Movies* had a different title, but it was largely the same show as *Sneak Previews*: the same basic format, the same mix of film clips and discussion, the same structure of individual reviews followed by crosstalk, even a variation of the same set that looked like a theater balcony. Ray Solley says the issue never went to court or yielded a lawsuit only because "two people on camera talking about something is not copyrightable."

Certain specific aspects of *Sneak Previews* were deemed to be WTTW's intellectual property, though. That meant Gene and Roger had to say goodbye to their rotating cast of dog sidekicks, along with the "Dog of the Week" segment. They wanted to continue covering bad movies on the new show, but struggled to find a suitable replacement—until Joe Antelo came into their office.

"Fellas, I have a terrific idea!" he announced. "Bring in Aroma!"

An animal trainer entered the room with Aroma the Educated Skunk—as in an actual, living, hopefully well-trained skunk.

"Instead of 'Dog of the Week,'" Antelo continued, "now we're gonna pick the 'Stinker of the Week.'"

Gene and Roger would try to incorporate Aroma into the show by petting him or feeding him nuts. (The skunk had been de-scented, so they were in no danger of getting sprayed.) But as animal sidekicks go, Aroma was a bit of a stinker himself. As you might have gathered from the pungent odors they give off when-ever someone comes near them, skunks are not social animals like dogs. When Aroma would arrive for his segment, he would imme-diately spin around in the Balcony and bury his face in the corner of his seat, away from the camera.

"This is when we knew that we couldn't take ourselves too ser-iously, because you didn't want to have the camera aimed at the back end of a skunk. It just didn't work. It wasn't telegenic," Siskel once recalled. "So we heard the director, Bob Varecha, over the transom at WGN say before each 'Stinker' segment began: 'Spin the skunk!'"

That was the animal trainer's cue. He'd leap up from his hiding spot in between the rows of seats in the Balcony, spin Aroma around so his face was visible on camera, then dart back down be-hind the chairs, while Gene and Roger would spit out their intro-duction as fast as possible, in the hopes of introducing Aroma before he could wedge his face back down into the seat cushion. Even then, Aroma could barely feign interest in the proceedings; during Roger and Gene's discussion of the worst Oscar nominations of 1984, Aroma yawned on camera during his big close-up.

After a year or so of trying to educate Aroma in the ways of television, *At the Movies* gave up and sent him packing. But Joe Antelo wasn't ready to abandon the "Stinker of the Week" segment yet. He called another meeting.

"Boys, I've got a fabulous idea!" he announced. "This is going to be so much better than the skunk! You're not going to believe it. We're going to do the 'Turkey of the Week'!"

"With a turkey?" Ebert asked.

"Even better!" Antelo replied. "A turkey *vulture!*"

Sharing a studio with a bird of prey was finally where Roger and Gene drew the line. The Dogs and Stinkers of the Week were gradually phased out completely, a decision Ebert later said became inevitable once they realized such "immaturities" were taking time away from movies that were "worthy of discussion."

Some weeks, Aroma's replacement was a new segment called "X-Ray," where Gene and Roger would examine a topic making headlines in the movie world. On a 1984 *At the Movies*, the hosts debated the newly proposed PG-13 rating, which Gene warned would have little impact on twelve-year-olds trying to go see *Indiana Jones and the Temple of Doom*. He instead advised that the rating should be advisory but not compulsory—which is exactly what the Motion Picture Association of America did when they officially introduced the PG-13 rating that July.

The *At the Movies* era also saw Gene and Roger looking beyond theaters for the first time to a new venue that was becoming increasingly important to the film world in the early 1980s: the video store. While the steady expansion of the home video market in the late 1970s went mostly undiscussed on *Sneak Previews*, the impact of VHS tapes on film culture became too big to ignore by the time Roger and Gene jumped to syndication. By 1984, nearly 10 million American families owned a VCR, and 25 percent of many movies' total revenue came from sales of videotapes. So starting in 1983, *At the Movies* occasionally abandoned its typical format of reviews of new theatrical releases to instead discuss the top ten best-selling videotapes.

These episodes offer a fascinating time capsule of a movie industry in flux. In the first of these "Top 10 Cassettes" episodes, both Roger and Gene revealed they didn't even own videocassette players, saying they still preferred to see movies in a movie theater—a comment that *At the Movies* sponsor (and VCR manufacturer) RCA must have loved hearing. A little under a year later, when *At the Movies* did a new "Top 10 Cassettes" episode in August 1984, both men admitted they now owned VCRs, although Gene insisted that he only rented tapes occasionally.

These episodes anticipated decades of debate about the financial and creative impact of home video on cinema as a whole. While Gene and Roger, like most of Hollywood, were initially wary of VHS leeching interest and grosses away from movie theaters, they soon observed that the opposite was happening. Video stores were fueling renewed interest in all kinds of movies, both new and old, and they were allowing people in suburbs and rural areas who didn't have access to art house theaters to discover foreign and independent films that were previously impossible to see. With that, Roger and Gene became ardent supporters of home video—with a few important caveats that will sound very familiar to cinephiles who follow modern debates about whether the convenience of home viewing represents a threat to the theatrical experience.

"We don't want to see the small screen become the primary viewing vehicle for pictures," Siskel said on one of these "Top 10 Cassettes" episodes. "It has to be the big screen, because if people start to say, 'I'll wait [to see it] at home,' then you'll never see *The Right Stuff* made. They'll never make a big-screen epic. They'll make these intense personal dramas which don't suffer as much, like *Terms of Endearment*, when you see them on a small screen. And that would be a disaster for the movie business. It wouldn't be the movies. It would be TV."

Because some of the best-selling tapes at the time were music video compilations, these shows also gave Gene and Roger the chance to review music videos right as MTV became an enormous force in popular culture. Although their opinions of music videos were often dismissive—they *both* gave negative reviews to Michael Jackson's *Thriller*—some of their remarks on the impact of music videos on popular culture were amazingly prescient.

Reviewing a tape of Duran Duran videos, Siskel predicted that their "high-energy films for a high-energy young audience" were "going to influence the way movies are made in the future, with faster cuts and a lot more happening on-screen." Their forecasts about videos' wider ramifications turned out to be absolutely correct.

Joe Antelo's forecasts about Gene and Roger's potential in syndication were correct as well. When the Tribune show launched in the fall of 1982, they hoped to get seventy stations to sign on in the first year. Instead, Antelo signed up that many in three months. By January of 1983, the show was up to 150 stations; by 1985, *At the Movies* had 11 million weekly viewers in 147 markets. (The number one ranked show on all of prime-time broadcast television in the summer of 2022, *America's Got Talent*, drew around 6 million weekly viewers.) Antelo later estimated that Siskel and Ebert each made $500,000 from their first year working on *At the Movies*. If there was any dispute who was the highest-paid dispensers of film reviews in the world before, there wasn't anymore.

Back at WTTW, *Sneak Previews* continued on without its now-extremely-well-paid former hosts. After an extensive casting process that involved hundreds of applicants from around the country (including a young journalism student from Illinois State University named Richard Roeper), the show replaced Siskel and Ebert with two New Yorkers: radio host and television film critic Jeffrey Lyons and critic Neal Gabler.

If Roger and Gene could be competitive with each other, they could be downright ruthless when it came to their *Sneak Previews* successors. About a year into their run at Tribune Entertainment, they gave a dismissive assessment of their old show in an interview with the *Washington Post*'s Tom Shales. Marveling at the fact that the new hosts of the Chicago-based *Sneak Previews* were now flown to the Windy City from New York every week, Ebert said, "There must have been people outside New York who could do that show well."

To which Siskel witheringly replied, "There might have been two people inside New York who could have done that show well, too." Gene and Roger weren't TV critics, but they made an exception in this case.

"Here's what I honestly think," Siskel added. "I don't find them interesting as individuals or as a couple. I find us mildly interesting as individuals and more than mildly interesting as a couple. And I believe that, I'm not embarrassed to say it, and I don't care what happens to me if I do say it."

Nothing happened, because audiences tended to agree with Gene's assessment. When *At the Movies* began airing in the fall of 1982, the two shows were programmed a half hour apart in Chicago on Saturday nights—with *At the Movies* drawing roughly three times as many viewers as *Sneak Previews*.

Because *Sneak Previews* continued on, albeit in less popular form, with the same "yes" or "no" ratings system for movies, Roger, Gene, and Nancy De Los Santos needed a different way to sum up *At the Movies*' reviews. Debating their options, Roger threw out an idea that Gene had offhandedly insulted just a few months before they left WTTW for syndication during their first *Late Night with David Letterman* appearance: "thumbs up" for good movies, "thumbs down" for bad ones.

"I would credit Roger with the thumbs," says De Los Santos, before adding with a laugh, "I would *never* say that in front of Gene. It wasn't Roger walking in the door and saying, 'I've got the idea! Let's use thumbs!' But I do think it first came out of Roger's mouth."

That's certainly the story Ebert told through the years—and one that even Siskel was hesitant to dispute. (Asked by *20/20* where the thumbs came from just six years after their introduction, Gene shrugged. "Boy, I don't remember.") When the subject came up, Siskel would sometimes try to claim credit for suggesting the popular variation "Two thumbs *way* up!"

Hand gestures involving thumbs date back at least to the days of ancient Rome, where—at least according to modern movies set in those days—thumbs up meant a gladiator would live, while a thumbs down from the emperor meant off with their heads. In fact, most historians believe thumbs up was the cue to kill a gladiator, while sparing a fighter involved no thumb raised up or down, but rather a thumb wrapped around the side of a clenched fist. But "Two clenched fists with a thumb wrapped around it!" doesn't have quite the same ring on television or in a newspaper ad—while "Two thumbs up!" quickly became a valuable commodity for marketers looking to sell potential customers on a movie's quality.

The use of "Two thumbs up!" in movie ads became a flash point among some in the film criticism community, who saw it as indicative of a trend toward the dumbing down of movie talk. When asked to defend his most famous creation, Ebert offered a simple rationale: "At least they can't misquote that." Siskel provided a cannier argument in favor of the thumbs. He noted that every single one of those "Two thumbs up!" quotes in commercials were as much advertisements for *At the Movies* as they were for whatever film they were actually being used to promote.

He was right. The thumbs weren't just *At the Movies*' rating system; it was a key part of Gene and Roger's brand—especially after the thumbs became so famous that Siskel and Ebert decided to trademark the phrase "Two thumbs up!" so that only they could use it, per the US Patent and Trademark Office, on "television programs and appearances in the field of motion picture critiques." (To this day, Siskel's and Ebert's estates still hold the trademark—so while "Two thumbs up!" might feel like the most appropriate way to review a tome on the history of *Siskel & Ebert*, kindly refrain from any such legally dubious outbursts.)

The thumbs became an intrinsic part of Gene's and Roger's personas, which were quickly taking on larger-than-life dimensions as *At the Movies*' ratings grew and the show spread to every corner of the country. Its hosts were no longer viewed as two reporters from Chicago who moonlighted on a television show. To the public, they were big TV stars in their own right. Not long after *At the Movies* debuted in syndication, Gene ran up to Joe Antelo at WGN.

"Joe!" Gene said. "I can't even walk down the street anymore without people bothering me!"

Roger, according to Chaz Ebert, had a slightly different reaction to his budding celebrity.

"Roger didn't think he was famous. He compartmentalized that. He would say things like, 'Elizabeth Taylor is famous. Paul Newman is famous. *That's* famous.' He'd say, 'Yeah, I've achieved some degree of fame,' or 'I'm well-paid, people know my work.' And he felt that if he could use his notoriety for anything, that was good—if there was some social justice issue he could weigh in on or support. He didn't think of himself as famous, but if you are going to be known, at least do something with it to help other people."

Roger may not have liked to acknowledge it, but he and Gene were quickly becoming *very* famous—famous enough, in fact, to get their own branded pizza at a local Chicago chain called Father & Son. While attending a lunch interview with *Vanity Fair*, the two raved about the "little edge pieces" of the pie—and were struck by an idea.

"How about this? Come up with a pizza that's all outer edges!" said Siskel.

"A doughnut pizza!" Ebert replied. "A doughnut-shaped pizza with nothing in the middle! Each piece has two edges!"

The kitchen quickly mocked up a prototype, which Ebert and Siskel adored. ("This moment could be as important as the day at Procter & Gamble when the Ivory soap floated," Ebert declared.) After debating a few titles—the Roger and Gene Pizza? The Gene and Roger Pizza? (Whose turn was it to go first, again?)—they settled on "the Double-Edged Pizza Ring," which actually became a menu item at the restaurant for a while.

Siskel loved pizza, even when it wasn't shaped like a doughnut, says Marlene Iglitzen, who laments that the pizza ring was "a brilliant idea that died the death of unrisen dough." Ebert himself admitted "it never caught on" in a 1995 column about Pizza Hut's stuffed-crust pizza, which he described as "exactly the wrong approach" to pizza innovation. (Almost thirty years later, "the wrong approach" is still a menu item at Pizza Huts around the world.)

Gene's and Roger's instincts about pizza may not have been as sharp as they were about movies—Who wants a pizza with *more* crust? Isn't that the part most people *don't* eat?—but the questionable foodstuff they created together made a perfect symbol of their relationship during the Tribune era. More and more, these guys who became famous as rivals were starting to look and work like a team. How that would affect their show's signature element— the cutthroat arguments—remained to be seen.

CHAPTER SEVEN

ACROSS THE AISLE

. . . .

I don't agree with you in
a single criticism of this film!

—GENE SISKEL

Well then, that makes it mutual.

—ROGER EBERT

. . . .

W*e've got to preserve this show!"*
In the history of *Siskel & Ebert,* Gene Siskel only said
that once, in February of 1990. At first glance, the episode that he
felt deserved to be saved for posterity did not seem particularly
extraordinary. The movies up for debate certainly weren't; of the
five, the only one that it is even slightly remembered some thirty
years later is *Cinema Paradiso,* the warm Italian drama that won
that year's Academy Award for Best Foreign Language Film.

The part of the show Gene wanted to preserve was not their
two-thumbs-up rave for *Cinema Paradiso.* It was their reviews of
two similar dramas to which the hosts had wildly different
responses. The first was *Stella,* an adaptation of the novel *Stella
Dallas,* which had previously been turned into a popular 1930s
melodrama starring Barbara Stanwyck. In the updated version,

Bette Midler played a single mother who stops at nothing to ensure her daughter's happiness. Roger called the new version "a great tearjerker with a big heart" with "a quality a lot of more sophisticated films lack, which is that it makes us really care about the characters." Then he quoted film historian Leslie Halliwell, who said of Stanwyck's *Stella Dallas,* "Audiences came to sneer and stayed to weep" and predicted the same might happen again with *Stella.*

Gene didn't see it that way. "I came to weep and sneered!" he replied, before adding, "We have a *wildly* big difference of opinion on this picture. I was really unhappy watching all of this. I was almost embarrassed for the people in the picture!"

After Gene ran down his list of complaints about *Stella*—primarily he didn't buy the modern actors in the film's flimsy period setting—Ebert tried to appeal to his cohost's emotional side.

"I never review the audience," Ebert said, before breaking his own rule. When he saw *Stella* at a local sneak preview in Chicago, "everybody in the theater was blowing their noses, honking."

"Well," Siskel shot back, "there's a lot of flu going around."

After a brief détente during a mutually negative review of the now-forgotten buddy comedy *Heart Condition,* tensions flared again a few minutes later when Gene and Roger turned their attention to a melodrama called *Men Don't Leave.* Like *Stella, Men Don't Leave* is a film about a down-on-her-luck single mother (this one played by Jessica Lange) who must weigh seeking her own happiness against what is best for her children. But unlike *Stella,* Roger hated *Men Don't Leave.* He accused it of lacking the courage to acknowledge that it was a manipulative tearjerker, and he said its mess of a screenplay was "cluttered up with the debris of unnecessary realism" and an unconvincing happy ending.

"I doubt if a fourth grader could ride his bicycle and hop a freight train out of Baltimore and wind up in a small town a two-hour drive away! I doubt that hot-air balloon rides are an instant cure for manic depression!" Ebert noted as he ran down some of his qualms with the movie's awkward plot.

Roger's dismissive pan of *Men Don't Leave* prompted Gene to suggest that this random episode of *Siskel & Ebert* needed to be preserved, "if only to say that I declare that *this* is the good, really fine movie, and that *Stella* is worthless."

"You're joking!" replied Ebert, looking genuinely stunned.

"That is exactly the way I saw these two pictures," said Gene. "People always want to know about our relationship? Look at these two pictures and see what you think."

Gene was correct. Maybe not about *Men Don't Leave*, which does indeed posit that a well-timed hot-air balloon ride can pull someone out of near-suicidal depression, but certainly about how these two back-to-back reviews succinctly encapsulated not only the differences in the two hosts' tastes and approaches to film criticism, but the very appeal of their show: the way Roger and Gene could turn *anything* into a passionate, heated, fascinating, and exciting debate—including the most frivolous or forgettable of movies, and even their lives together away from the cameras.

"A lot of times the press would say, 'They don't like each other,' and I'd go, 'That's not true,'" says Mary Kellogg, the former senior vice president at Buena Vista Television who oversaw *Siskel & Ebert* all through the series' tenure there. "They respected each other. Did they fight? Like cats and dogs! The first show I ever taped with them took ten hours for a half-hour show."

Those who knew them agree: the antagonism that fueled so much interest in the show was never an act. Robert Feder, the former *Chicago Sun-Times* media columnist and a friend of both Roger and Gene, says, "There was very little difference on camera and off, which you can't say about most TV people. Most people on TV become big phonies. These guys were totally the same. Nothing changed. Which could be wonderful, and it could be infuriating. But none of it was manufactured. None of it was for optics."

They might not have hated each other—at least not by the late 1980s—but they often projected the sense that they hated each other's *opinions*, or at least hated the notion that their own deeply held beliefs were being questioned on their own television series. As one staff member put it, "Each one of them thought it should be *their* show, and that the other guy shouldn't be there. And both of them were, every episode, basically trying to get the other guy off-stage."

Remember: There was a Roger Ebert and a Gene Siskel long before there was a *Siskel & Ebert*. And while they became even more successful together, they were both doing quite well on their own in the world of film criticism—which, until their television show came along, was an endeavor performed entirely alone.

In the days before *Sneak Previews*, a critic may have received feedback from readers or viewers. In rare instances, their work may have even sparked responses from peers, as when Andrew Sarris's 1962 essay "Notes on the Auteur Theory" (about the importance of considering directors as the singular creators of Holly-wood movies) prompted Pauline Kael's 1963 polemic "Circles and Squares," which strongly rejected Sarris's model for evaluating motion pictures—and even the phrases he chose to describe that model. ("Sarris believes that what makes an *auteur* is 'an élan of the soul,'" Kael lamented. "This critical language is barbarous. Where else should élan come from? It's like saying 'a digestion of the stomach.' A film critic need not be a theoretician, but it is necessary that he know how to use words.")

But those were exceptions. Siskel and Ebert each believed it

Roger Ebert (center) and Russ Meyer (far right) presenting a screening of
Beyond the Valley of the Dolls at Yale University in 1970.

Ebert at his desk, surrounded by a poster for *The Third Man*, a *Casablanca*
pillow, and several Mickey Mouse statuettes.

Gene Siskel, hailing a cab on Michigan Avenue.

Siskel at his desk, surrounded by issues of *American Film* magazine and a book on William Holden.

A Michael Loewenstein illustration for the *Sneak Previews* Balcony, dated November 11, 1975.

Another of Loewenstein's Balcony concepts.

The original shooting schedule for the *Opening Soon . . . at a Theater Near You* pilot.

"OPENING FRIDAY. . ."

Production Schedule

11-17 Monday

Dry run with talent
(24" riser, 2 chairs in studio-no FAX)

2:00-4:00 pm   VTR OPEN - 2 hours FAX time
3 cameras, 1 VTR (with editec), audio, switcher, 1 B&W film chain,
1 floor director, 1 asst. floor director, 1 TR video-tape

10:30a-12:30p   FILM TO TAPE TRANSFER-PREPARE ROLL-IN REEL - 2 hours FAX time
2 VTRs, 1 film chain color, count-down beeper, audio, switcher,
1-20 min reel video-tape

11-19 WEDNESDAY

Set-up & lite in studio
2:00 pm 1 color studio camera (not set-up) for set check,
switcher & chroma-key for set & lighting check

11-20 THURSDAY   **PRODUCTION DAY**   preproduction meeting @ 11:00a

FAX REQUIREMENTS   PRODUCTION SCHEDULE

4 cameras (cam # 2 on crane),   AM   Complete lite
(cam # 4 set-up in dark area   12:30p Make-up Talent
with Sony monitor)   1:00p FAX
1:00- Rehearse
2 VTRs (1 with editec)   2:30
1 colour film chain   2:30- Brk
1 B&W film chain   2:45
Audio   2:45- Touch-up
Switcher   3:00
1 Sony Trinitron Monitor (for Cam # 4)   3:00- Video-tape
(connected to Effects # 1 on G.V.)   4:30
1 Carosel projector with screen   4:30- Strike
(near ix Sony monitor & cam # 4)   5:00p
1 floor director
1 asst floor director
1 lighting director (& gaffers if necessary)
1 - ½ reel video-tape

11-23 SUNDAY

POSSIBLE POST-PRODUCTION (only if necessary) - 4 hours FAX time
2 VTRs (1 with editec), switcher, audio,
1- ½ hour video-tape

ABOVE: Producer Thea Flaum (center) with Gene Siskel and Roger Ebert on the set of *Opening Soon . . . at a Theater Near You* in 1976.

RIGHT: The show's entire original cast: Gene Siskel, Roger Ebert, and Spot the Wonder Dog.

As Gene and Roger prep for a taping of *At the Movies*, producer Nancy De Los Santos (center) kneels out of view of the cameras.

Gene's frustrations bubble over.

ABOVE: Although Roger and Gene were placed at opposite ends of the screening room for this photo shoot, Roger's preferred seat was an outside aisle twice as far back from the screen as the screen was wide.

RIGHT: By the mid-1980s, Gene and Roger were rarely photographed without their trademark thumbs.

A Michael Loewenstein and Mary Margaret Bartley design for the *Siskel & Ebert & the Movies* Balcony, which added the illusion of a third balcony to the set.

Roger and Gene dining at the Disney–MGM Studios theme park's replica of the Hollywood Brown Derby. After the move to Disney, *Siskel & Ebert* regularly taped special episodes at the resort.

Gene and Roger promote *Siskel & Ebert* at the 1994 NATPE conference alongside fellow Buena Vista stars Regis Philbin and Kathie Lee Gifford.

Roger Ebert receives his star on the Hollywood Walk of Fame in 2005.

Today, a plaque for Roger Ebert adorns the sidewalk outside the Chicago Theatre, while just across the street stands the Gene Siskel Film Center, one of Chicago's finest arthouse cinemas.

should be their show because they'd never had to share anything in their critical careers before. The readers of the *Tribune* and *Sun-Times* came for *their* opinions. *Siskel & Ebert* turned an art form that had previously only existed as a series of monologues into an ongoing dialogue.

Unlike all of Roger's and Gene's carefully considered print reviews in their respective newspapers, that dialogue emerged spontaneously. *Siskel & Ebert* debates were never rehearsed or scripted. The goal, whenever possible, was to capture their honest and sometimes surprised reactions to the other's reviews. (By their own admission, they periodically got so excited by a movie they couldn't contain their opinions until showtime. That happened in 1997, when Siskel leaped out of his seat immediately after the conclusion of *The Full Monty* press screening, raced over to Ebert, and yelled, "Perfect!")

You can see Roger's or Gene's genuine shock in many of their best debates, when they not only don't agree about the film but clearly hadn't even considered the possibility that the other might not agree. In 1993, Ebert gave a mildly positive review to *Cop and a Half*, a buddy-cop picture with Burt Reynolds as a gruff policeman who gets partnered with an eight-year-old who witnessed a murder. Ebert said the film, while not a masterpiece, was "not dumb and not boring, either," and he confessed, "somewhat, to my surprise, I liked it."

"Wow!" replied an incredulous Siskel. "Where's your big red suit and beard, Santa? You just gave them a gift!"

Not long after *Siskel & Ebert*'s review of *Cop and a Half* aired, a package arrived at the show's offices. It contained a signed photo of Norman D. Golden II, the little boy who had costarred with Reynolds in the movie, and who Ebert had praised as "a natural actor."

"Dear Mr. Ebert," the inscription on the photo read, "thank you for liking my film and giving it a thumbs up."

The photo quickly made its way onto the *Siskel & Ebert* office's Wall of Fame, a billboard filled with correspondence from notable movie stars and filmmakers. (The wall also included a slightly less positive letter from Marisa Tomei, advising the hosts how to correctly pronounce her last name.) A few days later, Roger glanced at the Wall of Fame as he passed and noticed the photo and the heartfelt inscription to him.

"Norman D. Golden just sent me this picture, and he thanked me for liking his film. See? That's a nice young man!" Ebert announced to the office.

Gene emerged from a nearby conference room where a production meeting was underway, laughing hysterically.

"What's so funny?" Roger asked.

"Doesn't that signature look familiar to you?" Gene answered.

Roger inspected the signature carefully.

"*I signed the picture!*" Gene declared.

Gene had a habit of messing with Roger's fan mail. During a review of the 1982 horror film *The Sender,* Roger enthusiastically compared the film's star, Kathryn Harrold, to Ingrid Bergman. Appalled by the comparison, Gene replied, "Roger, just ask her out for a date." Sometime later, a note appeared at the studio from Harrold saying the next time Roger was in New York, the two of them should get dinner. Suspicious, Roger asked Gene if he had sent the letter as a prank and Gene admitted he had been behind it.

"It was only two years later," Ebert later told *Playboy* magazine, "that I found out that he had *not* sent me the letter. It turns out that Kathryn Harrold thinks I'm extremely rude because I never answered her letter. Because Siskel told me that it was from him."

Siskel was often astonished by Ebert's reviews of children's films like *Cop and a Half,* which the latter would sometimes couch with an acknowledgment that his opinions should be taken with a grain of salt. After all, they came from someone well outside these movies' target audience. What should an adult's opinion matter of a movie expressly made for kids? Gene, on the other hand, felt a good movie was a good movie no matter who it was made by or intended for. Any kind of leniency toward a kids' film on Roger's part struck Gene as an affront to critical standards, and he regularly told him so on the air. He was infuriated when Roger gave a negative review to the kids' action movie *3 Ninjas Kick Back* with the caveat that he believed "younger children might find it entertaining."

"*Dim-witted* younger children," Siskel interjected.

When Ebert chided him for being unkind to kids and their still-unformed cinematic taste, Siskel added, "No! I *want* to be the cruel one!"

Their differing standards for kids' movies—and pretty much everything else—led to one of the longest arguments in the history of the show. Roger and Gene started a 1987 episode with a heated debate about Stanley Kubrick's *Full Metal Jacket.* Roger gave the movie a thumbs down, while claiming it was "not a bad movie, but it's not original and it's not a masterpiece." Siskel, who wound up putting *Full Metal Jacket* at number two on his list of the best films of that year, countered by stating, "I think it's *very* original and very close to being a masterpiece."

From there they began screaming at each other, with Roger calling the movie a cliché, and Gene announcing he'd "never felt a kill in a movie" quite like the ones in *Full Metal Jacket.*

"Well, in that case you're gonna love the late show because they have kills like that every night in black and white starring John Wayne!" Ebert shot back.

One advantage of the relatively short production schedule of *Siskel & Ebert* episodes in later years was that the two hosts didn't have time to calm down between reviews. As soon as a satisfactory take of a review was in the can, the crew immediately dove right into the next segment. As a result, the residual anger from a heated argument would often bubble up again later in the same episode. A couple movies after Gene and Roger discussed *Full Metal Jacket*, for example, they talked about *Benji the Hunted*, which Roger liked enough to recommend on its merits as a pleasant children's film, a fact Siskel could not abide.

"Roger, my rebuttal of this film is you're wrapping yourself in the flag of children," Siskel griped.

"Hold on, *I'm* not wrapping myself in the flag of children!" Ebert replied. "*You're* wrapping yourself in the flag of the sophisticated film critic who's seen it all!"

"No! Boredom! Boredom with Benji running!" Siskel screamed.

This episode-long feud continued into the week's home video segment, which was dedicated to other great works by director Stanley Kubrick. After recommending *Dr. Strangelove*, Siskel couldn't resist taking one last shot at Ebert.

"This is a show," he noted, "where you give *Benji the Hunted* a positive review and not Kubrick's film."

Gene's critical quirks could get under Roger's skin as well. Ebert hated when Siskel offered explicit suggestions for rewrites in his reviews. When the pair discussed Cameron Crowe's *Singles* in 1992, Siskel had hardly finished listing his complaints with the film—namely that Crowe had focused on three couples instead of one, meaning the film never spent enough time with any relationship to get really in-depth with any of the characters—before Ebert butted in to proclaim, "You're always trying to rewrite movies!

Why not let him make *this* movie about three couples and next time he can make a movie about *one* couple?"

Earlier that same year, they gave a split review to *The Hand That Rocks the Cradle*, which Gene argued was an implausible thriller. And to some extent it is; it's a psychological drama about a deranged woman who tries to get revenge against a family she blames for the death of her husband by becoming the nanny to their children and then pitting husband, wife, and newborn baby against one another. But like *Singles*, Roger felt *The Hand That Rocks the Cradle* should be judged on its own merits.

"This is the kind of argument we have very frequently because you find things that are implausible and so forth and other things you object to," Ebert said, not so much reviewing the movie as he was critiquing his partner's mental framework for evaluating art. "I found that this film worked and that's usually the way I approach it. I go to a thriller expecting to be thrilled. I don't go expecting to have all my sensibilities respected and all of my sensitivities honored because I know that in a movie like this I can almost anticipate exactly what is going to happen." He demanded that Gene at least grant the movie its premise.

"Let them write a better premise. Then I'll grant it," Siskel replied.

Ebert was not deterred. "I grant the premise. You can pick up the paper and read about killer nannies right now. All over the country!"

"Oh, Roger," Gene moaned. "What newspapers do you read?"

Siskel also loved being surprised, perhaps to a fault. If a movie *didn't* surprise him, even if it was well-made, he often held that against it. He felt the 1996 thriller *Primal Fear* was "standard stuff" because it wasn't surprising enough, to which Ebert replied,

"There is such a thing as good genre stuff and bad genre stuff, and if you're a movie lover you love genre stuff if it's done well!" Siskel didn't see it that way—or think *Primal Fear* was genre stuff done well—although he did admire and single out the debut performance of a twenty-six-year-old Edward Norton. (After Siskel pointed out that Norton was a graduate of Yale like Siskel, Ebert snidely quipped, "Well, that explains it.")

Ebert also took issue with the way Siskel would compare new releases to time-tested classics as proof that whatever they were reviewing wasn't up to snuff. Siskel felt the 1984 period teen drama *Racing with the Moon* was "nothing very substantial," and after Ebert insisted he was being unfair to it, Siskel tried to compare the new film unfavorably to Peter Bogdanovich's 1971 masterpiece of teen alienation, *The Last Picture Show.* At that, Ebert got really hot.

"What you do is you take the ten greatest films of all time and go compare them to every movie we're reviewing this week to show it's not as good!" Ebert griped, his voice getting louder as his arms waved more and more frantically.

Siskel didn't see the problem. "I think that's not a bad way to operate," he replied. "Take the paradigm case, the best film of the kind, and see how it stacks up!"

The hosts sometimes looked sick as they endured their counterpart's arguments—and on one occasion, Ebert *literally* got sick during a review and threw up all over the set. As you might imagine, the footage did not make it on air, but Gene liked to needle Roger by reminding him what he said right after he hurled: "You really didn't like that one, did you, Roger?"

The men didn't just have different taste, they had totally different approaches to their job. Those different points of view were not limited to movies, and they sometimes caused tensions behind the scenes of the show as well.

By the late 1980s, the *Siskel & Ebert* brand became strong enough to expand beyond its weekly syndicated time slot. Once or twice each year, the show released a prime-time special, typically compilations of interviews with major Hollywood stars and film-makers. The task of cutting these *Siskel & Ebert* specials fell to Jim Murphy, then *Siskel & Ebert*'s director and supervising producer. But in order to finish the edit, he had to get Gene *and* Roger to sign off on the same version of the show—which was next to impossible.

First, Murphy would show the cut to Siskel. He would demand Murphy take certain things out and put other things in. Ebert would look at the cut next. Then he'd demand Murphy put back the material he'd cut out, and trim other parts that Siskel had requested. And around and around it went.

One special featuring an interview with Steven Spielberg proved especially tough to finish. After the tenth cut, Murphy was summoned to the office of *Siskel & Ebert* executive producer Larry Dieckhaus. Roger and Gene still weren't happy.

"You're going to have to cut it again," Dieckhaus said.

Murphy took a Betamax tape and hurled it at the wall of Dieck-haus's office. He threw it so hard it left a hole.

"You people are fucking crazy!" Murphy screamed as he walked back to the editing room.

While no one says Roger and Gene were necessarily bad bosses, many former staffers say they could be difficult at times, especially when they were jockeying with one another for control of something. Who would get their hair and makeup done before the other became a battle—not because either wanted to be first, but because *neither* wanted to be ready and sitting around on the set waiting for the other.

The longer Gene and Roger waited around, the more likely

some argument would erupt. During a break on a particularly long taping day in the *Sneak Previews* era of the show, Gene decided to take a nap in his favorite spot at WTTW: on the carpeted floor beneath the large table in the main conference room.

Ignoring *Sneak Previews* assistant producer John Davies seated at the conference room table typing up the next episode's script, Gene folded his sports coat under his head and closed his eyes. A few minutes later, Roger entered the room to use the phone. After the taping wrapped, he was headed to New York, where he was going to interview Nastassja Kinski, then one of the hottest young actresses in the film business thanks to her work in movies like Francis Ford Coppola's quirky musical *One from the Heart* and Paul Schrader's erotic horror thriller *Cat People*. Both Gene and Roger had noticed Kinski's prodigious talents—not to mention her prodigious beauty—and were big fans.

Roger called Kinski's publicist and confirmed the interview for later that week. Then he turned to Davies, told him he was off to get lunch downstairs, and left.

There was just one problem: he never noticed Gene Siskel lying under the table. And Roger's phone call had woken him from his nap. He heard the entire conversation.

As soon as Roger left the room, Gene darted out from under the table.

He hit redial on the telephone.

"Hello? Yes, this is Mr. Ebert's assistant," Siskel said when the publicist answered the phone. "Yes, unfortunately, Mr. Ebert needs to cancel the meeting in New York. Thank you."

Gene then turned to Davies, who had witnessed his prank.

"Not one word, fucker."

(Siskel told a different version of the same story to *Chicago* magazine in 1987. In that version, Ebert was setting up interviews with George Burns, Art Carney, and Lee Strasberg all at once. In Siskel's telling, he [Gene] immediately flies to both coasts and by Sunday he has interviews with all three actors in the *Tribune*. "I have the ability," he bragged, "to look this guy straight in the eye and lie to him and he can't tell.")

Paying close attention to Ebert's schedule—and sometimes using that information to try to scoop him—was a pastime of Siskel's all through the *Sneak Previews* era. If he suspected his cohost might have booked a chat with a major star, he would call his secretary at the *Chicago Tribune* and tell her to call Roger at a certain number at a certain time to get him to answer a phone away from his desk.

"And then," says *Sneak Previews* assistant director Laura C. Hernández, "Gene would go through Roger's appointment book to see who he was interviewing."

If that didn't work, he would employ a technique Roger referred to as "blind man's chess." If he thought Ebert might be traveling to New York on a certain day for an important interview, he would intentionally suggest scheduling an equally important press screening on the same day, then watch Ebert's reaction to see if he demanded they reschedule. "He was so often right," Ebert recalled, "that I would sometimes fake an out-of-town trip to throw him off the scent." Siskel's instincts for Ebert's schedule were so consistently correct that the latter began to wonder if his rival was secretly calling airlines and impersonating him while "confirming" flights in order to figure out when and where he was headed.

Although Roger was generally the butt of Gene's pranks and not vice versa, Roger did occasionally strike back. In 1997, the pair were invited to speak at the Harvard Law School Forum. During their visit to Cambridge, Ebert also had a book signing at the Harvard Coop—which for some reason, is spelled and pronounced like "chicken coop." *Siskel & Ebert* executive producer Stuart Cleland informed Roger of the strange pronunciation.

"Okay, but don't say anything to Gene about this," Ebert told Cleland.

Toward the end of their appearance at the Forum, Roger mentioned his book signing at the "coop"—and Gene, never one to pass up an opportunity to tease his partner, began needling him for being a bumpkin from Urbana, Illinois, and mispronouncing the word *co-op.*

Roger giddily looked to the students to back him up, and they did. When that happened, says Cleland, Gene had to "backpedal frantically."

On at least one occasion, Roger and Gene's off-screen arguments got so intense they got covered in *TV Guide.* Starting in the Tribune days, Roger and Gene made a tradition of revealing their picks for the annual Academy Awards on a one-hour special titled *If We Picked the Oscars,* and later *If We Picked the Winners.* By their time on Buena Vista Television, the *If We Picked the Winners* special had ballooned from a fairly routine episode of the show with Roger and Gene sitting in the Balcony in tuxedos to a lavish production complete with a studio audience and a live band, all synergistically recorded live at the new Disney–MGM Studios theme park in Orlando at the behest of Disney CEO Michael Eisner.

The 1993 edition of *If We Picked the Winners* was the one that made *TV Guide*'s "Grapevine" column, thanks to Roger and Gene's fierce fight over the movie *The Crying Game.* During their discussion of the nominees for Best Supporting Actor, Gene decided to reveal the film's big twist: that Jaye Davidson's character, Dil, was a transgender woman. Before he discussed the secret within the context of explaining why that made Davidson especially worthy of awards consideration, Siskel did warn viewers, "You might want to turn down the audio on your set."

Ebert immediately scolded him for even thinking of doing such a thing, and after Siskel did reveal Dil's identity, Ebert accused him of "cheating" viewers out of one of *The Crying Game*'s great pleasures.

From that point on in the special, there's palpable friction between the two hosts. When Ebert names Al Pacino as his preference in the Best Supporting Actor category for his role as Ricky Roma in *Glengarry Glen Ross*, Siskel objects on the grounds that there were dozens of actors who could have played the role as well as or better than Pacino did.

"John Barrymore could have done a good job, too, and it's too bad Laurence Olivier isn't around, but among the people who were nominated, the best performance was by Al Pacino!" an exasperated Ebert said in response.

But Siskel didn't let the point go. "But I got news for you: Lionel Barrymore, or John Barrymore, or *Ethel* Barrymore couldn't have done the role of Jaye Davidson as well as Jaye Davidson did the role."

According to *TV Guide*, Ebert's "tirade" against Siskel's unilateral choice to spoil *The Crying Game* continued even after the show had concluded filming.

"The program is *Siskel & Ebert*. A decision like that should have been discussed beforehand. It was arrogant of him," Ebert told *TV Guide*.

"Arrogant?" replied Siskel in the same news item. "That's a strange choice of words. We never discuss our opinions in advance. I was simply making a case for one of my picks." Siskel then accused Roger of getting "as angry as a 50-year-old child" before taking a shot at Ebert's physical fitness. Asked whether he was worried the two might come to blows over this *Crying Game* incident, Siskel said, "That is not possible. There's not enough motor coordination."

In more than twenty years and hundreds of on-screen debates, neither Siskel nor Ebert ever convinced the other to change their vote on a movie—except once. In 1996, Siskel gave a marginally positive review to the bombastic action film *Broken Arrow,* while criticizing star John Travolta's performance and a lazy script that dragged on for way too long. When it was Ebert's turn to speak, he disagreed with Siskel's vote but agreed with most of his criticisms, including his comments about the film's length and the lack of a compelling story.

Then Gene spoke again, and found himself echoing all of Roger's complaints.

"You know," Siskel said as a tiny smile crept onto his lips, "I don't think I've ever done this on this show in twenty years, but . . . I'm gonna twist my thumb."

Ebert was hysterical. "I talked you into it?!"

"Well, because listen, it was a half-hearted endorsement," Siskel said. "What am I really defending here? I'm defending some colorful action scenes—and they *are* colorful action scenes—but really I can't recommend it."

"I'm amazed," a stunned Ebert remarked.

"I know you're amazed," Siskel said. "Do me a favor. Look in the camera and say, 'I was wrong about *Cop and a Half,* it wasn't a very good movie.'"

"No, I won't do that," Ebert replied.

"What?!" Now Siskel was amazed.

"Listen, I saw things in *Cop and a Half* that I admired."

"Yeah, that no one else did."

"Well, in any event, you've done a very good thing, and I've done a very good thing by sticking to my guns."

Broken Arrow notwithstanding, the debates on *Siskel & Ebert* were never really about the hosts trying to change each other's minds. They weren't just there for drama and excitement on a show where a couple of guys in blazers looked at clips from new movies, either. Gene and Roger's back-and-forth invented an entirely new kind of film criticism—one that, ironically, may have been purer to the concept's roots than the solitary kind that had been practiced until that time.

"The root of criticism, the essence of criticism, is when you walk out of the movies with your friends and you talk about what you just saw and you argue with them about it," says former *New York Times* film critic A. O. Scott, who's also written a book on the history, theory, and practice of criticism. "That's kind of where criticism starts. And Siskel and Ebert are the representation of that."

"By turning criticism into a debate, by turning it into a conversation, Siskel and Ebert found two things," says Robert Thompson, the director of the Bleier Center for Television and Popular Culture at Syracuse University. "One: that people found it interesting to hear people talk about movies, and two: *arguing* about movies seriously, which is presumably what *we* do whenever we walk out of the theater. They carved out that space. That was so groundbreaking."

"One of the things I grew to appreciate about them once I became a critic myself," Scott adds, "is that idea of criticism as an argument; that actually the ideal critic is two critics, and that it's a sort of back-and-forth." Through that back-and-forth, Roger and Gene brought the essence of criticism to a mass audience that numbered in the millions all through the 1980s and '90s.

Their perpetual disputes subliminally told their viewers that there wasn't any singular correct opinion about movies—no matter what any one critic, Siskel and Ebert included, wrote about it. All art is subjective, and in injecting criticism with a heaping dose of lively debate, they created a show that was itself a persuasive argument in favor of the subjective experience of cinema.

As successful as *At the Movies* was, as Gene and Roger neared the end of their contract at Tribune, they began to feel unappreciated again. They believed they deserved more attention and a bigger piece of the show's financial pie. *At the Movies* had grown into a hefty moneymaker for Tribune Entertainment; this was no Mickey Mouse operation they were running. Or at least it wasn't until they got an offer from Mickey Mouse's home to jump ship yet again.

CHAPTER EIGHT

HOORAY FOR HOLLYWOOD

· ·

We'll also take a look at a new film about
a friendship between a boy and a whale.
I'm Roger Ebert of the *Chicago Sun-Times*.

—ROGER EBERT

Sort of reminds me of our relationship.
And I'm Gene Siskel of the *Chicago Tribune*.

—GENE SISKEL

· ·

or those in the TV syndication industry, the National Association of Television Program Executives' annual conference is
one of the most important weeks of the year. Producers head to the
NATPE convention to sell their shows to local broadcast networks;
executives at those networks go to NATPE to find new content to
license for their airwaves. NATPE held its first annual conference
in New York City in May of 1964. Back then, just seventy-four
TV professionals and producers attended. By 1986, NATPE had
swelled to a massive industry-wide summit with over 7,100 guests
and 250 exhibitors spread out across 180,000 square feet of trade
show space. The World Wrestling Federation set up a wrestling
ring in their booth and held exhibition matches. Jackie Gleason

received the NATPE Award of the Year. Anyone and everyone in syndication was there. (Film critic Richard Roeper, who attended a few times in the 2000s, describes it as "grown-up Comic-Con.")

Once *At the Movies* became a part of the Tribune Entertainment empire in 1983, that included Gene Siskel and Roger Ebert. Every year, they were expected to show up at NATPE and help drum up business for the show. While there, *At the Movies* executive producer Joe Antelo gave them one specific instruction: when they walked the floor of the convention, they *had* to be together.

"Together, you're stars," Antelo said. "Separately, you don't mean shit."

Walking the floor of NATPE (together) Siskel and Ebert would rub elbows with stars like Soupy Sales and Regis Philbin. One time, they bumped into an older man who said, "Boys, I wish you all the best. I hope you have half the success in syndication that I've had over the years." When Roger and Gene replied with a few mumbled pleasantries, the old man said, "You don't recognize me, do you? I'm Bozo the Clown!"

If two schlubby film critics from Chicago didn't already feel out of place hobnobbing with professional wrestlers and aging clowns, the 1986 NATPE convention left Gene and Roger uncomfortable for another reason: they were there promoting a show that didn't have them under contract. Their initial deal to host *At the Movies with Gene Siskel and Roger Ebert* (it still wasn't the other way around) was set to end with the 1985–86 season. After several successful years, they were looking for an extension to include a significant bump in pay. The budget-conscious Tribune was reluctant to give in.

For weeks leading up to NATPE, Gene repeatedly pressed Joe about their deal: "You know, Joe, we're going down to New Orleans. You better get that contract signed before we go down there."

"I'm calling upstairs every day," Antelo replied. "They're dragging their feet." The contract was supposedly sitting on the desk of someone above Antelo's pay grade at Tribune. It just needed a signature.

"Tribune people at the time had kind of an arrogant attitude about everything," says Liza Antelo, Joe's widow. "They just felt, 'They're making so much money with us they'll never leave.'" Tribune was *so* confident Gene and Roger weren't going anywhere that they never did get around to signing their renewal before they sent the duo down to the 1986 NATPE conference.

That decision, in Joe Antelo's words, "was a big boo-boo."

Working the convention floor at NATPE, Siskel stuck a note on the inside of his sports coat that read "Working without a Contract." When he bumped into an executive from a rival syndicator, he would subtly open his jacket and show it off. At least that was the story Gene and Roger told.

Jamie Bennett, the head of Buena Vista Television at the Walt Disney Company at the time, says he never saw Gene's note, although he has heard that story. But Bennett admits he also might not have seen the sign hidden inside Gene's coat because he blurted out his interest in syndicating *At the Movies* so fast that Gene might not have had time to show it to him before they were deep into a conversation about the show's future.

Bennett knew Siskel from their time working together at WBBM in Chicago. As the station's business director, he was the one who'd sent Gene the "color TV" during his contract negotiations. Later, when Bennett moved into a programming job at WBBM, he hired Gene to chat about movies on the station's noontime talk show.

Both single at the time, Bennett and Siskel would socialize together in their off-hours. "It was fun to hang out with Gene,"

Bennett says, laughing, "because it meant that you'd go to the movies and it didn't cost you anything."

Bennett eventually left WBBM and moved to Los Angeles to become the general manager of KCBS, but he and Siskel stayed in touch. When Gene and Roger came to LA to appear on the *Tonight Show*, they'd all go out to dinner together. So Bennett was very comfortable with Siskel and Ebert—but he had no idea that their contract at Tribune Entertainment had not been renewed when he bumped into Gene in the elevator lobby of the Windsor Court hotel in New Orleans.

"When's your deal up?" Bennett asked Siskel.

"It's up right now," Siskel says, grinning. "Tribune is foolish bringing us here. This is like bringing your fiancée to a singles bar. They brought us here to schmooze, but they don't even have the show under contract."

The timing was fortuitous, for Siskel and for Bennett. The mid-1980s were a time of major changes all over the Walt Disney Company. In 1984, Michael Eisner was brought over from Paramount Pictures to become the new CEO, with Jeffrey Katzenberg hired to serve as chairman of Walt Disney Studios. They set about restoring Disney's reputation after years of middling movies—and saw Gene and Roger as a way to simultaneously prove their commitment to quality and solidify the company's new syndication division, Buena Vista Television. Although Siskel and Ebert would be a relatively modest moneymaker at Disney—the big syndication profits came from five-day-a-week shows like *Live with Regis and Kathie Lee*—Bennett says they were important to Disney as a "prestige item" as they worked toward rehabbing Disney's image.

"Gene and Roger stood for quality as critics, and so if they're picking a studio to distribute their show, and they chose us as opposed to Paramount or someone else, it was an implicit endorsement," he notes.

Siskel explained the full situation at Tribune to Bennett and walked off. Within seconds of his departure, the elevator doors in the Windsor Court opened again. This time, Jeffrey Katzenberg walked out—Bennett's new boss. Bennett immediately relayed what Siskel had told him to Katzenberg.

"This is something we should do, but we better move quickly," Bennett said.

"Don't waste any time. Just get it done," Katzenberg replied.

They did. By the time Gene and Roger were on a plane heading home, the deal was basically complete. Bennett flew back to Los Angeles by way of Chicago, and spent the first leg of his trip seated next to Don Hacker, Tribune's executive vice president of TV production.

"He didn't know me, but I knew who he was," Bennett recalls. "I literally rode all the way back sitting next to the guy, and he didn't realize that I had just picked his pocket."

Gene and Roger's main condition for leaving Tribune for Disney—besides enormous raises, which reportedly saw them each earn around $1 million a year—was a contractual guarantee of freedom to review whatever they wanted however they wanted, especially Disney movies. Press releases announcing the new show guaranteed Gene and Roger would have "complete independence and autonomy" from Disney's movie division. Mary Kellogg, the Buena Vista executive who oversaw the show for Disney from its debut through the early 2000s, says the rule governing the show was "church and state."

"And to their credit," she adds, "I never got a call from Michael [Eisner] or Jeffrey [Katzenberg] or any of their minions asking,

'How did they vote?' They honored that the entire time they were at Disney."

In Gene and Roger's first appearance on *Late Night with David Letterman* after they jumped ship to Disney, Ebert declared he couldn't wait "for Disney to make a movie that we hate," before wryly joking, "It just so happens, the first four movies they made since we made the change have been very good." (In a more serious interview with the *Los Angeles Times*, Ebert insisted accusations of potential conflicts of interest were misplaced, saying, "We will have total autonomy over what we say and what we cover. . . . I will say exactly what I want about any film Disney makes.")

Gene, Roger, and Mary Kellogg may not have heard from Katzenberg, but Jamie Bennett did. Katzenberg would sometimes ask him, "Can't you get those guys to say *something* nice?" about whatever new Disney production was hitting theaters that week. Bennett told him no, and never mentioned the calls to Gene and Roger, though he also says, "Jeffrey knew. He may have asked, but he also knew the answer would be no."

Left without hosts for their successful movie review show, Tribune Entertainment announced on March 26, 1986, that they would "revamp" *At the Movies* the following fall and fired a few shots at the departing stars. Tribune's Don Hacker said that the company was "unable to reach an acceptable agreement" with Siskel and Ebert because, while "the ratings of the show remain good, the most recent ratings erosion could not justify the monies the two hosts were asking for over a long term contract." In an interview with *Crain's Chicago Business* on March 31, another Tribune executive compared the show to a rusty car—not worth the money the drivers wanted for it. (According to Nielsen, the show was averaging a 3.7 rating in November of 1985, and ranked seventy-fourth among all syndicated TV shows. In November 1984, *At the*

Movies had average a 4.2 rating, and was the fifty-fifth-ranked syndicated television show.) Tribune also claimed that they had tried to "spice up" the series to boost ratings and Siskel and Ebert refused to entertain their ideas. Their "revamped" *At the Movies*, hosted by Rex Reed and Bill Harris, and later by Reed and Dixie Whatley, continued for another four years and was canceled for good in 1990.

Gene and Roger faced no such pressure at Disney to retool their time-tested formula of movie reviews and crosstalk. As they had when they moved from PBS to Tribune, they recruited a handful of trusted staffers to join them in their new venture, most importantly Andrea Gronvall, who had joined *At the Movies* in its first season, eventually replaced Nancy De Los Santos as the show's producer, and then remained with the Disney version of the series until the early 2000s. Don Voigt, who had directed Gene and Roger during their *Sneak Previews* days at WTTW, became the new show's first director.

Disney also brought back Michael Loewenstein, the designer of the original *Sneak Previews* Balcony, to create the new set for the series with his partner, Mary Margaret Bartley. After ten years reviewing movies in two different theater balconies, Gene and Roger were at least willing to entertain new concepts for their set, and Bartley and Loewenstein obliged with some very unusual designs.

"It was an opportunity to think crazy, because sometimes you come up with something really good," explains Bartley. "We asked, 'Are they in their own screening room? Do they have this private jet where they fly around the country or the world to see the newest movies?' I was trying to think out of the box a little bit."

"I do remember spending a lot of money with that scenic designer trying on everyone's cockamamy idea of what we should do," Jamie Bennett says. "Literally, I remember it costing money and we wound up with essentially the same set that had been used previously."

Eventually, Gene and Roger did return to the classic concept of a movie theater balcony. While Bartley says they discussed integrating Disney characters into the theater design in honor of the show's new home, producers eventually settled on a grander and more colorful version of the same sort of theater balconies they had used in their previous series. The Disney set wasn't much larger than the previous versions, but it looked like it was thanks to another of Loewenstein's forced-perspective illusions, which made it appear that Gene and Roger were actually sitting in the mezzanine of an enormous movie palace with three levels, one above the hosts and one below.

When it launched in the fall of 1986, Buena Vista's version of the show was called—much to the annoyance of Roger—*Siskel & Ebert & the Movies*. The following season, "*& the Movies*" was dropped; an acknowledgment that after more than a decade on the air, viewers were tuning in as much for the critics as the clips of the latest films in theaters. *Siskel & Ebert* arrived with an amusing new opening-title sequence that saw Gene and Roger at work in their respective newspaper offices before hustling through Chicago to arrive at a movie theater to watch (and argue about) the latest movie in town.

The opening sequence played up the two men's differences and their oil-and-water chemistry. Roger worked on an old-fashioned typewriter, while Gene pounded out a review on a cutting-edge word processor; Roger walked to the theater, and Gene hailed a cab. It cast the pair as a real-life version of Neil Simon's *The Odd Couple*. Perhaps it's not shocking, then, that TV executives tried to seize on that idea by literally turning them into *The Odd Couple*— by giving Gene and Roger their own sitcom.

Titled *Best Enemies*, the proposed show would have mined the critics' famous rivalry for fictional TV fodder. Two distinct concepts were discussed, according to Chaz Ebert: one in which actors would have portrayed fictionalized versions of Siskel and Ebert and another where Gene and Roger would have played themselves in what would have been one of the earliest reality television shows. (From a certain perspective, *Siskel & Ebert* itself was one of the earliest reality television shows: it starred two people as they performed their real-life jobs and engaged in a series of unscripted conversations.)

Best Enemies never happened, but if it had, it would have had plenty of dramatic real-life story lines to adapt in the 1980s, as Gene and Roger's move to a new TV distributor had massive repercussions for Siskel's career as a print journalist. When Gene and Roger left PBS for Tribune, the fact that their show was now produced and syndicated by the corporate owners of Siskel's paper was auspicious; the *Chicago Tribune* could promote its lead critic's television show, and Tribune Entertainment could encourage people to read its star's reviews in the *Tribune* newspaper. When Roger and Gene departed Tribune, that synergy vanished—and the company decided to demote him in response.

The first article about Siskel's uncertain job status appeared in *Variety* on April 2, 1986, under the headline "Drop Siskel as Chi Trib Critic; TV Pact Cited." The article reported that Siskel had been asked to "step down" as the paper's movie critic by editor Jim Squires. The reason for the decision, according to Squires, was that Siskel's commitments to the television series, a series of prime-time specials that were part of the new deal with Disney, and his various promotional responsibilities "just spread Gene too thin." Squires also claimed that with the show now distributed by Disney, the same company that produced many of the pictures Siskel would review on the show, there was the potential for "conflict of interest"—or at least the perception of one by the audience and other studios.

"If I were 20th Century Fox, or some other movie-maker, and if they gave me a bad review," Squires said, "I might feel that they are in competition."

Siskel refused to comment on the situation all through the spring and summer as he continued to negotiate with the *Tribune* for a new position at the paper. Instead, a surprising advocate began speaking in public on his behalf: Roger Ebert.

In a joint appearance on *Late Night*, David Letterman asked about the public fight over Siskel's job. Ebert leaped to defend his partner. "Our previous show was syndicated by the Tribune Company and so when we left the Tribune Company, I can say—I don't think Gene would even necessarily vocally agree with this—the *Tribune* was mad at him. They said he was overworked. And my question is, if he had renewed with the Tribune Company, would he have been overworked or would he still be the *Tribune*'s film critic? And my answer to that is yes." In a marked change from their usual *Letterman* appearances, Siskel didn't interrupt or disagree with anything Ebert said. Instead, he sat silently through his partner's assessment of the situation with a wry smile on his face.

"If they'd renewed their deal with Tribune Entertainment, Gene's status would not have changed. I'm convinced of that," says Robert Feder, who covered the kerfuffle over Siskel's status at the *Tribune* as the *Chicago Sun-Times*' media columnist. "All the excuses were excuses. There were no *real* reasons other than that, and therefore I think it's reasonable to say that it was punitive."

A week after the initial *Variety* article about Siskel's issues at the *Tribune*, a second column—"Chi Film Critic Plot Thickens in Trib Circus"—included even more comments from Siskel's supposed rival and competitor. This time, Ebert not only defended Siskel from accusations of being spread too thin, he lashed out at his former TV home, accusing them of unfair business practices.

"It looks to me," Ebert said, "that Gene is being punished for leaving Tribune Entertainment, an absolute violation of the FCC's 'concentration of media' policies. Look, we made $12,000,000 dollars for them in net profit over four years and we were their only success.

"Gene supplies more column inches per week than any other writer on the paper and he would have continued to do so under his new contract," Ebert added. "Why, if not out of a fit of anger, is the *Tribune* demoting him at the same time that it is nominating him—for the third time—for a Pulitzer for his film reviewing?" Those remarks led to a third piece in *Variety*, where Squires shot back, "Roger Ebert doesn't know a goddamn thing about the *Tribune*," while encouraging the press to look into Ebert's new role at Disney while simultaneously working at the *Sun-Times*, a paper that had recently been acquired by 20th Century Fox chief executive Rupert Murdoch.

Gene's relationship with his print home for almost twenty years may have hit an all-time low, but his partnership with Roger had clearly evolved from one forged purely out of begrudging necessity. And as publicly protective as Roger was of Gene, he was even more supportive in private. While Siskel wrangled with *Tribune* management over a new job, Ebert went to his own bosses at the *Sun-Times* and lobbied them to bring Siskel over. He was worried about Gene's future at the *Tribune*—and he was angry about the way they were treating him after years of loyal service. *Sun-Times* editors were willing to entertain the idea of teaming Siskel and Ebert at the paper, as long as Ebert was willing to share the movie section with Siskel. He said he was.

The idea of Gene Siskel and Roger Ebert working side by side at one newspaper would have been unfathomable just a few years earlier. Their whole public image—which was essentially accurate in the days they hosted *Sneak Previews* together—was of two mortal foes locked in an endless struggle to destroy the other. While they continued playing those roles on television, and while they did still annoy the shit out of each other on occasion, they had clearly come to appreciate their importance in each other's lives. Even the title of their Disney show pointed to the fact that, despite their on-air disagreements, they really were a team.

"Roger came to understand that they were so much more powerful together. And it was in Roger's best interests to keep Gene viable," says Robert Feder. As Jamie Bennett puts it, "They knew that this thing was the goose, and they were not going to kill it for the golden egg."

Most people who knew Siskel believe he never seriously considered going to the *Sun-Times*. But an offer to unite the most famous film critics in the country under a competitor's masthead made for a potent bargaining chip. And regardless of any bitterness about Siskel and Ebert abandoning *At the Movies*, the *Tribune* still had a lot invested in their longtime critic. While Dave Kehr soon became the paper's official film critic, Gene continued working under the new title of "syndicated film columnist," contributing capsule reviews and weekend features. And despite the demotion, Gene's picture was the one at the top of the *Tribune* front page on Fridays.

Gene and Roger's feud with *Tribune* management became part of a pattern in the late 1980s and into the early 1990s as the co-hosts increasingly found themselves making news together instead of just reporting on it separately. While the stories about Gene's issues at the *Tribune* were largely confined to Hollywood trade journals, the pair got even more mainstream publicity a few years later when they pissed off—and then essentially defeated—a touchy movie studio.

The source of the controversy was, of all things, a comedy called *Nuns on the Run*. The now-forgotten film starred Eric Idle and Robbie Coltrane as a couple of crooks who disguise themselves as nuns to escape a Mob hit. While appearing on *Live with Regis and Kathie Lee* to promote their annual special about the Academy Awards, Roger and Gene made fun of a *Nuns on the Run* newspaper ad with a pull quote that declared it "the funniest anti-clerical transvestite movie of the decade!"

"This is 1990!" Ebert quipped. "How many other transvestite clerical comedies have there been so far in this decade?"

The film's distributor, 20th Century Fox, was furious, and they responded by officially banning both men from all advanced screenings of future Fox movies. Fox marketing executive Bob Harper told the *Hollywood Reporter* that the company supposedly objected less to their two-thumbs-down vote for the film, and more the fact that they showed up on *Regis and Kathie Lee* "in the capacity of entertainers—not critics—promoting their Oscar special and wound up making fun of *Nuns on the Run,* which, as you might imagine, was decidedly not an Oscar contender. "From now on," Harper added, "they can catch up with our films in the theater."

That suited Gene and Roger just fine. They predicted the ban wouldn't last, accused Fox of not having a sense of humor, and vowed to watch any of their movies in the meantime by buying their own tickets. Subsequent articles in newspapers and magazines around the country tracked the fallout from Fox's decision, but after all the attention, Gene and Roger were banned for a total of three weeks, until the very next time Fox released a new movie to theaters. Assuming the ban was in place, Ebert had left town on a trip before the Chicago preview screening of Fox's *Vital Signs*. Siskel, meanwhile, called Fox to inquire if he could attend, and was told that he could. In subsequent coverage of the ban's end, Gene insisted that "no understanding was achieved" between the show and the studio before Fox decided to allow them back into screenings. He also said the only thing he was disappointed about regarding the whole affair was that he predicted Fox would keep them out of one screening, while Roger anticipated they would change their minds as soon as they had a film to promote. Roger was right, and he was sure to let Gene hear about it.

"He's going to be hard to deal with when he gets home," Siskel groaned.

It was the first and last time a studio tried to ban Gene and Roger from their screenings—and the speed with which the prohibition was overturned showed just how powerful *Siskel & Ebert* had grown. A negative review from the pair could certainly hurt a movie like *Nuns on the Run*, but a "Two Thumbs Up!" review was incredibly valuable as a marketing tool in print and television ads. Studios needed (and filmmakers wanted) the critics' endorsement.

In fact, later that same year, *Spy* magazine attempted to ascertain which film critics exerted the greatest influence over the movie business by comparing their reviews to box office totals and pull quotes in ads. According to their calculations, Siskel and Ebert were clearly the two most influential film critics in the country—although which of the two was most powerful was a subject of much debate, especially among Gene and Roger.

Upon being told that he ranked second on *Spy*'s list of most influential critics, right after Siskel at number one, Ebert whined, "How could he have *possibly* edged me out? Did you know that I'm in 190 papers and he's in 16? That I'm on the number-one-rated network in Chicago and he's on number three? I'm in the [New

York] *Daily News* and he isn't—that's another million every day."
Technically, Siskel was in seventy-five papers, but the point stood.
Unfortunately for Ebert, so did the ranking.

Gene and Roger's collective impact on the film world grew so
large in this period that they began drawing comparisons to the
most influential people in all of the entertainment business, not
just other film critics. When *Entertainment Weekly* ranked the "101
Most Powerful People in Entertainment" in 1990, Gene and Roger
came in tenth place, in part because of their perceived victory over
Fox's publicity department without so much as an apology. ("We
came out of that stronger than ever, because Fox was seen as firing
from the hip and shooting themselves in the toe," Ebert said in
EW's list.) Siskel and Ebert ranked behind Disney CEO Michael
Eisner and Hollywood superagent Michael Ovitz of Creative Artists Agency, but ahead of Hollywood moguls like David Geffen and
Ted Turner, stars like Madonna, directors like Steven Spielberg
and Spike Lee, and even their own boss at Disney, Jeffrey Katzenberg, who didn't appear on the list until number twenty. (No
wonder they weren't worried about him trying to influence their
reviews.)

As their power grew, so did their targets. In 1995, Senator Bob
Dole made attacks against Hollywood a centerpiece of his early
presidential campaign. In a stump speech that May, he claimed the
nation's "popular culture threatens to undermine our character as
a nation" and directly accused the movie business of unleashing
"nightmares of depravity" on the American public. In response,
Siskel & Ebert devoted an entire segment of a June 1995 episode to
Dole's comments, and to the hosts' reactions to his diatribe.

Gene and Roger were hardly horror fans themselves. A decade
earlier, *they* were the ones attacking movies for their excessive and
wanton violence, particularly against women, in a special episode

of *Sneak Previews*. But while Siskel and Ebert were often critical of movies with crass and misogynistic gore, they were incensed that Dole made his comments while admitting he hadn't actually seen or heard any of the so-called nightmares of depravity he'd targeted in his speech.

They continued their criticism of Dole at a National Press Club luncheon that same summer—where Siskel proudly declared that they "probably have dumped on Hollywood, and the bad films and bad artistic values of those films, more than any other people in this country for the last twenty years," while at the same time accusing Dole of making an error that no journalism student would ever be permitted to attempt: confusing, in Ebert's words, "the inventory with the analysis."

"To say that a movie or a song contains something is not to make a meaningful statement about it, except simply to say what it contains," Ebert explained. "I think you have to look a little further into tone, mood, message, purpose, context, and origin in order to understand whether a movie or a song has a message that's worthwhile or whether it's simply negative and destructive. And that's something I think that Senator Dole and other people who have joined his cause have not been willing to do."

Instead, Siskel said, Dole was trying to "divide people" by creating a "boogeyman" for people to fear—one, Ebert argued, that deliberately invoked rap music as "code words" designed to make his core constituency think of "drug-crazed young Black men in the ghetto with guns shooting cops."

"That's what he wants us to think of," Ebert said. "He's probably not interested in the fact that ninety-five percent of rap music doesn't have anything to do with the kinds of targets he's singled out. What he's doing basically is, he's trying to draw a wedge. He's trying to say those terrible people over there are perverting our central American values with their bad ideas about violence and about the family."

In other words, they were as much offended by Dole's divisive partisan politics as they were by his shabby film criticism. In attacking movies he'd never watched, Dole violated the number one rule of Siskel and Ebert's chosen profession: you have to see it before you criticize it. If Dole had spent any time watching *Siskel & Ebert,* he would have known there was a big difference between a movie showing a subject and endorsing it.

If Dole *had* watched the show, he also would have seen *Siskel & Ebert* begin to experiment with a variety of new segments to augment the old *Sneak Previews* format. In 1996, the series added "The Revolving Thumb," a place for Gene and Roger to pontificate on issues in the world of film—and to give thumbs up or down to things besides the latest movies opening in theaters. One week, they might give a thumbs up to actor Jeff Daniels for showing impressive range in films like *Dumb and Dumber, Speed, Fly Away Home,* and *2 Days in the Valley.* The next, they might vote thumbs down on the trend toward generic action-movie titles like *Extreme Measures, Chain Reaction,* and *Maximum Risk.*

In 1996, the show also introduced "The Viewer's Thumb," which gave the audience the chance to join the show's conversation by mailing in video rebuttals to Gene and Roger's reviews. In the mid-1990s, recording yourself on video was still an arduous and complicated task. There were no consumer-grade digital cameras to speak of, much less smartphones and emails with video attachments. (When *Siskel & Ebert* launched its own website around this time, dial-up internet access was so slow that the original Siskel-Ebert.com could only offer audio versions of the show's reviews.) Making a "Viewer's Thumb" video required expensive equipment, plus the motivation to then physically mail a VHS tape to Chicago. The idea, which drew on the early energy of interactive internet message boards, was at least a decade ahead of its time.

Still, some viewers were passionate enough to go to the trouble and mail in their videos. But if they were expecting Gene and Roger to welcome them into the debate with open arms, they had another think coming. In fact, Siskel and Ebert were just as hard on viewers as they were on each other. Gene told a young teenager who mailed in a tape complaining about *Siskel & Ebert*'s positive reviews of documentaries like *Hoop Dreams* and *Microcosmos* that the younger generation's "lack of reading and watching frenetic television" was ruining their attention spans. "The Viewer's Thumb" appeared on the show a few times before it was retired; executive producer Stuart Cleland believes it was doomed by a combination of a lack of submissions, the poor technical quality of the submissions they did get, and Gene and Roger's preference not to share the spotlight on their show.

New segments came and went, but the bedrock of *Siskel & Ebert* remained the hosts' reviews and debates, which were still fiery even as the men's animosity toward one another behind the scenes cooled considerably. The biggest change between the two during their time at Disney was Roger's marriage, at age fifty, to Chaz Hammel Smith, a Chicago attorney. According to Roger's memoir, they met in a Chicago restaurant, when he spotted her at a nearby table while he was sharing a meal with Eppie Lederer— aka advice columnist Ann Landers. (In the documentary version of *Life Itself*, Chaz says Roger saw her for the first time at an Alcoholics Anonymous meeting.)

Chaz Ebert says she and Gene "got along right from the beginning." Even as Roger and Gene warmed to each other all through the 1980s, they still didn't socialize very often—but that began to change with Chaz's arrival. She remembers one conversation with

Gene after she and Roger got engaged where he thanked her for bringing love into Roger's life.

"Gene and Marlene gave us a nice prenuptial party," she adds. "We would call ourselves . . . like, if he and Roger were brothers, he was my brother-in-law. He would say things like that, that made it feel like we were all in this together, the four of us: Gene and Marlene, and me and Roger."

"Gene was delighted to hear of Roger's engagement and so excited about the wedding," says Marlene Iglitzen. "Gene said he wanted the same happiness and sense of completion he felt with our life as a couple and family to be Roger's own experience as well. It definitely created a tighter bond between them."

Roger and Chaz married at the Fourth Presbyterian Church in Chicago on July 18, 1992. Gene wasn't Roger's best man—but his and Marlene's daughters were the couple's flower girls. Friends and colleagues in attendance noted changes in Gene and Roger's relationship at the wedding.

"It was an amazing day," Robert Feder says, "when Gene and Marlene's two daughters were the flower girls at the wedding. It was clear that there was a lot of love between these two families, and that Gene and Marlene were truly thrilled for Roger, that he had found someone in Chaz. To me, that was a real moment. It had always been fraught with this competition; the stress and the one-upmanship and the jealousy. And it all just sort of melted away—at least publicly, from what I could see. And from that point on there was no pretext that these guys didn't love each other. And it was so unlikely at the beginning, but that's kind of what made it so sweet when it finally happened."

"Unlikely" was putting it mildly. Just a few years earlier, Ebert had called his relationship with Siskel "unnatural"—because critics by their very nature are meant to be "solitary creatures. They go to the event, they think about the event, they write about the event, and that's it." At times, he confessed that he saw himself as "a complete film critic—one-stop shopping" who could do the show just fine without Gene. Thea Flaum says that while the world came to see Siskel and Ebert as a two-person act, they both "never, ever saw themselves, thought of themselves, as part of a duo. They *resented* the idea that they were joined at the hip."

Still, if Gene and Roger insisted on maintaining their separate identities as journalists, they could no longer deny that they had collectively built one of the most durable and imitated franchises on television. They'd come a long way from the guys who had to be reminded by Joe Antelo that they *had* to walk the NATPE floor together.

"I noticed in the wedding speeches that Gene and Roger had grown closer together," says Jim Murphy, the supervising producer and director of *Siskel & Ebert* from 1988 to 1993. "They had been fighting for so many years over what, when it comes to the bigger picture of your humanity and your life, they knew intrinsically just didn't matter that much. 'My hatred of his beating me or getting a Pulitzer is nowhere near as big as my love for what we've built together.' That overcame a lot."

CHAPTER NINE

GET TO THE CROSSTALK

We firmly believe that the show is not about us.
It's about the movies. And we know how popular
our relationship is, and special. But I tell you:
the show is about the movies.

—GENE SISKEL

Why do we go to the movies in the first place?
To have a vicarious experience. For two hours we
sit there and if the movie works we stop being
ourselves to some degree and become the
characters on the screen. And then a review
to some degree should talk about whether we
enjoyed that vicarious experience.

—ROGER EBERT

In the early 2010s, film critics up for consideration as hosts of the final version of *At the Movies* were given a document titled "Roger's Primer." In seven points, it laid out Ebert's guidelines for writing a film review the *Siskel & Ebert* way.

While Roger and Gene always encouraged aspiring critics, they never formalized their advice as clearly or succinctly as in this primer. Here are Ebert's instructions, along with illustrations of its

recommendations (and some examples of Gene and Roger breaking their own rules) from throughout the history of *Sneak Previews, At the Movies,* and *Siskel & Ebert.*

1. The key to the show is to get moving quickly and get to the crosstalk.

Shortly after landing his job as the *Chicago Tribune's* film critic in
1969, Gene Siskel went to his editor, Clayton Kirkpatrick, and
asked for advice. He was struggling with a review.

"Imagine what the headline would be, and start with that,"
Kirkpatrick said.

Siskel took those words to heart and kept them close throughout
his career. No wonder Siskel's reviews convey such a great sense of
urgency, even if all he's talking about is his take on *Jetsons: The
Movie.* (He didn't like it, by the way.) Asked at a public seminar
what he admired about Siskel, Ebert once complimented his partner's ability to do exactly that, to "find the lede in a review." Rather
than simply regurgitate the facts about where a movie takes place
or who is in it, Ebert explained, Siskel would get right into "the
reason you might want to see it, why it might be important, why it
might *not* be important, in a way that is very clear so that people
who are watching the show can understand."

That kind of urgency was especially crucial on television. Even
in the earliest days of *Sneak Previews,* when the show ran about
twenty-eight minutes with no commercials—compared to the
twenty-two minutes of the Buena Vista years—the on-air reviews
were far shorter than most newspaper pieces on the same movies.
According to Siskel, by the mid-1980s a typical review on the show
would contain about twenty sentences. (The sample review included with the primer, of the 2005 Albert Brooks film *Looking for*

Comedy in the Muslim World, includes just thirteen sentences. Roger's print review of the same movie was fifty-two sentences long.)

In other words, a *Siskel & Ebert* review needed to get moving quickly because every second of airtime was precious. Conversely, there was no louder way Gene and Roger could signal a film's importance than by delaying the crosstalk to show additional clips with further context and commentary from one of the two hosts. These extremely rare double-size reviews were reserved for the most culturally and artistically significant movies; a few examples include Spike Lee's *Malcolm X* and Steven Spielberg's *Schindler's List* and *Saving Private Ryan.*

2. In a typical segment, there is an intro on prompter, one to three reads on prompter, and an outro. Then the crosstalk.

"Sound a little excited, Gene."

"Sound *less* excited, Roger. That's why we're redoing it. Because of something *you* did."

In 2013, nearly fourteen years after its last episode was taped, *Siskel & Ebert* went viral. Someone had uploaded a series of outtakes from a promo recording session in 1987. While Gene and Roger *should* have been focused on hyping their reviews of the thrillers *No Way Out, The Big Easy,* and *The Fourth Protocol,* all they could concentrate on was each other. And the start of all the problems was the teleprompter.

First, Roger complains that Siskel sounds jaded as he reads the copy about their next episode. Then Ebert gets frustrated that the script mentions two thrillers when the episode actually includes three. After a quick rewrite of the script—"You can't ad-lib, Gene!"—they're back at it, even more annoyed at each other than before.

"It's Thriller Week on *Siskel & Ebert at the Movies* and we've got three new ones," announces Siskel.

"It's called *And the Movies*, not *At the Movies*. And that's why we're doing it *this* time," Ebert spits back.

The studio goes quiet. The tension is worthy of any of the selections on Thriller Week. Siskel starts again. (It must be said, this time he does sound a little more excited.)

"It's Thriller Week on *Siskel & Ebert and the Movies* and we've got three new ones!"

Next, it's Ebert's turn. "Dennis Quaid in *The Big Easy*! Michael Caine in *The Fourth Protocol*! And Kevin Costner and Gene Hackman in *No Way Out*!"

Back to Siskel, who now takes a slight pause after each part of the show's title. "That's this week on *Siskel . . . and Ebert . . . and the Movies*."

"Great!" a stage manager says from off camera. But Gene's not done.

". . . and the Asshole!" he grumbles, before adding, "And that's Roger!"

Oh, the teleprompter. It was a source of major struggle in the early years of the show and, as the battle over Thriller Week suggests, was never the hosts' favorite aspect of TV production. Even by the mid-1990s, when *Siskel & Ebert* ran like a well-oiled machine, with many full episodes recorded in less than a handful of takes, there were still occasional slipups. In 1996, a taping ground to a halt when Ebert struggled to read the name of an Italian filmmaker off of the teleprompter. Hoping to avoid future issues, Siskel suggested that, in the future, the crew should warn them of any name that could be tough to pronounce. A frustrated Ebert commented, "Whenever any kind of plan is settled on, some mysterious little gnawing thing begins to grow within Gene, compelling him to change it." (No such plan was ever implemented.)

3. The intro is a setup, and it may or may not reveal the critic's opinion.

While Roger's primer says that revealing an opinion in a review's introduction is optional, Siskel and Ebert usually did. And the more they loved or hated a movie, the more likely they were to get right to the point and announce it at the start of their review. For instance:

> "Our next movie is named *This Is Spinal Tap*. I just want to start out by saying: This is a good movie. This is not only one of the funniest movies I've seen in a long time, it's also one of the smartest and most clever."
>
> —ROGER EBERT

> "*Jagged Edge* is both a terrific courtroom drama and a genuinely scary thriller. How scary? Well, I got a whole new movie critic's test I think for a scary movie. Roger, I call it the Backseat Test. It works this way: Do you, after leaving the theater and getting in your car, look in the backseat just to make sure no one is hiding back there ready to stab you? *Jagged Edge*, I'm embarrassed to admit, made me do that."
>
> —GENE SISKEL

> "Our next movie is named *Stealing Home*, but this is a movie that probably couldn't even steal second. It's one of the sappiest, most pathetic movies of the year."
>
> —ROGER EBERT

"Our next film is a candidate for the year's worst . . . *any* year's worst."

—GENE SISKEL ON *LITTLE INDIAN, BIG CITY*

4. The interior reads are very brief, written to video, furthering the plot or mentioning important characters and actors.

The Hollywood marketing machine grew increasingly sophisticated over the life of *Siskel & Ebert.* By the show's final years, nearly every major release came with its own "electronic press kit" (or EPK) containing preselected clips available to broadcast journalists looking to cover movies on television. When *Opening Soon . . . at a Theater Near You* first debuted on WTTW, it was a totally different world. At that time, almost every clip for every movie had to be personally chosen by Gene and Roger and then made by one of the show's staff members.

The advent of EPKs made the process easier on the producers, but it also gave studios more control about how their movies were presented on the show, something Gene and Roger were understandably displeased about. Sometimes, studios tried to place conditions on how their clips were used, or which clips could be shown—and the hosts were not above publicly shaming anyone that tried it. In 1986, they called out the distributors of the low-rent sequel *King Kong Lives* for attempting to force them to sign a document promising that any clips released to them for use on their local Chicago news broadcasts would not also be used on their nationally syndicated review show. Incensed, Siskel included *King Kong Lives* on his list of the worst movies of 1986. He showed no clips of the film, but he did include this warning: "If you don't believe me or Roger, believe the film company that, think about it, couldn't find a single scene that it wanted you to see."

In the distributors' defense: Roger and Gene could wield clips like deadly weapons when they chose, ruthlessly turning a movie against itself to make their points for them. In 1995, the show reviewed the seemingly harmless children's film *The Pebble and the Penguin*. But Ebert felt the movie—and its near-subliminal suggestion that "if you have a darker complexion you're the bad guy"— might not be so harmless. To prove it, he simply played clips from *The Pebble and the Penguin*, which did confirm that its heroic characters had predominantly white faces, while the villain's face was almost entirely dark brown. In a handful of seconds, Ebert presented a damning case against racial stereotyping in animation.

While Ebert's primer warns to keep interior reads "brief" and focus on important plot or character elements, that was also dependent on the clips available—and sometimes on Roger's and Gene's moods. If clips displayed evidence of ridiculous clichés, the focus on plot or character could go out the window very quickly. While narrating the clips from the 1987 thriller *Death Before Dishonor*, Ebert paused his plot synopsis to describe "the Rule of the Suspicious Pedestrian," which states that anytime a hero hits a woman with their car in a thriller, that woman is inevitably a man in disguise. It should go without saying that the clip from *Death Before Dishonor* does not violate Ebert's rule. (Siskel hated the movie so much he then violated *Siskel & Ebert*'s rules and relinquished his own rebuttal time to instead show additional clips and mock more of their clichés.)

5. The outro forcibly expresses the critic's opinion.

Does it ever. Whether they adored or loathed a picture, neither Siskel nor Ebert ever had a problem with mincing their words. It was not uncommon for Gene and Roger to end reviews they felt particularly strongly about with a note that whatever they had just discussed was one of the year's best or worst films—even if it was only March and the year still had nine months and hundreds of titles to go.

When Gene and Roger enjoyed something, their enthusiasm was palpable—like Roger's when he reviewed *Pulp Fiction* for the first time in 1994 and said it was "charged up with the exhilaration of pure filmmaking, with colorful characters and screwy dialogue and unbelievable situations and violence and comedy all trying to shoulder each other off the screen."

When a movie left them disgusted, that was palpable, too. Gene Siskel concluded his review of the abysmal 1992 comedy *Frozen Assets*—about a snooty bank manager who gets reassigned as the manager of, you guessed it, a sperm bank—with the declaration, "I don't think I can adequately describe to you how unpleasant the remaining ninety-five minutes were or will be for you. It was as depressing an experience as I've ever had going to the movies. That's twenty-three years of going to the movies professionally. Maybe six or seven thousand pictures?"

"Well, Gene," Roger replied, "I was going to the movies professionally for two or three years before you were there and nothing I saw during that time even approached this in its abysmal awfulness. This is perhaps the worst comedy ever made."

6. The key to the show is in the crosstalk, which is ad-lib.

While Gene might have insisted the series was about the movies and not his relationship with Roger, most fans will tell you they cared about both. Let's face it: the final version of the show was called *Siskel & Ebert* for a reason.

The place where that relationship was most purely expressed was during the crosstalk. Even though Gene and Roger were critics, not creators, they seemed to take it very personally when their partner sided against them. Ebert once said that he believed the intensity of their arguments came from their roles as newspapermen. By the time they showed up at WTTW or WBBM to record their show, they had already written full-length reviews or columns about the movies up for debate. In doing so, they had fully cemented their own opinions. "We're not just getting there and winging it," Ebert explained. "We already have a position and we're defending it."

In a *20/20* interview, he took things even further. "When you disagree on a movie," Ebert said, "you're *not* disagreeing on the movie. You're disagreeing on who you are. If I don't like a movie and he does, then I'm not saying that the movie is flawed, I'm saying that *he's* flawed."

Because the crosstalk was unplanned and unscripted, it occasionally ventured off into fascinating tangents. A *Siskel & Ebert* movie review could mutate at a moment's notice into a debate about philosophy, morality, or spirituality. The occasion of the 1987 fantasy film *Made in Heaven*, about a young man who dies, meets his soulmate in heaven, then must return to Earth to find her when she is reincarnated in a new human body, inspired Roger and Gene to talk less about the movie than their own beliefs about the afterlife.

"I believe," Siskel revealed, "that if you think of someone, whether it be here or in someplace else, that they come alive. I think the film had a religious content to it. So I found the film beautiful."

"Yeah, but, of course, whether or not you believe in this doesn't have anything to do with whether the movie is good or not," Ebert countered.

"For me, it does," Siskel responded.

"Okay, well, in that case you think every movie you agree with is good!" Ebert said.

"I have for years," Siskel replied.

7. At the end of the crosstalk, there is NEVER a sentence like "so we both agree."

Although this is the most emphatic of the primer's points, this is also the guideline that Gene and Roger violated most frequently. For example, Roger and Gene had a major disagreement about 1989's *The Return of Swamp Thing*. Roger gave the movie a thumbs up and Gene gave it a thumbs down, right after they had given the opposite votes to a dark indie film called *Lost Angels*. As with their dispute over *Full Metal Jacket* and *Benji the Hunted*, Siskel was flabbergasted that Ebert could give a recommendation to a trifle like *The Return of Swamp Thing* while voting thumbs down on an ambitious (if flawed) movie like *Lost Angels*. And so, for two straight minutes, they bantered back and forth—less about the two specific films than the larger theoretical concepts of good and bad in cinema.

"I expected to see more or less what I saw at *Return of Swamp Thing*. I thought they did a pretty good job of it," Ebert explained. "I felt on its much higher level of ambition and achievement, *Lost Angels* didn't quite make it over the edge."

"And so in other words," Siskel replied, "if you had to see one of these two films again you'd rather see *Swamp Thing*, right?"

Ebert paused. "I'm not sure. I'm really not sure about that."

Eventually, Siskel did get around to knocking *The Return of Swamp Thing*, claiming that unlike the first movie (which earned two yes votes from Gene and Roger on *Sneak Previews*), he felt no sympathy for "Swampy" and thought villain Louis Jourdan looked so "stiff" he was concerned for the actor's health. ("You're supposed to! After all, this man only has twenty-four hours to live unless he can get this injection of new genes!" Ebert replied, which, one must admit, is a very solid argument for an actor looking a little peaked.)

After all that back-and-forth—after Siskel was unable to get Ebert to concede that his choice to rate films relative to their ambitions was flawed, and after Ebert was unable to convince Siskel that *Swamp Thing* was a fun frivolity—Ebert finally declared, "I guess we have a disagreement." To which Siskel derisively chuckled, and said, "No kidding!"

Siskel & Ebert's reviews made the show the gold standard of film criticism on television, which, for a period of about ten years, from the mid-1980s to the mid-'90s, became its own improbable television subgenre. Every time Roger and Gene left a show—*Sneak Previews* for *At the Movies, At the Movies* for *Siskel & Ebert*—their previous series carried on with new hosts. *Sneak Previews* continued with critics Jeffrey Lyons and Neal Gabler; when Gabler left the show in 1985, he was replaced by Michael Medved. Around that same time, Roger and Gene jumped to Disney, and Tribune tried pairing one of the most famous film critics in the country, Rex Reed, with *Entertainment Tonight*'s Bill Harris. When Harris left after two seasons, his replacement, Dixie Whatley, was another *Entertainment Tonight* contributor. (*Entertainment Tonight* also had its own film critic, Leonard Maltin, who filed solo reviews on the celebrity news show for thirty years.)

The public's interest in movie criticism grew so great that even nonprofessionals got into the act. The kids' cable channel Nickelodeon had its own movie review show in the mid-1980s called

Rated K: For Kids by Kids; Gene and Roger sat in on one episode and a dismissive Ebert asked one of the enthusiastic kid hosts, "Have you ever in your travels encountered the word 'hyperbole'?"

Meanwhile, baseball legend Yogi Berra starred in a surreal series of beer commercials called "Yogi at the Movies." Berra, sporting a comb-over to rival Gene Siskel's, would briefly review films (i.e., "*Moonstruck* is a romantic comedy about a Brooklyn Italian family that gets moonstruck!") and give baseball-themed ratings (*Moonstruck* earned a "triple") while hawking Stroh's beer.

By this time, *Siskel & Ebert* aired in hundreds of markets to an audience of several million viewers every week. But not everyone was a fan of the show—or its role in inspiring so much TV talk about the movie business. Some hard-core cinephiles accused *Siskel & Ebert* of dumbing down the conversation around cinema, reducing nuanced discourse to a series of binary yes or no votes.

A lengthy 1988 piece in the *Los Angeles Times* decried "Siskbert," along with the wave of "TV film critics," and actively accused television of "killing film criticism." *Times* critic Patrick Goldstein was particularly put off by the show's use of clips from movies, which he likened to free advertising, whether the critics liked the movies they were discussing or not. He also slammed *Siskel & Ebert* for having the same "heightened visual sensibility" as MTV, adding, "Its economics are a dead ringer for MTV, a seamless sales medium where it's virtually impossible to tell where the videos end and the advertising begins." In a sidebar in the same issue of the *Times*, Ebert defended the show and its use of clips. "When a newspaper film critic reviews a movie, isn't that advertisement for the movie?" he noted. "Have you ever noticed that interviews with famous stars appear in newspapers just at the time the movie is coming out? Why do you time it like that? Don't you just give free publicity when their movie comes out?" Maybe things hadn't changed that much in the criticism business since the days of Frank E. Woods and D. W. Griffith.

One of the most notable attacks on the show came in a 1990 issue of *Film Comment*, one of the country's oldest and most respected forums for long-form film criticism. In an essay titled "All Thumbs: Or, Is There a Future for Film Criticism?" the magazine's former editor in chief, Richard Corliss, penned a three-thousand-word tirade against the sorry state of film culture, claiming that the world of criticism was increasingly a place where "less is more" and "shorter is sweeter." The consumer of film criticism of 1990, Corliss claimed, was only interested in "an opinion that can be codified in numbers, letters, or thumbs."

Corliss, who once named *Beyond the Valley of the Dolls* one of the greatest movies of the 1960s in *Time* magazine, now longed for the days of what he called "elevated" movie criticism practiced by Andrew Sarris of the *Village Voice* and Pauline Kael of the *New Yorker* (both of whom were still regularly writing at the time of this column). Those glory days, when Sarris and Kael regularly lobbed lengthy broadsides at one another about their respective tastes and critical theories, "made film criticism sexy" and "lured people to see new films, and to see old (especially old Hollywood) movies in a new way. They opened eyes, awakened curiosity, aroused intelligence." By 1990, Corliss argued, that sort of criticism was "an endangered species."

Although Corliss's targets were primarily Siskel and Ebert's colleagues and imitators—as well as mainstream media as a whole—he didn't entirely spare Gene and Roger from blame. *Siskel & Ebert*, Corliss wrote, "does not dwell on shot analysis, or any other kind of analysis. It is a sitcom (with its own noodling, toodling theme song) starring two guys who live in a movie theater and argue all the time. Oscar Ebert and Felix Siskel. 'The fat guy and the bald guy.' *S&E&TM* is every kind of TV and no kind of film criticism."

Corliss blamed the dumbing down of film criticism on recent developments in journalism and pop culture, but "All Thumbs" actually revived an argument about the nature of criticism that predated the invention of motion pictures. According to A. O. Scott, "the idea that there's a good kind of criticism that needs to be protected from the bad kind—and the bad kind is always about there being too much of it and it being disseminated in the 'wrong' ways—that was something that was being complained about by Coleridge in the early nineteenth century. In a way, Corliss's attack on *Siskel & Ebert,* and the idea that they pose an existential threat to the integrity and seriousness of film criticism, is the latest version of that kind of attempt to protect what you imagine the serious enterprise of criticism to be from the vulgar version."

Vulgar critics or not, Gene and Roger were the first to admit that *Siskel & Ebert* did not provide the same sort of rigorous analysis as a venue like *Film Comment*—but they were proud of the show, and the good work it did exposing its audience to all kinds of movies from around the world and throughout history. So in the next *Film Comment,* Ebert penned a response titled "All Stars: Or, Is There a Cure for Criticism of Film Criticism?" and rebutted Corliss point by point.

Although Roger agreed that "the age of the packaged instant review is here" and that very few people took the time "to read the good, serious critics," he also pushed back against the notion that the early '90s were some kind of apocalyptic era for film discourse. On the contrary, Ebert wrote, film criticism was "thriving." In the halcyon days that Corliss romanticized, film criticism was a niche within a niche, practiced largely by academics writing for a selfsame audience. By the early 1990s, magazines like *Premiere* and

Entertainment Weekly thrived on newsstands, and most major newspapers and many general interest magazines employed their own film critics. While the audience for "serious film criticism" was still present, a far broader segment of the population was reading and watching movie talk than ever before.

Ebert argued instead that the blame for the film world's issues should be placed at the feet of Hollywood marketing campaigns, which were growing louder and more expensive all the time. "The sad fact," Ebert wrote, "is that film criticism, serious or popular, good or bad, printed or on TV, has precious little power in the face of a national publicity juggernaut for a clever mass-market entertainment."

This is an interesting debate to look back on some thirty years later. Corliss's larger points about the rise of "opinion-mongering" on television and newscasts that offer "more but briefer stories: not news in depth—news in shallow" feel especially prescient. TV news is shallower than ever, but it's practically an Edward R. Murrow broadcast compared to the biased and outright fake "journalism" that spreads on the internet through social media.

Still, pointing a finger at Siskel's and Ebert's thumbs feels like blaming a minor symptom for a much larger disease. It seems especially strange in hindsight that Corliss accused Gene and Roger of doing nothing to open eyes, awaken curiosity, and arouse intelligence, when an entire generation of filmmakers and critics first discovered their love of movies from the show.

"I think *Siskel & Ebert* really had a major influence in upping the ante of the discourse of the American movie," says Robert Thompson, a Syracuse University professor and TV historian. "As idiosyncratic as they were, they knew a lot about film, very much loved film, and very much wanted to be evangelists to get others to take it seriously.

"You can't walk into a place like MIT without having a bunch of people tell you that they got their start getting interested in that kind of thing by watching *Star Trek*," Thompson adds. "What *Star Trek* did for budding young scientists in the sixties, *Siskel & Ebert* did to budding young film people in the 1980s and '90s."

Siskel & Ebert may have looked like a sitcom to Richard Corliss, but to a generation of up-and-coming cinephiles, it was their first taste of film school. And as Gene and Roger settled into their highest-profile gig yet as the hosts of Buena Vista's *Siskel & Ebert*, they seized the opportunity to teach their ever-broadening audience even more, and to advocate for serious, positive change in the world of cinema.

CHAPTER TEN

THE FUTURE OF THE MOVIES

. . . .

You and I have devoted our adult lives—all of our
adult lives—to the movies. Because we love movies.

—GENE SISKEL

Traditional movies are expensive to make,
but the day is coming when features can be
shot in high-def video by virtually anyone.
How will this affect the future of the movies?

—ROGER EBERT

. . . .

Gene Siskel and Roger Ebert hosted hundreds of television
shows and reviewed thousands of movies together. They
only ever collaborated on one book.

It wasn't for lack of interest. After they moved to Disney, the
company's publishing arm reached out to the duo to jointly write a
history of their partnership. (A history of *Siskel & Ebert*? Who
would read something like that?!)

"They offered them a lot of money to do it," Chaz Ebert says.
"And Roger turned it down. He said, 'I'll write a book and you can
have Gene write a book. I don't want to write a book with Gene."
Gene would occasionally pitch such ideas, says Chaz, and Roger

always resisted. "He would say, 'I'm a better writer than Gene. I need a partner on the show, but not as a writer.'"

The lone book they *did* collaborate on happened mostly by accident. After a glitzy event at the American Film Institute in Washington, DC, in 1989, Roger and Gene decided to check out the bar at their hotel, where they happened to bump into three of the AFI's other VIPs: George Lucas, Steven Spielberg, and Martin Scorsese.

Although Siskel typically preferred not to fraternize with filmmakers—he felt doing so might cloud his critical judgment—Ebert felt no such pressure to maintain an appearance of objective detachment, or to give filmmakers he was on good terms with positive reviews. (After growing close with director Robert Altman, Ebert said to him, "You know, I'm still going to review your films exactly how I see them," to which Altman replied, "If you never gave me a bad review, why would I care about the good ones?") So on that night in Washington, DC, arguably the three most powerful directors in the country hung out with inarguably the two most powerful film critics in the world.

As Roger and Gene approached their table, Lucas, Spielberg, and Scorsese were already discussing the subject of film preservation. The rise of home video in the 1980s had sparked renewed interest in classic cinema. It had also sparked an increasing awareness that the negatives of many old movies, including some of the most beloved titles in history, had been so poorly maintained through the years that many were in danger of being lost forever. To that end, Scorsese would soon create the Film Foundation, a nonprofit group dedicated to preserving and restoring classic films.

Film preservation and restoration was a subject close to Siskel's and Ebert's hearts as well. By 1989, they'd begun discussing notable restorations and theatrical rereleases on their show, and they regularly talked about the importance of protecting old movies during the show's weekly home video segment. But while film studios had a financial incentive to invest in restoration, many were reluctant to do so due to high cost. The five men agreed that it would be mutually beneficial to create a television special highlighting these issues. Siskel and Ebert would interview Lucas, Spielberg, and Scorsese about film preservation and other matters vital to the ongoing health of the movie business. *Siskel & Ebert* would get a star-studded special episode full of exclusive interviews with three titans of the film industry. In exchange, the directors got what amounted to an extremely well-made infomercial about their passion project broadcast to millions of people around the country.

The show was called *The Future of the Movies*, and thirty years later, we live in the future it predicted. Asked what home viewing would evolve into, Spielberg boldly announced there would be a world of "made-for-home movies" shot in "high definition . . . bypassing film and the process of the chemicals in film . . . right into an HDTV receiver." At the time, consumer-grade HDTV sets were still about eight years away—and Netflix's online video player was about seventeen years away.

Lucas was even more prophetic. In the same year that the World Wide Web was first invented, the architect of *Star Wars* essentially anticipated the world of streaming movies, and how it would change the theatrical landscape forever, telling Ebert, "I think the marketplace will shift dramatically. I think certain kinds of movies will be made directly for the home and certain kinds of movies will be made for theater presentation . . . the larger, more spectacular ones will end up in the theater and the more personal ones will end up on the screen." The degree to which the show correctly forecast the exact state of cinema circa the early 2020s is almost eerie.

After *The Future of the Movies* TV special premiered in 1990, Roger and Gene turned the transcripts of the three directors' interviews into a companion book of the same name. They believed in Scorsese and the importance of film preservation enough to donate the book's profits to his newly launched Film Foundation.

In the years that followed, Siskel and Ebert embraced their roles as the moviegoing public's chief advocates—of both movies that they felt deserved a wider audience and of causes they believed would improve the world of cinema and how their audience experienced it. For two people who frequently disagreed, Roger and Gene saw eye to eye on many of these issues. Their fights may have been famous, but Siskel and Ebert were far more powerful when they worked together. The positive, lasting changes they helped bring to the film world have outlived *Siskel & Ebert,* and both of its hosts.

Many of these changes arose from what were initially called "Take 2" episodes of *Sneak Previews,* and later became referred to as "Special Editions" of *Siskel & Ebert.* Rather than review four or five new releases, a "Take 2" or "Special Edition" would feature Gene and Roger discussing one important topic in the world of cinema.

These episodes were borne out of necessity. In the early days of *Sneak Previews,* PBS affiliates wanted as many episodes of their biggest hit show as they could get. Crazy as it sounds, says producer Thea Flaum, "there weren't enough movies to fill up fifty-two weeks, or forty-eight weeks, or however many we would have done. There just weren't enough, especially at certain times of the year. So I came up with the idea to do *Sneak Previews* Take 2."

These themed shows were the TV equivalent of one of Roger's or Gene's Sunday columns in the *Sun-Times* or the *Tribune.* Introducing the concept before a "Take 2" episode dedicated to the topic of midnight movies and cult films, Siskel said the occasional specials would "take a more in-depth look at movie genres, issues, and trends; where the movies are now, and where they are headed." A decade before *The Future of the Movies* book and special, the subject was already on their minds.

Some of these shows were fairly innocuous; many were dedicated to recommending overlooked titles that could be found in repertory houses or video stores. But occasionally Roger and Gene would get out their soapbox and lobby for a topic they felt needed addressing. In 1980, they dedicated a full half hour of *Sneak Previews* to decrying what they dubbed "Extreme Violence Directed at Women," which had become an increasingly prevalent trend in cinema after the massive success of John Carpenter's slasher film *Halloween*.

Both Gene and Roger liked and recommended *Halloween*. But they felt that the copycats that followed in its wake, in Ebert's words, "hate women" and "portray them as helpless victims." Showing numerous illustrative clips from violent horror movies, they argued that these films' point-of-view shots from the perspective of sadistic killers were subliminally encouraging audiences to relate to misogynistic murderers, a development Siskel called "depressing."

They didn't just diagnose the problem; they also tried to identify its cause. Siskel tied the rise of violent, hateful slasher movies to a "primordial response" to the women's movement of the 1960s and '70s. The films, he claimed, represented angry men "saying, 'Get back in your place, women!'" Most of the female victims enjoyed an independent, sexually active lifestyle, while most of the killers were sexually frustrated men.

"What was being sold," Siskel later recalled, "for five dollars a ticket price, is a rape fantasy. And it was awful." Responses poured in from women's groups, thanking the show for addressing the issue.

"The response that we got emboldened us," Siskel said. "And we continued to focus on issues."

Whether you agreed or disagreed with Roger and Gene's

premise, they presented a compelling argument against these movies. And whether this episode had an effect on stanching the flow of violent slasher movies pouring into theaters in the late 1970s and early '80s, the episode pushed viewers to reassess their reactions to supposedly harmless entertainments. In other words, this episode of *Sneak Previews* was about as serious a work of film criticism as you're going to find.

As the show's audience grew, so did the hosts' boldness when it came to pushing for change in Hollywood. Any concern that Siskel and Ebert might temper their criticism of the movie studios when they began working for one was squashed by the third week of the Disney-syndicated *Siskel & Ebert*. That's when Gene and Roger released a "Special Edition" episode titled "Colorization: Hollywood's New Vandalism." In it, they lambasted every distributor in Hollywood for a practice that was growing increasingly popular in the mid-'80s, but that Roger and Gene found insidious: the addition of artificial color into old black-and-white movies.

Gene and Roger first encountered a demonstration of colorization at the NATPE convention of television syndicators. Some networks wouldn't air black-and-white movies in prime time—but if those old movies could be given color, they might be sold far more widely. Representatives from the Hal Roach Company had developed a process that added color to its library of old Westerns and Laurel and Hardy films, and they wanted to show the results to the famous film critics.

"They were waiting for us to burst into applause, and we kind of nodded and thanked them for the demonstration," Ebert remembered at a public talk years later. As soon as they got away from the booth, they agreed: it looked awful.

Ebert called the practice an "abomination" that looked like cheap postcards and disrespected the intentions of the artists who'd made the films in the first place. To Gene and Roger, this was the dark side of film preservation—rather than restoring a film to the exact specifications its director intended, greedy distributors were adding colors to movies that never had them and didn't need them, purely to make more money.

Siskel & Ebert was uniquely situated to argue against colorization in ways print film critics never could. A print critic—even one as deft as Roger or Gene—could describe why colorization was bad. But on television they could actually show the problem with outrageous examples of bad artificial color in black-and-white movies. Some of their complaints were humorous—Gene mocked a cheaply colorized version of the Frank Sinatra film *Suddenly* by noting that they had given Ol' Blue Eyes brown eyes—but others were angry. "I don't think anybody has the right to obliterate a person's artistic creation," Siskel explained during one of the more intense parts of the episode.

"Literally what we were saying was, 'You know what? Somebody is defaming what we love,'" Siskel said later of the episode. "In other words, if you're in a museum and someone throws a bucket of paint on a great painting, do you stand there, do you tell the guard, or do you try and tackle the person and arrest them? Well, we wanted to tackle them and knock them out. And I think we were, in part, successful."

"There was a time when colorization was poised to go somewhere," Ebert agreed. "Ted Turner was busy colorizing everything he could find that was both black and white and didn't star Henry Fonda. And our show just turned that around a little bit. People who were informed began to tell each other, 'You know, that's not right.' And Turner wound up with a warehouse full of *Casablanca* tapes that were colorized that he couldn't move."

Even after they helped end the rise of colorized movies by

educating the public that they were a rip-off rather than a bonus, Gene and Roger continued to argue for the beauty of black-and-white movies. Two years after their screed against colorization, they made what they both considered one of their greatest episodes ever: a tribute to the glory of black-and-white photography, shot entirely in black and white.

"Hail, Hail, Black and White!" showed clips from more than two dozen black-and-white movies, while Roger and Gene, wearing tuxedos instead of their usual blazers over sweaters, tried to persuade their viewers that black-and-white films were not "missing" color, because they were rich in qualities that color movies could never replicate. Ebert said black and white "distills" things down to their essence. Siskel revealed he dreamed in black and white. Ebert claimed women look sexier in black and white. And Gene got in at least one dig at Roger's expense; when Ebert noted that black-and-white movies look better than color on television, Siskel quipped, "For example, *you* look halfway decent right now." (Put-downs aside, they were particularly proud that WBBM had brought back the retired gaffer who had lit the 1960 presidential debate between John Kennedy and Richard Nixon—which was recorded in the same studio where they shot their weekly show— to light the Balcony in black and white for the episode.)

Another "Special Edition" put them in direct conflict with their new bosses at Disney. Walt Disney had made *Snow White and the Seven Dwarfs* in the standard aspect ratio of the 1930s: 4:3, roughly the same dimensions of a boxy tube TV set. With the popularization of television in the 1950s, film studios responded to the increased competition by shooting new productions in wide-screen: 1.85:1 or 2.35:1, images that were much wider than they were tall, and could only be fully appreciated when projected in a movie theater. So when Disney rereleased *Snow White and the Seven*

Dwarfs in 1987, they cropped the top and bottom of the print to fit on modern theater screens.

During their review, Siskel and Ebert didn't just point this out, they illustrated the problem by superimposing black bars over the top and bottom of a close-up of Ebert's face in order to show how Disney was robbing their paying customers of the full *Snow White* experience. Then Ebert went further, wagging his finger and saying, "Shame on Disney!" (the company sending him a paycheck every two weeks) for butchering their own masterpiece. Once again, Roger and Gene used the unique qualities of a TV show to do film criticism in ways print film critics couldn't.

Week after week, *Siskel & Ebert* educated its viewers about matters that ranged from the gravely important to the amusingly trivial. Ebert once wrote that if *Siskel & Ebert* had a theme, it was the belief "that movies should always be seen, as nearly as possible, in exactly the form their makers intended." That thinking led the hosts to attack the Motion Picture Association of America for its lack of a legitimate, commercially viable adults-only rating, and helped spark the conversation that led to the introduction of the NC-17. They dedicated a whole episode to silent cinema, encouraging their viewers to discover the works of Charlie Chaplin, Sergei Eisenstein, and Abel Gance. And they produced a series of "Special Editions" called "They'll Do It Every Time," where they delighted in pointing out the most egregious clichés in modern movies, backing up their criticism with hilarious clips of trucks flying into fruit stands and killers explaining their evil plans in enough detail that their movies' heroes could foil their schemes just in the nick of time.

Gene and Roger were particularly clued in to movie clichés because they saw so many films; upward of half a dozen every single week. They were also attuned to movies that bucked clichés, and those were the films they wound up championing the loudest and longest. When they loved an original movie that they felt needed their support, they wouldn't just review it; they would discuss it over and over again, any chance they got, in an effort to drum up attention and boost its box office numbers. Their support sometimes made the difference between a flop and a hit—and between a filmmaker receding into a life of anonymity and going on to a prolific Hollywood career.

In 1978, a tiny independent documentary about two California pet cemeteries premiered at the New York Film Festival. The movie didn't get good reviews, because it essentially didn't get *any* reviews; the 1978 New York Film Festival fell during a newspaper strike, with the city's three biggest papers, the *New York Times*, the *New York Post*, and the New York *Daily News* all shut down from mid-August to early November. As a result, *Gates of Heaven* came and went from the festival very quietly.

The film's director, Errol Morris, moved on to other projects. *Gates of Heaven* played a few other festivals. In the summer of 1981, Gene Siskel and Roger Ebert saw it—today, Morris says he isn't even sure how or why. But however they saw it, they loved it. And they went on to give it one of the most enthusiastic reviews in the history of *Sneak Previews*. Ebert called it a masterpiece. Siskel said that while he liked all five movies on that week's episode, you could add the other four films up and "together they don't equal the beauty, the poetry, the directorial imagination" of *Gates of Heaven*.

Morris had no idea the review was coming, and he watched the episode of *Sneak Previews* in utter disbelief. "It was like being hit by lightning," he says. "Except, not having had the other experience, I believe far more pleasant."

A few months later, Siskel and Ebert discussed the movie again, in a "Take 2" episode called "Buried Treasures." A month after that, *Gates of Heaven* appeared on both their lists of the best movies of 1981. Morris says their constant praise and discussion of the movie helped the film find an audience. He believes their reviews changed his life.

"This sounds hyperbolic, but I don't think it is. They gave me a career," he explains. "They gave me a reason to go on with it at all. They had an inherent understanding of me and what I was trying to do. They were for me, and I think for a lot of other people, a force for good. They gave me something which is in terribly short supply in my life: they gave me hope. Quite simply, I loved them." In 1998, Siskel said receiving "letters of appreciation" from the filmmaking community for their work promoting lesser-known and up-and-coming talents was "among the most satisfying aspects of our job."

The same year Siskel and Ebert went to bat for *Gates of Heaven*, they also threw their weight behind an independently financed drama about the most mundane of subjects: two old acquaintances talking over a meal. The film, *My Dinner with Andre*, starred and was written by two real-life friends, André Gregory and Wallace Shawn, and was inspired by real events and real conversations between the two. But the finished product amounted to little more than eavesdropping on a 110-minute conversation. The sheer concept—two people just sit and *talk* for almost two hours straight—flew in the face of every rule of movies. Maybe that's why Roger and Gene loved it so much. (The fact that two people sitting and talking was the same concept that had turned Siskel and Ebert into television stars may have helped their appreciation of it just a smidge.)

"This, to me, knocks all of the notions about what movies have to be into a cocked hat," raved Siskel. "We have Hollywood spending tens of millions of dollars to faithfully re-create towns and villages and everything else. And here, with people talking at a dinner table, it's just as fascinating. More so! This is what I want films to be like."

"I've never seen another film like this, and I don't know if there *could* be another film like this," Ebert countered. "But I'm glad *this* film is like this."

By the time that review of *My Dinner with Andre* aired on a Thursday night in New York City, the movie was on the verge of closing at the local Lincoln Plaza Cinema. "The fact was that the film was selling very few tickets," admits Wallace Shawn. "We kept trying to convince Dan [Talbot, *My Dinner with Andre*'s distributor] that the film would catch on, that word of mouth would soon provide an audience, because people who saw it loved it." Talbot was unmoved, and began placing ads counting down the days until *My Dinner with Andre* would close.

Then that *Sneak Previews* review aired. The very next screening of *My Dinner with Andre* later that night sold out. Then the next and the next. The countdown ads stopped running in the New York papers. Instead of closing, *My Dinner with Andre* stayed at the Lincoln Plaza Cinema for a year straight, and it wound up playing in more than nine hundred theaters all over the United States. When it finally closed in Manhattan, Shawn and Gregory invited Siskel and Ebert to join them onstage for a post-screening Q&A, where they credited the show with helping transform *My Dinner with Andre*'s financial fortunes overnight. ("There's no question that if it hadn't been for Siskel and Ebert, the film would not only have been financially unsuccessful, but everyone would have remembered it as one more avant-garde experiment that just didn't work," Shawn says.) Siskel called the night "a fabulous thrill and the ultimate point of being a critic."

Siskel and Ebert's magic took a little longer in the case of *Hoop Dreams*. It was also perhaps the most improbable smash they helped to engineer. It featured no stars, no famous filmmakers, and a prodigious run time of three hours. It was also a serious documentary about life in Chicago's inner city for two high school basketball prospects and their families, shot on video, made at a time when most nonfiction movies were lucky if they got played on public television. Wide theatrical releases for films of its kind were almost unheard of.

It was also unheard of for *Siskel & Ebert* to review a movie before it had even premiered at a film festival, but that was precisely what the show did with *Hoop Dreams*. Shortly before the documentary was set to debut at the 1994 Sundance Film Festival, the movie's publicist, John Iltis, slipped a copy to Gene and Roger. Gene rarely traveled to festivals, so the show seldom discussed them outside of occasional dispatches hosted by Roger. But according to *Hoop Dreams* director Steve James, Iltis believed they might make an exception to that rule for his movie. Gene loved basketball, and both were obviously passionate about life in Chicago. Why not give it a shot?

"Somehow, [Iltis] convinced those guys to watch it," says James. "And I remember talking to John after the screening was over. I said, 'How'd it go?' He says, 'Well, you know, critics never want to tell you anything. They're very stone-faced about it. I think they liked it, but they didn't talk about it.' And then he says, as they headed for the elevator, the door opened and he heard Roger say, 'You know, one thing I thought was really interesting—' and then the door closed."

They might have had their poker faces on when Iltis was around, but Chaz Ebert says that by the end of their private *Hoop Dreams* screening, Gene and Roger were high-fiving in the theater. They loved the film more than almost any other in all of the years working together. (Both picked it as the number one movie of 1994, ahead of Quentin Tarantino's *Pulp Fiction*. At the end of the '90s, Ebert would pick it as his number one movie of the entire decade.) The week that *Hoop Dreams* debuted in Park City, Utah, at the Sundance Film Festival, *Siskel & Ebert* dedicated a segment of their show to it, hailing it as "a very special documentary" and one of the best films about American life that they had ever seen.

The review wound up airing during Sundance, after the movie had already played once. *Hoop Dreams'* first screening after the *Siskel & Ebert* review was at a terrible time slot for a three-hour documentary: 10:30 p.m. But because of the review, James says the screening was packed with distributors who couldn't stop telling him how excited they were to see the film. "And showing up at all for a ten-thirty screening," he adds, "which normally they would not do.

"You have to remember," James says almost thirty years later, "that at that time maybe one documentary a year would get a legitimate theatrical release. *Roger & Me*, or *The Thin Blue Line,* or *Brother's Keeper.* Maybe one doc a year would get that. And they were all shot on film, too. *Hoop Dreams* was shot on video. I remember Iltis saying to us at the time, 'If people ask you what it's shot on, tell them it was shot on film,' because there was a fear that the fact that it originated on video would be the death knell of any kind of potential theatrical release. That coupled with the fact that it was three hours long about two guys nobody had ever heard of. The *Siskel & Ebert* review was what galvanized all of it for distributors to think, 'Well, maybe this *is* a theatrical film.'"

As with *Gates of Heaven*, Siskel and Ebert's continued support ensured it was. In fact, James says despite the fact that *Siskel & Ebert* reviewed the film prior to Sundance and then again when it opened in theaters in the fall of 1994, *Hoop Dreams* still wasn't performing all that well until the film got snubbed for an Academy Award nomination for Best Documentary in the spring of 1995. At that point, Roger and Gene talked about the movie *again* in a segment, where they excoriated the Academy of Motion Picture Arts and Sciences' documentary branch. "This situation stinks! It's rotten!" Ebert said of *Hoop Dreams'* lack of a Best Documentary nomination.

James watched the Oscar nomination announcements from the offices of *Hoop Dreams*' production company in Chicago. After the movie was totally shut out beyond a nomination for Best Editing, James returned home. As soon as he got there, his phone rang.

"It's Roger Ebert," James says. "And he goes, 'I am outraged!'" Ironically, *Hoop Dreams*' omission from the Best Documentary category, and all of the publicity it drummed up for the film, finally turned it into a box office hit.

"I think at the time when the nominations were announced, it had done like a million dollars in the theaters," James says. "And after that, it did six to seven million." (Siskel and Ebert's outrage may have had another impact; within a year, the Academy had changed the rules surrounding how movies were nominated in the Best Documentary category.)

While Gene and Roger's Oscar prognostications could be hit or miss—Roger once forecast a Best Picture nomination for Michael Moore's *Roger & Me* and it wound up not even getting nominated for Best Documentary—their predictions about actors' and directors' careers were usually right on target. One of the more remarkable things about watching vintage *Siskel & Ebert* episodes today is how often they correctly divined which young artists were destined for greatness. Siskel declared that future *Gravity* and *Roma* director Alfonso Cuarón was a "find" after his first English-language effort, *A Little Princess*, and correctly speculated that Hollywood would "swarm" Oscar-winner Guillermo del Toro after he watched his low-budget horror movie *Mimic*. Ebert recognized that Jennifer Lopez was a star in the making when she appeared in the title role of 1997's *Selena*, and said he expected computer animation "to create entire movies" with "breathtaking" visual possibilities in 1992, three years before *Toy Story* opened in movie theaters.

Two years before that prediction, Gene Siskel wrote in his afterword to *The Future of the Movies* book that he was concerned about the "tailspin" that movies seemed to be in. Everywhere he looked, he saw motion pictures that were "shrinking in size and spirit to become little more than oversized television." He predicted that things wouldn't improve or get more exciting in the world of movies "until we have some good old-fashioned upheaval in this country and the world beyond." And he wrote that somewhere out there ("right now, perhaps reading this book") was a young film student who viewed *The Future of the Movies*' three interview subjects as "tired, as complacent, as the establishment.

"That person," Siskel added, "is the future of the movies."

Gene Siskel was always fascinated by the future. And while he was often pessimistic about the evolution of cinema, as in that passage, he was excited about the future of mankind as a whole. One of his most consistent complaints on *Siskel & Ebert* was the way movies about the future depicted it as a miserable place. "Why make the future so bleak?" Siskel wondered while reviewing the sci-fi film *Screamers*. "I'm tired of it! Break the rule! Please!"

In contrast, in 1992, Roger and Gene reviewed a Russian movie called *Close to Eden,* about a family of Mongolian farmers that encounters a Russian truck driver and has to grapple with modernity encroaching on their ancient ways. While Roger dismissed the movie's "tacked-on ending" about pollution and the modern world, Gene said he loved the conclusion and found *Close to Eden* to be "a very hopeful film in a strange way about what life will be like in the twenty-first century. I think things are going to get better, not worse.

"We're going to be okay as a civilization," Siskel mused. "And I like that."

Sadly, Gene Siskel would not live to see whether that prediction came true.

CHAPTER ELEVEN

THE BALCONY IS CLOSED

. . . .

There's a line late in the picture where in talking
about a character someone says, "Some people
die. And some people don't." And I thought how
beautiful a line that was. That you can live a life
in a fashion so that you will never die.

—GENE SISKEL

Gene told me . . . it wasn't necessary to think too
much about an afterlife. What was important was
this life, how we live it, what we contribute, our
families, and the memories we leave.

—ROGER EBERT

. . . .

I n the spring of 1989, Gene Siskel and Roger Ebert delivered the
single harshest review of their careers together. The occasion
was *She's Out of Control*, in Siskel's words a "trash, TV-style"
comedy about a father (Tony Danza) who becomes obsessed with
guarding his teenage daughter's budding sexuality.

As Siskel described it, it was even ickier than it sounded.
"When I saw *She's Out of Control,* I became so depressed I actually
thought about quitting my job as a film critic, feeling as though the
movies had abandoned me," he confessed. "Fortunately, however,

I would see the movie *Say Anything*... later in the same day, and all is right with the world. I'm still on the job."

"People probably think you're joking when you're saying you were really thinking of quitting your job, but I know what you felt," Ebert replied. "Because I sat there and I thought, 'Life is precious! Life is short! And the idiots who made this film are taking two hours of my life and robbing it from me in order to give me less than nothing!'"

That was pretty tough stuff, even by *Siskel & Ebert*'s standards—and Roger still wasn't done. "A movie like this is a *crime*," he continued. "What it does is it robs life from people by requiring to spend two hours having such a terrible experience happen to them."

Film critics have a unique relationship with time. All movies are, in one way or another, about time: how it moves and how it is perceived. A great film can make us hyperaware of time's passing by lingering on a shot for minutes or hours—like the unforgettable opening shot of Orson Welles's *Touch of Evil,* which follows a car with a bomb in its trunk for three full minutes as the audience waits in breathless anticipation for an explosion. Or movies can leap thousands of years in the span of a single edit—as Stanley Kubrick did when he cut from a hominid at the dawn of man tossing a bone into the air to a highly advanced satellite gliding through space in the future of *2001: A Space Odyssey,* a favorite film of both Gene's and Roger's.

But while time flows in strange ways on a theater screen, it always marches inexorably forward for the men and women in the audience. Of all the complaints Roger and Gene were apt to lob at a bad movie, accusing it of wasting the audience's time was by far the most severe. Calling out a Tony Danza comedy for the crime-of-life theft may have been a tad hyperbolic, but it was not inaccurate from Gene's and Roger's perspective.

By the late 1990s, Gene Siskel and Roger Ebert had both worked as film critics for three decades. Busy reviewers see upward of 250 movies every single year—so Roger and Gene watched at least 7,500 movies over that period. Assuming those movies had an average run time of an hour and forty-five minutes, that means they spent about 13,125 hours in theaters and screening rooms over that period. A single year contains 8,760 hours—so they had logged far more than a full calendar year of their lives watching movies in the dark. It couldn't have felt great to recognize you'd given over that much of your precious time on Earth to dreck like *Leonard Part 6* or *Highlander II: The Quickening.*

The longer they stayed on the job, the more Siskel and Ebert talked about the hours they felt had been stolen by the movies. In a 1996 interview, Siskel said that he told readers that by going to movies they "are spending something more valuable than money—your life," and if a movie didn't work after an hour they should "get up and leave." Of the crummy 1990 thriller *Lisa*, Ebert mused, "If the two hours you spend in front of the screen are not as interesting as two hours you could spend outside the theater, why spend your money?" (Siskel suggested potential viewers could enjoy themselves more "just in the lobby of the theater, overpaying for refreshments.") Discussing 1997's wannabe children's adventure film *Masterminds*, Siskel announced, "We know we have one of the great jobs of all time. But this is when it's rough, because you're being robbed of your life."

"Two hours. Gone forever," Ebert agreed, before dramatically repeating, "Gone. For. *EVER.*"

That episode aired in August of 1997. In April of 1998, Chicago's Museum of Broadcast Communications honored the pair with a special benefit dinner celebrating their twenty-three years as two of the city's biggest television stars. During their final speech of the evening, among their thank-yous to Thea Flaum, Eliot Wald, Joe Antelo, and others, Gene Siskel made a point to deliver some pointed remarks to his daughters, Kate and Callie, in the audience.

"If they're wondering why all this has happened, we've given lots of reasons," he said. "I want you girls to know that the one thing that *hasn't* been mentioned is that we found a job that we love. And as you go out into the world and get a job, I want you to know that the most important thing is loving your work. And Roger and I love more than just doing a television show. It started with love of newspapers as kids even younger than you. When you feel passion about one aspect of your job, it's easy to translate it to another—and then we fell in love with the movies, and we found jobs. And I loved watching TV as a kid. I was born in '46, I grew up with television literally, so think about it: our job combines three things that I love—newspapers, television, and movies.

"And I hope that the work that you do, the work that you choose, that you will take a very quick inventory of it and decide, 'Do I love this? *Can* I love this?' And I don't mean like a lot, I mean passionately love. That you would hate having it taken away from you. That's a very good test.

"In a few years," he added, "I hope you remember this and tell your younger brother what I said. I'd appreciate that very, very much." (Siskel's son, Will, was still a toddler at the time.)

For weeks leading up to that speech, Gene had been suffering from unexplained headaches. At first, he would complain to the *Siskel & Ebert* staff that his beloved Starbucks must have screwed up his coffee order, because he felt off. But the headaches didn't go away.

The month after the benefit dinner, *The Tonight Show with Jay Leno* came to Chicago to record a week of shows at the Rosemont Theatre. One night, Gene and Roger were Leno's second guests, following Arsenio Hall and preceding a performance by the Blue Man Group. By the end of the '90s, the pair were seasoned talk show veterans; they had already been on Leno's version of the *Tonight Show* nine times. The appearance, in their hometown no less, should have been a piece of cake.

But the day of the *Tonight Show* taping, Gene and Roger had shot two *Siskel & Ebert* episodes back-to-back to cover for Roger's impending trip to the Cannes Film Festival. Gene struggled with a headache the entire time. Then, on the limo ride over to the *Tonight Show*, the pain became unbearable.

As was Leno's custom every time Gene and Roger were on the show, the host stopped by their dressing room prior to the taping to say hello and catch up. He found Siskel lying in the dark with a cold compress over his eyes.

"Jeez, why don't you just go?" Leno asked.

"No, no. I want to finish what we're doing," Siskel replied.

That night on the *Tonight Show*, Gene and Roger were supposed to take part in a comedy sketch involving a bunch of Jay Leno look-alikes. They would be the judges.

"My headache is too bad to focus on it," Siskel told Ebert. "You do it and I'll agree with everything you say. You can look amazed. We can make it a schtick."

They got through the show, at which point Roger and *Siskel & Ebert* executive producer Stuart Cleland told Siskel they thought he should go to the hospital. No way, he said, the Bulls had a big playoff game that night, and he had tickets. And off he went, to watch the Bulls lose to the Charlotte Hornets, 78–76.

That was May 6, 1998. On May 8, Gene Siskel was diagnosed with terminal brain cancer.

But five days later, the *Chicago Tribune* reported that Siskel had undergone a procedure it described in vague terms as "the removal of a growth in the brain." It also claimed his prognosis was "good" and that Siskel "expects to be back taping his syndicated TV program, *Siskel & Ebert*, when his colleague Roger Ebert returns from the Cannes Film Festival." That same week Siskel released a statement of his own that read "People deal with these things successfully all the time, and not just in the movies."

None of the articles or press releases made mention of brain cancer, terminal or otherwise. That's because the only people who knew the truth about Gene Siskel's condition were a handful of his immediate family members. No one at *Siskel & Ebert* realized how serious his health crisis was. Not even Roger Ebert. On May 13, Ebert emailed a colleague that he was "relieved that [Gene] came through surgery with flying colors and is mending quickly. The outlook is good, and he plans to be in the balcony for our next scheduled program." He wasn't putting a bold face on bad news— that's genuinely what he believed based on the limited information he'd been given.

Instead, the staff was told a variation of the same information in the *Tribune* article. Stuart Cleland relayed the limited details he had: that Siskel had had surgery to remove a "growth" and that he planned to return to hosting the show. Associate producer Carie Lovstad—a confidant of Siskel's and something like an unofficial personal assistant—only knew he was going to get some "tests" done. It wasn't until much later that she learned that in fact Gene was getting tests at Memorial Sloan Kettering in New York City, one of the leading centers for cancer treatment in the United States.

The strict code of secrecy around Siskel's condition even extended into the upper ranks of Buena Vista Television, *Siskel & Ebert*'s syndication company. "I didn't know how bad it was," says Mary Kellogg, the executive who oversaw *Siskel & Ebert* for Disney all through the 1990s. "It was very secretive. There was no dialogue between the family and us. And I'm respectful of that, but it put me in a terrible position. Because the studio was saying, 'Well, what's going on? What's happening?' And all I could say is 'It's not good.' But I couldn't give them any facts because I didn't have them."

"What I remember is knowing that things weren't good, but not knowing *how* bad they were," says David Plummer, a relatively new addition to *Siskel & Ebert* in 1998 as the show's production secretary. "I don't know that *anyone* really knew what was going on."

In twenty-three years of hosting the show together, neither Gene nor Roger had ever filmed an episode without the other. Apart from the occasional broken bone here or there, and Roger's 1987 surgery to remove a benign tumor in his right jaw, they had both stayed in remarkably good health since the late 1970s. ("Cal Ripken has nothing on us," Siskel quipped in 1995.) Siskel was determined to prove he was still capable of doing his job, and he returned to work less than a month after his surgery. While in the midst of his recovery, he joined the show via telephone to offer his thoughts on *Fear and Loathing in Las Vegas* and *Godzilla*—a blockbuster that included the characters of Mayor Ebert and his sidekick, Gene, a dig that Siskel found "petty." To visually cover his absence, director Don DuPree used stills of Gene in split screen with Roger live in the Balcony. ("I hope our producers have selected a really good photo of me that our audience will be forced to stare at for the next few minutes," Gene joked.)

For a show recorded by two men in totally separate locations who couldn't see each other—while one of them was still recuperating from brain surgery—the phone system worked surprisingly well. Reviewing his own performance in an interview with the *Chicago Tribune*, Siskel said he felt "perfectly fine" and asserted the show "didn't feel any different" than it had before his illness.

That was a testament to the strength of the rapport Gene and Roger had honed through their years together. Still, Roger did occasionally look uncomfortable in the Balcony for the first time in decades. Delivering comments about Warren Beatty's political satire *Bulworth*, he seemed unsure where to look and how to relate to the camera without Gene to bounce off of. And in an interview with the *Chicago Sun-Times*, Ebert admitted that while he was "really happy with how the show went," he had no "medical details at all" about Gene and "no idea" where he was calling from.

"I don't even know what city he was in," he confessed.

When the episode was over, Ebert went to give their customary sign-off—"That's next week and until then, the Balcony is closed"—when Gene interrupted.

"Roger, I just have one question: Has anyone tried to sit in my seat?"

"Nobody," Ebert said as the camera cut to a close-up of Gene's empty chair in the Balcony.

"Good," Siskel replied. "Keep them out."

Gene delivered the line like a joke, but it also seemed to reveal some of his own worries about his tenuous position at the show during his illness.

"I suspect he and Marlene knew he had a disease that might prove fatal, and that they wanted to keep living the same life—personally and professionally—as long as possible," Stuart Cleland said in a 2012 interview. "That meant releasing very little information, even to us, and treating his illness as just a temporary bump in the road."

So Gene kept the severity of his prognosis secret and carried on. That first episode with Gene live via telephone from his hospital room ended with Roger announcing that his cohost hoped to be "back in the Balcony very soon." Very soon came just three

weeks later, when Gene returned to the set at WBBM to debate titles like the big-screen version of *The X-Files* and Disney's animated
film *Mulan*. Reintroducing himself to the audience after his absence he quipped, "To Hollywood, I just want to say: just when you
thought it was safe to make a bad movie."

Hollywood, though, was pleased to have Siskel back. During
his recuperation, he'd received get-well notes from prominent
Hollywood filmmakers as well as from fans. Dustin Hoffman sent
flowers with a note: "I need you to review *Ishtar II*." (Gene and
Roger had put the notorious bomb on their list of the worst movies
of 1987. Siskel wrote Hoffman back, suggesting this time they
should call the movie *Ishtar II: The Comedy*.)

"My recovery has been rapid and, if I can say it, enjoyable,"
Siskel said in an interview. "I'm happy to have done it. I've always
read about people who have a medical problem, [and] through
hard work and attention to their physical therapy, have come back
strong and surprised their doctors. I never wanted to be one of
those people who didn't do that. I achieved that goal."

The production team at *Siskel & Ebert* wasn't so sure. With Siskel back in the Balcony, the motto around the office became "Good
and Great and Fine"—as in "How's Gene doing?" "Good! Yeah,
great! Fine. Good, great, fine." No one knew how he was actually
doing, but they knew enough about Gene's desire for privacy not
to ask too many questions.

"He worked really hard to try to get back up to speed," Carie
Lovstad says. "But seeing him every day, I could tell that he was
struggling. He was not quite the same as he was before he had his
surgery."

Viewers noticed as well. In a cab with Lovstad, Gene was
furious to read a letter published in the *Chicago Tribune*'s *Parade*
section. "I was watching *Siskel & Ebert* and noticed that Siskel

seemed to have difficulty with his speech and reacted slower to Ebert's comments," a viewer named Glen Dettwiler wrote. "Did he have a stroke, or is there some other problem?"

The letter, published in Walter Scott's "Personality Parade" column, noted that "doctors reportedly discovered a brain tumor and removed a benign growth" and even included a comment from the critic himself: "Siskel, 52, who won't provide medical details and has tried to make light of his ailment, told us: 'I think things are going so well because of my balanced diet—popcorn, Dots and Raisinets.'"

For someone who had always been known for his quickness and intellect, not to mention the tenacity with which he engaged his cohost in spirited conversation, seeing that letter in print stung. Siskel's frustration made sense, but because he never told viewers the precise nature of his health issues, so did their curiosity and speculation. Lovstad tried to calm him down by explaining that his fans' concern was understandable. But that only made Siskel angrier, Lovstad says.

"It was really hard to see that," she adds. "He seemed like somebody who was so invincible. And for a while he really seemed like he was. He bounced back so quickly."

But only so far. Gene's illness had taken its toll, and it was becoming noticeable on camera. His producer at *CBS This Morning*, Al Berman, says the single most painful moment of his entire professional career came when he had to have a conversation with Siskel about his performance a short time after his brain surgery.

"I had to tell Gene that the problem he was having was starting to show up on-screen, and it was turning into a negative for him," recalls Berman. "He said, 'Really?' And I said, 'Really. We've been noticing it. But I just want to tell you for your sake that it's become very noticeable and kind of distracting. I'm not sure you want to be in that situation.' And he said, 'You're right. I don't.' And that was it for him appearing [on *CBS This Morning*]. . . . That's the toughest thing I've ever had to do. I've laid off people, been in other very difficult situations, but that was it. He was such a young guy, in his early fifties. That spoke to his character and to the tragedy that was the end of his life, and the graceful way he went about it."

Gene's health was beginning to affect *Siskel & Ebert* as well. The key to the show had always been an intellectual battle of wills between equals. After Siskel got sick, the central dynamic fell off-kilter; it no longer felt like a fair fight. Still, while Gene did speak a little slower upon his return in the summer of 1998—and while he and Roger never really went at it like they used to from that point on—Siskel's reviews arguably got more personal and profound after his diagnosis. After sounding so disheartened about the state of American cinema a few years earlier in his afterword to *The Future of the Movies* book, he was thrilled by the risk-taking films he saw in 1998. He called *The Truman Show*, the timely and insightful story of a man who discovers his entire life takes place inside a television show, "nothing less than a watershed movie" and declared that cinema was finally returning to "the way things used to be that made us want to be film critics in the first place thirty years ago when we were in college, and that is films of ideas."

With the benefit of hindsight, Siskel's final episodes take on deeply moving dimensions. He never told anyone outside his family that he was dying. But a series of confessional reviews sometimes hinted at the gravity of the situation. Siskel's deteriorating condition, for example, gives particular poignancy to his remarks about *Meet Joe Black*, a glossy romantic drama about an extremely handsome Grim Reaper (Brad Pitt), who falls in love with a young woman and helps an aging businessman (Anthony Hopkins) come to terms with his own imminent death.

"I like this film's message," Gene mused. "The message is: Love intensely. And take your life seriously."

At the opposite end of the spectrum, when it came time to select the single worst movie of 1998, Gene chose *Patch Adams*, a treacly comedy about an eccentric doctor, played by Robin Williams, who believes laughter is the best medicine. Siskel had a lot of personal experience with doctors in 1998, and he openly declared he "couldn't stand this character," and promised that if "[Patch Adams] ever tried to get near me, I'd switch HMOs in an instant."

Just one week later, in late January of 1999, Gene Siskel appeared on his namesake television show for the final time—although even then, no one outside of Siskel's closest family knew it would be his last episode. Physically, Siskel was in rough shape. By the end of 1998, he needed assistance getting to his seat in the Balcony—and requested to be seated on set before Roger arrived.

Mentally, though, Gene was still capable of the same insights and wit. That last *Siskel & Ebert* appearance saw Gene deliver a showbiz joke with perfect timing: "Two goats are eating cans of films on the back lot of MGM. . . . One goat says, 'This film is pretty good.' The other goat looks up, chewing: 'Not as good as the book!'"

The final movie Gene Siskel and Roger Ebert ever reviewed together was *The Theory of Flight*, an early work by future *Bloody Sunday* and *The Bourne Supremacy* director Paul Greengrass. Fittingly, the film, which starred Helena Bonham Carter and Kenneth Branagh, was about illness, with Bonham Carter playing a woman with amyotrophic lateral sclerosis who wishes to lose her virginity. Also fittingly, Gene and Roger split on the movie, with Siskel giving a thumbs up to its unpredictable love story and Ebert voting thumbs down because it played to him like the "lite version" of a similar picture that debuted at Cannes the prior year called *Dance*

Me to My Song. Siskel and Ebert disagreed to the very end—to the very last review on their very last show.

Gene Siskel ended his twenty-year tenure on *Siskel & Ebert* not with a maudlin speech about his life and career or a grateful tribute to his viewers or his partner, but with a correction. Two weeks earlier on *Siskel & Ebert's* annual "Memo to the Academy" show, where Roger and Gene lobbied Oscar voters on behalf of their favorite movies and artists, Gene had argued for one of his favorite actors, James Woods, to get a long-shot Oscar nomination for his work in the horror film *John Carpenter's Vampires*. Siskel claimed that Woods was especially deserving because he had given so many great performances through the years that had gone unrecognized by the Academy, which had only given him a single Oscar nomination to that point. In fact, Woods had earned two nominations, one for Oliver Stone's *Salvador* and one for Rob Reiner's *Ghosts of Mississippi*, which Siskel acknowledged shortly before the episode's credits rolled. He never stopped being a newspaperman dedicated to the truth and accurately reporting the facts.

On February 3, Siskel announced he was taking a "leave of absence" from the show for the remainder of the 1998–99 season—although he still refused to reveal his diagnosis. Instead, the release claimed he was taking more time off to heal from his brain surgery the prior spring, and he would return for next season's premiere. ("I'm in a hurry to get well," Siskel added, "because I don't want Roger to get more screen time than I. Also, this experience will give me a chance to work out my left thumb—the stunt double.") The report on Siskel's condition in the February 4 *Chicago Sun-Times* called his time off an "intermission." It quoted Ebert wishing Gene "a speedy continued recovery."

Roger wasn't just going along with Siskel's story for the sake of being a good friend. While others on staff suspected the worst,

Chaz Ebert says Roger truly did not know that he'd already re-corded his final episode of *Siskel & Ebert* with his longtime partner.

"We were all so happy that day," says Chaz Ebert. "Gene came and did the show. He was very happy he was able to get through it. Roger and Gene joked a little bit." She adds that while she and Roger thought returning in September sounded like a "long time," they genuinely believed that he would be back in the fall.

Seventeen days later, Gene Siskel died at Evanston Hospital, surrounded by his family. He was only fifty-three years old.

Publicly, Roger Ebert gave one moving tribute after another to his rival turned professional partner. His first public statement on the news read "Gene was a lifelong friend, and our professional competition only strengthened that bond. He showed great brav-ery in the months after his surgery, continuing to work as long as he could. As a critic, he was passionate and exacting. As a husband and a father, his love knew no bounds." In *Star* magazine, he said Gene "kept private about the state of his health in the months after surgery and I understand why. He wanted to protect his family from the attention that might result."

Privately, Roger was heartbroken that Gene never told him the full extent of his illness. "Even to this day," Chaz Ebert says, "it's kind of stunning to me, because I remember how hurt Roger was. He was devastated." She says that the first inkling they got of Gene's real status was just a few days before his death, when someone in Siskel's family called Roger.

"I think you should know," the caller said. "You think Gene's coming back to the show, but he's not. He's dying. And if you want to see him, you should go see him now."

Roger and Chaz immediately made plans to visit Gene in the hospital the following Monday, February 22. Instead, Ebert spent the day as one of the pallbearers at Siskel's funeral, an event attended by 1,500 family, friends, and colleagues—including such luminaries as Chicago mayor Richard Daley and Oprah Winfrey—at Synagogue Beth El in Highland Park. It was the same synagogue where Siskel's aunt and uncle had been among the founding members in the 1940s, and where Siskel had his bar mitzvah forty years earlier. Just a few weeks earlier, Siskel had attended his daughter Callie's bat mitzvah there as well. Those there that day noted he was "obviously in great pain," but Siskel would only concede "his back hurt."

The next episode of *Siskel & Ebert* broke from its time-tested format to pay tribute to Siskel. After the same old opening credits with Gene and Roger wandering the streets of Chicago and squabbling under a theater marquee emblazoned with their names, a somber Ebert in a black suit noted that Siskel "continued as long as he could to do the job he loved [because] he had a real passion for his job and thought it was worth doing." Of the cause of his partner's death, he only noted Gene "died from an illness he'd been fighting since last May."

The tribute episode focused on Siskel's life and accomplishments as a critic and journalist and showed Gene and Roger's most famous debates, their guest spots on other television series like *The Critic*, and some of the spoofs of themselves they enjoyed, like an appearance in *MAD* magazine that Gene considered one of the great honors of his life. After various interviews and clips, the show concluded with a monologue from Roger, quoting a question that Siskel asked everyone he interviewed: "What do you know for sure?"

"Okay, Gene, what do *I* know for sure about you?" he continued. "Well, you were one of the smartest, funniest, quickest men I've ever known, and one of the best reporters. It was almost impossible to tell you anything you didn't already know. Your friend Bob Greene wrote in the paper that sometimes you seemed like a wise old man and on other days you seemed about eleven years old. And I know for sure that seeing a truly great movie made you so happy that you'd tell me a week later your spirits were still high."

Before the closing credits rolled, Ebert added, "People always asked if we hated each other. And one thing I know for sure is that we didn't."

At the Museum of Broadcast Communications' benefit dinner in Gene and Roger's honor back in April of 1998, just weeks before Siskel's initial trip to the hospital, the two men set aside their public persona as disagreeable rivals to spend a few moments acknowledging each other's importance in their own success.

Foreshadowing what he would say in his tribute to Siskel less than a year later, Ebert yet again asked the rhetorical question: Did they like each other or not?

"The answer, for me at least: most of the times yes, occasionally very much so, sometimes not at all," Ebert mused. "But we value each other, and we need each other, and we have a working relationship that has lasted for twenty-three years.

"Gene is a very smart, intelligent, perceptive, and ferociously ethical critic who just doesn't want to let anything shoddy get past him and it's great to have him across the aisle from me. He keeps me on my toes."

Gene was equally complimentary, telling Ebert, "Without you this doesn't happen. *Siskel & Siskel*, jumping between the two seats, it wouldn't have flown. I just don't think it would have been that interesting. And so I thank you, my dear friend, my colleague, at times mentor. This is a wonderful opportunity to declare that. Thank you."

CHAPTER TWELVE

EBERT & ROEPER & LYONS & MANKIEWICZ & PHILLIPS & SCOTT & LEMIRE & VISHNEVETSKY

. . . .

I do prefer challenging endings. . . . I want to see a film that I can talk about after I leave the theater. And a happy ending doesn't always provide that.

—GENE SISKEL

The only true ending is death.
Any other movie ending is arbitrary.

—ROGER EBERT

. . . .

Say the words *Siskel and Ebert* to most people, and the image called to mind is probably two men arguing with one another about a movie. And there was some truth to that image, especially in their days cohosting *Sneak Previews* on PBS. Gene and Roger continued to squabble and pester each other well into the 1990s, after they had worked together for more than two decades.

But never—not one single time—did they ever get into a fight big enough to threaten their partnership. No one who knew or worked with them can recall an instance when things got so rough between Roger and Gene that one or the other stormed out of the office in a rage or threatened to quit the show. They worked together from late 1975 to early 1999, a little over twenty-three years. They were partners more than twice as long as Dean Martin and Jerry Lewis, and exactly as many years as Bud Abbott and Lou Costello, the comedy duo whose mismatched physicality earned them frequent comparisons. And even then, *Siskel & Ebert* only ended because of Siskel's death.

Publicly and privately, both men insisted they had no plans or desires to ever end the show. In fact, in a 1995 *Chicago Sun-Times* interview commemorating their twentieth anniversary on the air together, a reporter specifically asked, "What happens if one of you says, 'I don't want to do the show anymore'?" Gene and Roger both had the same response: they had never discussed it.

"My fantasy is that in another 40 years we'll be in wheelchairs and we'll have attendant nurses and we'll do the show," Siskel said.

"Every time I see pictures of Anna Nicole Smith with her late husband," Ebert added, "I think that's Gene and myself doing the show in 40 years."

"You're going to have the implants?" Siskel quipped.

"Um yes, no no no."

"You don't need 'em."

Tragically, *Siskel & Ebert* didn't last another four years, much less forty. But the end of *Siskel & Ebert* was not the end of their movie review show. For the duration of the 1998–99 television season, Ebert cohosted with a rotating crew of guest critics, including NPR's Elvis Mitchell, the *Los Angeles Times*' Kenneth Turan, and, for a special tribute to the late Stanley Kubrick, a roundtable of Chicago film critics including Ray Pride of *Newcity*, Jonathan Rosenbaum of the *Chicago Reader*, Dann Gire of the Chicago *Daily*

Herald, and Michael Wilmington, who held Siskel's old job as film critic of the *Chicago Tribune*. When the television season ended in August 1999, the *Siskel & Ebert* title was retired for good. Gene's seat in the Balcony was removed and given to his wife, Marlene, who still has it to this day. ("Who else could fill it? I had to take it," she says.) On the very last episode under the *Siskel & Ebert* banner, Roger paid one final tribute to Gene with another montage of clips, this one set to the Bee Gees' "How Deep Is Your Love" from Siskel's beloved *Saturday Night Fever.*

"There isn't a lot of real film criticism on TV anymore," Ebert noted, wistfully and accurately. Both of the other series Gene and Roger had started—*Sneak Previews* at PBS and *At the Movies* at Tribune Entertainment—had continued without them for years, but they were long since canceled by 1999. *Sneak Previews* actually carried on until 1996; the show aired for far more years without Gene and Roger than with them.

As Ebert threw one final video tribute to his late partner, he made the audience a promise. "Gene stood for the very best critical standards. This program *will* continue in that tradition."

When the series returned for the 1999–2000 season, it had a new title—*Roger Ebert & the Movies*—and the same old format of lively movie reviews and discussion. As suggested by the title, the show now had only one star; a different guest critic took Gene's old spot each week. In fact, when the show rebranded there was some consideration given to never hiring a new permanent cohost.

"We can never find a replacement for Gene Siskel," Buena Vista executive Mary Kellogg told the *Hollywood Reporter* shortly before *Roger Ebert & the Movies* premiered. "I think it is fair to say that the odds are against us ever going back to a one-on-one formula that made the original *Siskel & Ebert* so original." Instead, the new show initially alternated between a trio of regulars who had stood out from the rest of the guests who filled in on *Siskel & Ebert* in the weeks after Gene's death: CNN's Jeff Greenfield, *Good Morning America* critic Joel Siegel, and Joyce Kulhawik, the arts and entertainment anchor for CBS's Boston affiliate, WBZ-TV.

"Gene cannot be replaced," echoed Ebert in an interview in mid-1999. "We are trying to carry on in a way we hope he would have approved of. In choosing co-hosts, I've tried to cast a very wide net, choosing people from national and local media, above ground and underground, print, TV and radio, and the web." Thea Flaum believes that asking Ebert to find a replacement for Siskel at that time would have been "like saying to a widower, 'Find somebody else who can take the place of your late wife.' Good luck with that."

As *Roger Ebert & the Movies* continued into the 1999–2000 season, that wide net brought in other guests as well. Some came from the world of print criticism, like Janet Maslin from the *New York Times*, and others from TV, like Michaela Pereira, a television anchor and host of the cable series *Internet Tonight*. The show also drew upon cohosts from the burgeoning world of online criticism like David Poland and Harry Knowles, the editor of the controversial geek gossip website Ain't It Cool News. Supposedly, only one person turned down the chance to guest-host beside Roger in the Balcony: Manohla Dargis, then of *LA Weekly* and later the film critic of the *New York Times*.

Some of these pairs worked quite well, and it was a little exciting to tune in week to week; you never knew who might show up in the Balcony next. (Director Martin Scorsese appeared for a special episode dedicated to picking the best films of the 1990s; he named Chinese filmmaker Tian Zhuangzhuang's drama *The Horse Thief* as the decade's best.) But bringing in new critics every single week was costly, time-consuming, and difficult; guests not only had to be flown in to Chicago for tapings, they also had to make time to see four to five new movies, sometimes well in advance of their actual release in theaters. On at least a few occasions, a planned guest would cancel last minute because of travel issues or scheduling problems.

When that happened, the show tended to call in a colleague of Roger's at the *Sun-Times*, columnist Richard Roeper—who, in a curious twist of fate, had been the journalist who interviewed Siskel and Ebert for that twentieth-anniversary piece and asked about their backup plans if one or the other ever decided to leave the show. At the time, Roeper had zero inkling that he might one day sit in Siskel's seat in the Balcony.

"I grew up a huge movie fan, but I never thought of being a film critic, especially because I grew up in Chicago, and by the time I was old enough to really start pursuing writing about entertainment, we had Gene Siskel and Roger Ebert," Roeper says. "It wasn't 'Oh well, I wanted it, but those guys have it.' It just didn't occur to me. And there was certainly plenty of room to write about popular culture in a column that wasn't always about movies. But I could never say that I really wanted to be a film critic, which I know drives a lot of other film critics nuts because of the good fortune I've had." Of course, neither Siskel nor Ebert had wanted to be film critics when they were children, either.

Roeper joined the *Sun-Times* in 1986 and within a year was writing a regular column. By the late '90s, Roeper was up to five columns a week, along with work in local radio and television. Unlike Ebert's prickly relationship with Siskel, he and Roeper hit it off immediately—although, Roeper says, in his early years at the *Sun-Times* he was actually closer with Gene than with Roger because of his and Gene's mutual love of the Chicago Bulls (and occasional trips to the off-track betting parlor). In fact, it was Siskel's idea to have Roeper interview him and Roger in the *Sun-Times* for their twentieth anniversary—according to Roeper, Siskel said he liked him better than anyone on staff at the *Tribune* at the time.

Ebert and Roeper grew closer after Roger's marriage to Chaz; she and Richard began chatting regularly before movies in Chicago's screening room for critics on Lake Street. Eventually, Roeper even spent time with the couple at their home in Michigan, where they often invited colleagues for summer parties. As Roger and Richard grew closer, the former championed the latter as his backup at the *Sun-Times*; if Ebert went out of town to cover a film festival or interview a star, he suggested the entertainment editor have Roeper review the movies he couldn't see.

Still, when the show began looking for guests to replace Siskel, it wasn't Roger who suggested Richard; it was Chaz. While running on the treadmill one morning, she happened to see Richard doing a spot about movies on a morning talk show on the local Fox affiliate. She thought he was smart and with just the sort of attitude that might make him a good foil for Roger.

"Why don't you try Richard? Give Richard a chance to sit in the chair," she told Roger after she finished her workout.

"I can't," he replied. "We both work at the *Sun-Times*."

"So what? You don't have to be rivals from this point. It doesn't have to be somebody from the *Tribune*; just somebody who would stand up to you and know enough and respect enough about movies and be prepared. *That's* what you need."

Ebert relented, and Roeper was invited to appear as a critic in March of 2000. According to Chaz, at his first audition, "everybody on the set said, 'Oh my God, he's the one.'" According to Roeper, he was "blissfully ignorant" that there even was an audition—at least for any sort of permanent role on the show.

"When they had me come on as a guest on the show, I thought, 'What an amazing experience. I'll always get to say I sat in the Balcony and I got to go back and forth with Roger on movies,'" Roeper explains. His first appearance went well enough that they asked him to return a few weeks later. And then, because Roeper was based in Chicago, he became the show's unofficial understudy. If a Chicago snowstorm made it impossible for the planned guest to fly in and tape the show, they'd have Richard see that week's movies and fill in. Without any sort of conscious plan on his part, he'd soon appeared on the show eleven times. Even then, Roeper says, it never occurred to him that he might be in the running to become the permanent cohost.

"[*Sun-Times* media reporter] Robert Feder was actually one of the first people to say to me, 'You know you're on the short list, right?'" Roeper says. "I'm like, 'For what?' So by the time it got down to two or three people under consideration and there was some press about it, I was like, 'Oh, *I'm* one of those people.' And I think honestly that's probably one of the reasons why [I did well]. I didn't think I was auditioning. A lot of critics, they *knew* they were auditioning. And I remember Roger telling me after two or three tapings, 'A lot of these folks are great, but they're comporting themselves as if they're guests on *The Roger Ebert Show* and they don't want to be impolite. You don't have any problem with that. I *need* someone who will disagree with me, get in my face, and argue with me instead of just saying, 'Gosh, I'm just so happy to be here.'"

Amid heavy speculation over the fate of the cohosting spot—the *Chicago Sun-Times* called it "the summer's hottest movie deal"—Disney and *Roger Ebert & the Movies* producers narrowed the list of candidates down to three finalists: Kulhawik, Pereira, and Roeper. In the end, Disney left the final decision up to Ebert—and Ebert wanted Roeper. Amid all the coverage of the competition for the seat opposite him in the Balcony, Ebert privately pulled

Roeper aside in between press screenings one day and asked him to take a walk with him.

They turned right out of the screening room's building and came to the corner of Lake and Wabash. Ebert stopped.

"You're the guy," he said.

"What do you mean?" Roeper replied.

"You're gonna get offered the job. I'll get fired if you tell anyone. But I can't have you thinking, 'What's going on?' They're going to come to you in a couple of weeks. Act surprised when they offer you the job. I just feel like you should know this so we can move forward—but you can't tell anybody."

Roeper kept quiet. And sure enough, two weeks later, Disney executives invited him over to a meeting at the Four Seasons Hotel, where they "surprised" him and offered him the full-time gig cohosting *Roger Ebert & the Movies*—or, as it was soon called, *Ebert & Roeper & the Movies*. (Roeper says he tried his best to act shocked.) The news was made official on July 13, 2000, in a front-page *Sun-Times* article. Explaining why he chose the one male finalist over the two female ones, Ebert said, "It's my fault that it's a little hard to take off the gloves with a woman. I felt a different kind of freedom with Richard. I felt comfortable with him. As we had him back several more times, it became increasingly clear that he would be the best choice." To colleagues at the *Sun-Times*, Ebert joked, "It's all in the family."

Ebert's new cohost was a colleague instead of a competitor, and the duo's relationship off camera reflected that stark difference. In a 2005 interview, Ebert noted that he and Richard had never had an argument in five and a half years hosting the show together, while he and Gene "hardly went five and a half minutes" without one. ("Nevertheless, that's not a complaint about Gene," he added.)

The difference between Gene and Richard—and between both

and Roger—was made very apparent during an incident early in Richard's tenure as the new cohost. Richard was reviewing a foreign movie, and when he went to say the director's name, Roger took issue.

"I think you're wrong," Ebert said. "It's pronounced *this* way"—and then he demonstrated.

Disagreements over the pronunciation of foreign filmmakers' names were not uncommon on the set of *Siskel & Ebert*, but they typically escalated into all-out fights. Among the show's crew, Gene and Roger's dispute over the pronunciation of the word *gauntlet* is legendary—even though, to this author's knowledge, there is only one correct pronunciation of "gauntlet."

When Richard and Roger disagreed on the pronunciation of this director's name, everyone on set braced for another blowup. But it didn't come. Instead, Roeper proposed an idea: shoot the review twice, with both pronunciations, figure out which one was correct later, and then use that version in the final edit.

Ebert was delighted. "That makes things so much easier!"

But while a peaceful set might make for a better working environment, it didn't necessarily produce a better television product—or better ratings. In 2005, *Ebert & Roeper* was still a syndicated television staple airing on two hundred stations across the United States. But it was only watched weekly by about 2.5 million people—down from 8 million in its early days at Buena Vista, and from about 3.3 million during Gene Siskel's final year as cohost. And after more than twenty years doling out occasionally nasty reviews on television, Roger Ebert's show became the target of some bad reviews of its own.

The *Boston Herald* claimed that Roeper "has a tendency to speak in sound bites and cliches" and was "too willing to kowtow to Ebert," resulting in a show that was "flat and not very insightful."

Entertainment Weekly was similarly unimpressed, and gave the updated series a C grade, mostly because of the way Roeper looked and spoke, calling him "a post-boomer who recites his devotion to art but who looks like he spends more time in the gym than in theaters."

"I probably would have given myself a negative review," Roeper admits, before adding, "I also understand there were dozens upon dozens of movie critics who had more experience as print critics, whether or not they were going to be great on television. So I could certainly understand the resentment on some folks' part. The bottom line was: Roger thought I was the best person for the job. So I was good with that."

When critics complained that Roeper was too in shape for the part, it was another way of saying he wasn't Gene Siskel—and of course he wasn't, and never could be. For one thing, Roeper had the misfortune of being compared to the most popular and successful film critic duo in history—and of learning on the job in front of a national audience of millions, instead of on a single PBS station in Chicago the way Gene and Roger did in their rocky early days. What was far more important, though largely unsaid in these reviews of *Ebert & Roeper*, was not a cosmetic difference between Gene and Richard but a temporal one. Where Siskel and Ebert were peers, born just a couple years apart, Roeper was seventeen years younger than Ebert. By Roeper's own admission, he and Ebert had "much more a father-son, or at least older brother–younger brother dynamic" on camera.

That created an imbalance between the two critics that was difficult to overcome. The *Siskel & Ebert* formula thrived on parity; that sense that you were watching the journalistic equivalent of two top-ranked boxers duking it out to be crowned the champion of the world of criticism. The same issue occurred when Gene Siskel had first become ill; it no longer seemed like a battle between equally matched competitors. It wasn't so much that Roeper was inexperienced—he'd been a columnist for well over a decade and written books about movies—it was that the audience *perceived* that he didn't have the same knowledge base, experience, or authority as Ebert, who they'd watched on television for a quarter century.

Within a few years, something else was missing from *Ebert & Roeper* as well: Roger Ebert himself. On February 21, 2002— exactly three years and one day after Gene Siskel's death—Ebert announced he was suffering from cancer. The next day, he had surgery to remove a malignant tumor on his thyroid gland. A press release from Northwestern Memorial Hospital noted he was "expected to make a complete recovery"; a note from the Ebert family encouraged anyone who wanted to help to go out with a group of family or friends to a movie ("one recommended by Roger") and then discuss it over dinner, give it a big thumbs up, and send out good thoughts and prayers for Roger.

The following Wednesday, Ebert sent *Sun-Times* media columnist Robert Feder an update on his recovery: "I had surgery on Friday, came home Sunday, wrote a review Monday, attended two screenings on Tuesday, and leave today (Wed) for the Ebert & Roeper Floating Film Festival aboard the *Disney Wonder* out of Port Canaveral. Reports from the doctors could not be more positive. This type of thyroid tumor is fairly common, and in many cases childhood radiation is suspected as the cause. Yes, I had radiation treatments as a kid for tonsillitis and ear infections."

As strange as it sounds today, this sort of treatment—which was also used to help patients suffering from everything from fungus infections to pimples—was not unusual when Ebert was a child in the 1940s and '50s. By the time the practice ended in the 1970s, more than 1 million children had been irradiated, including babies. Those who'd received the treatments like Ebert were at far higher risk of thyroid cancer than the general public. A prophetic March 2002 article in the *Chicago Sun-Times* about Ebert's thyroid surgery and its links to childhood radiation treatments noted that "other possible long-term effects of radiation include cancer of the salivary gland."

Ebert & Roeper prepared for Roger's surgery by taping several weeks of shows in advance, and he was able to return to work by the time the episodes were aired. ("I will not miss a single movie!" he boasted in the email to Robert Feder.) But in February 2003, Ebert had a second surgery, this time on his salivary gland, followed by a third that September. Each time, Ebert and his doctors insisted his prognosis was good, that these sorts of cancers were not aggressive or considered life-threatening. And each time, Ebert prepared for his surgeries by taping episodes that could run during his recovery.

The cancer may not have been aggressive, but it was persistent. While Ebert did have a few periods in the 2000s of uninterrupted TV appearances—and he was healthy enough in 2004 to receive a star on the Hollywood Walk of Fame, an honor that had him giddily write a colleague, "To think I am in the company of Patricia Neal and Tom Brokaw! And Donald Duck and Soupy Sales!"—they didn't last long. In June of 2006, he had yet another surgery on his salivary gland. And this time, his recovery was not as swift.

Doctors discovered the cancer had spread from his salivary gland to his lower jaw, and a portion of the bone had to be removed. After several weeks of recovery, he was given the all-clear to return home, but before he and Chaz left the hospital, Ebert put on one of his favorite songs, Leonard Cohen's "I'm Your Man." Suddenly, Ebert's carotid artery burst; it had been weakened from countless operations and rounds of radiation treatments in the area. Doctors rushed him into surgery and barely stanched the bleeding in time. If he'd left the hospital just a few minutes earlier, he'd have been in a car when the incident occurred and almost certainly would have died. Ebert credited Leonard Cohen with inadvertently saving his life.

But Cohen couldn't save Ebert's television career. Starting in the summer of 2006, Roger endured a string of unsuccessful surgeries designed to repair the damage to his jaw and face. In the fallout of his carotid artery's collapse, Ebert also underwent a tracheostomy in order to ensure his breathing even if he had another burst artery. All of the procedures left Ebert unable to eat (he was fed a liquid diet through a G-tube into his stomach) and, more important, unable to speak. His mind was as sharp as ever. But he was physically incapable of returning to the show.

That left *Ebert & Roeper* without one of its two titular stars, and it put the other in a strange position. Just a couple years after he had been the guest host himself, Roeper was now the show's stalwart veteran, and it was up to him to carry on in Roger's absence opposite a new slew of guest critics. The very first cohost was the *Tonight Show*'s Jay Leno, a longtime viewer of *Siskel & Ebert* and *Ebert & Roeper*, and a big movie fan. (His appearance fee: five pies from his favorite pizza joint.)

His appearance garnered so much media coverage that it inspired Disney to expand their search for guests beyond the ranks of film critics, to other celebrities like director Kevin Smith, screenwriter John Ridley, and comedian Fred Willard.

"Some people were very eager to help, but not necessarily suited for the actual gig," says Roeper, who cites actress Aisha Tyler as his favorite cohost from this period. ("If she didn't have seventeen other jobs, I would have loved to have eventually done a show with her.") Roeper had a very surreal encounter with John

Mellencamp, whose team contacted the show saying he would love to be a guest. On his episode, Mellencamp and Roeper reviewed a drama called *In the Land of Women*. At one point, Mellencamp turned to Roeper and asked, "Now, what's the name of that one actress?" referring to Meg Ryan, who starred in the film opposite Adam Brody and Kristen Stewart. A few years later, Roeper was gobsmacked when he read that Mellencamp and Ryan were dating. ("I'm like, *You didn't even know her name when we did the show!*")

Even as Ebert's absence stretched on for months, Roeper still believed the guest hosts were a temporary fix and that Roger would eventually return to his seat in the Balcony. But a series of attempts to restore Ebert's jaw and voice proved unsuccessful. (Ebert had so many operations during this period, he claimed he lost count of the exact number.) Doctors removed segments of bone from other parts of Ebert's body and attempted to use them to reconstruct his jaw, all to no avail. When he reemerged in the public eye in the spring of 2007 to appear at his annual Overlooked Film Festival in Champaign-Urbana, he wore a large bandage to cover the damage to his lower jaw and neck.

"I'm told the paparazzi will take unflattering pictures, people will be unkind, etc.," Ebert wrote in a column in the *Sun-Times*. "Frankly, my dear, I don't give a damn. As a journalist I can take it as well as dish it out. . . . Being sick is no fun. But you can have fun while you're sick. I wouldn't miss the Festival for anything!"

For another full year, Ebert continued with a cycle of surgeries and rehabilitation, while *Ebert & Roeper* continued with a cycle of guest critics. When Ebert's Overlooked Film Festival rolled around again in April of 2008, Ebert penned another letter in the *Sun-Times*, admitting that after yet another unsuccessful procedure the previous January, he would require even more surgery to fix his voice—and he was "not ready to think about more surgery at this time." Instead, he decided to be "content with the abundance I have," announcing his imminent return to reviewing movies in print in the *Sun-Times*.

"I still have all my other abilities," Ebert wrote, "including the love of viewing movies and writing about them. And at my side I have my angelic wife, Chaz."

What Ebert did not explicitly state had been tragically obvious to Roeper for months: Roger Ebert would never speak again. And that meant the television show he had hosted for more than thirty years would either have to end or it would have to go on without him. Buena Vista executives didn't want to cancel *Ebert & Roeper*, which had been retitled yet again to *At the Movies with Ebert & Roeper* during the former host's long absence. But with the loss of its central star and the most famous film critic in the country, they did want to make some major changes.

Roeper says he wasn't privy to a lot of the behind-the-scenes discussions that followed, but it was clear that the show would go in one of two directions: either he would continue on in some sort of reduced capacity or Disney was going to make even more drastic alterations in order to create "a different type of show." Eventually, both sides agreed it was time to start fresh with new hosts. On his final episode, Roeper pointedly wore all black: black jacket, black shirt, and black tie, a choice he now says may have been "a little overdramatic" but was absolutely intentional.

"That was my way of saying that I knew they were going to try other things, but I felt like I had, to the best of my abilities, honorably carried on the tradition of *Siskel & Ebert*. That was me saying, 'They can do whatever they want; it's their show. But *At the Movies, Siskel & Ebert, Ebert & Roeper*, this is the last show.'" Roeper also says he doesn't harbor any ill will toward those who followed him;

they were offered an opportunity and they took it. A few years earlier, he'd been in the same situation.

"And I don't fault them for this," he adds. "To do *Roeper & Somebody* . . . I think they felt, 'Let's just bring in two younger guys.'"

The two younger guys turned out to be Ben Mankiewicz, forty-one, a host on Turner Classic Movies, and Ben Lyons, twenty-seven, a reporter for *E! News*. On July 21, Buena Vista Television announced that both Ebert and Roeper would leave *At the Movies*; one day later, Mankiewicz and Lyons were introduced as the show's new stars. Mankiewicz called his hiring "an awesome responsibility," while Lyons promised the Associated Press that as a Los Angeles resident who spent time in "studio lots and meetings with executives," he had "insider information that will make the show grow and continue its legacy."

Although he says he is proud to have been "part of something iconic," Lyons now admits he "struggled creatively" during his time hosting *At the Movies*. He pressed producers to add filmmaker interviews to the series—something *Siskel & Ebert* did try for a period in the mid-'90s—but the idea was repeatedly rejected. He recalls being told, "We're a movie review show, we can't have interviews with actors," to which he would reply, "We're trying to make this television show an entertaining product.

"I believe that show had a real opportunity to cement itself as a brand in the film conversation beyond traditional movie reviews," Lyons adds. "I wanted to bring the access and the film relationships I built at the E! channel to the show, and it didn't really fit what they were trying to do. And that's unfortunate."

The *At the Movies* format probably did deserve a serious reconsideration by the mid-2000s. The pop culture of that era looked almost nothing like the one that had first birthed *Opening Soon* . . .

at a Theater Near You. By all accounts, the initial creation of the show had very little to do with Siskel and Ebert's rivalry (and even less to do with their on-air talents); WTTW made the show to reach an audience of moviegoers who were interested in news on the latest films playing in theaters. By 2008, that audience didn't need a weekly television show airing in syndication at odd hours of the weekend to get their movie news, because the information they wanted could be found daily on television shows like *Entertainment Tonight* and Lyons's own *E! News*, or at any time of the day or night on the internet.

Plus, the film clips that were once so rare and unique when *Opening Soon* first launched were now easily accessible on social media, which was exploding in popularity right as Lyons and Mankiewicz's *At the Movies* debuted. Their version of the show would have to compete with YouTube, where thousands upon thousands of movie trailers from throughout the history of cinema could be viewed at the click of a button, and with Twitter, where viewers could broadcast their own reviews to millions of people. (Lyons says he spent months "fighting, fighting, fighting" to get the show an official Twitter account.) Simply put, viewers didn't need *At the Movies* to tell them what was going on at the movies. Odds were, most of them already knew.

Beyond the fact that Lyons and Mankiewicz were still a pair of white men, Disney could not have found two hosts less like Gene and Roger if they had tried. Siskel and Ebert were Hollywood outsiders; born and raised in the Midwest, headquartered in Chicago. Mankiewicz and Lyons both hailed from showbiz families. Mankiewicz's grandfather Herman cowrote *Citizen Kane*; his great-uncle, Joseph L. Mankiewicz, wrote and directed the Oscar-winning *All About Eve*. Lyons's grandfather Leonard was a prolific entertainment news columnist; his father, Jeffrey, spent decades

as a film critic in New York City and was one of the men who replaced Siskel and Ebert when they left *Sneak Previews* for syndication in 1982. Gene and Roger were newspapermen who stumbled
into television stardom. By the time they landed the hosting jobs
on *At the Movies*, Mankiewicz and Lyons were both extremely polished on-camera hosts.

But neither were film critics, a fact that Mankiewicz openly
admits. "I was just a guy who talked about movies," Mankiewicz
says. "So I had to learn the language of criticism. I was really concerned that it felt authentic; am I just trying to sound like what a
movie critic says? I think it's fair to say in criticizing the work Ben
and I did that we didn't have strong points of view. It just didn't
come across right. He was too friendly and I was not comfortable
criticizing."

Mankiewicz pinpoints the day he found out he would be hired
to host *At the Movies* as "the high point" of his time with the show.
"Right from the start," he adds, "it was apparent that it was going
to be a struggle to make this a long-term success."

Although the show was still taped in Chicago in the same
studio at the local ABC affiliate where *Ebert & Roeper* had been
filmed, the look of the show was totally reconfigured. Gone was
the Balcony that had given Siskel, Ebert, and Roeper a home for
three decades. Instead, Lyons and Mankiewicz spent large parts
of the show standing on a wood-paneled set decorated with a pair
of plush leather armchairs and an enormous flat-screen television.
It was an attractive design in the abstract, but an odd choice given
the show's title. Right as the show reverted to the name *At the Movies*, Disney abandoned the set that actually made it look like the
two hosts were hanging out at the movies.

Also gone were the fabled thumbs, which were trademarked
by Ebert's and Siskel's estates; when Ebert left the show for good,

so did his digits. Instead, Lyons and Mankiewicz employed a three-pronged "See It/Rent It/Skip It" rating system with corresponding green, yellow, and red lights like a traffic signal. They also added a rotating cast of remote guest critics, who would join select reviews live via satellite for a "Critics Roundup," in a segment that was reminiscent of talking-head roundtables on CNN.

Lyons believes the changes didn't go far enough, leaving his *At the Movies* looking like a pop culture anachronism. "Oftentimes we'd review a movie poorly and it would open at number one, which makes our show look irrelevant," he explains. "Oftentimes we would review a movie and say, 'That was the greatest film we've ever seen—and *you'll* see it in a month.' It just didn't feel timely. And then you're wondering why the ratings are down in Wisconsin."

Indeed, Disney's half-hearted attempts to modernize the show did not attract younger viewers. Instead, they only served to alienate *At the Movies'* core audience of loyal cinephiles; ratings hovered around 1.8 million total weekly viewers. And if the reviews for *Ebert & Roeper* were mixed, the reviews for Mankiewicz and Lyons's *At the Movies* were downright savage. Four months into the series' run, the *Los Angeles Times* published an article about the show with the lede: "Is Ben Lyons the most hated film critic in America?" Based on the rest of the piece, the answer appeared to be a resounding yes. Other critics quoted in the piece referred to Lyons as "a joke" with "no taste." One launched an entire website named StopBenLyons.com dedicated to trying to remove him from the show.

"That was a lot," Lyons admits. "My thoughts on it back then were, 'Well, someone's watching. That's cool. That's a validation of your success on some level, that the words come out of your mouth and create a reaction.' But it was to be expected. To be honest, Roger never liked my father. He never wanted to play nice with my dad. My memory was growing up that they were always nasty to my dad. They'd talk shit about him on panels with him." (They also talked shit about him in the press, as seen in chapter six of this book.)

Although Ebert later called Lyons a "victim of a mistaken hiring decision," in October 2008 he penned a highly critical blog post titled "Roger's Little Rule Book." While never mentioning Lyons by name, it quoted from his *At the Movies* reviews, while railing against the rise of what he called "Celeb Info-Nuggets that will pimp to the mouth-breathers."

"Look, I get it," Mankiewicz says. "It's Ebert's show, and there's something refreshing about Ebert's honesty about it." Mankiewicz also acknowledges that while he knew the show was "revered," he wasn't prepared for the way viewers came to see him and Lyons as not "honoring the show but betraying it. That's what became clear pretty quickly, is that people thought we were the anti–Siskel and Ebert. But with Ben, it did feel personal. I continue to like and admire Roger. But I just felt bad for Ben. He suggested that it was not that big a deal, but I find it hard to believe."

Lyons says he was "surprised and disappointed" by the extent of Ebert's public criticism, but insists he refused to let the negativity define his time on the show. "It got to the point," he explains, "where no matter what I said or did, I realized this whole community wasn't going to let up. So what am I going to do? I just had to take it."

But not for long. With so-so ratings and terrible press, Mankiewicz says he quickly saw the writing on the wall. "Ben and I didn't have the right set of skills together," he adds. "I think both of us might have done well in a different setting—we both *have* done well in different settings. . . . But I think we were doomed. The show needed Roger Ebert, period."

But with Roger Ebert still unable to speak, *At the Movies* was retooled again after just one year hosted by Lyons and Mankiewicz. Instead of trying to modernize the show or make it cool, Disney took it back to its roots, hiring two men who were more in the Siskel and Ebert mold of legitimate print critics who'd dabbled in television: A. O. Scott of the *New York Times* and Michael Phillips of the *Chicago Tribune.* Both had guest-hosted during Ebert's long illness, and now both returned to the show to, if nothing else, restore some critical credibility to *At the Movies.*

While Buena Vista had largely taken a hands-off approach with *Siskel & Ebert*, the gradual departure of its longtime stars began to affect its independence in the company. Scott says he was astonished after he took the job to see "the full insanity of the Disney corporate structure, and the sort of weird micromanaging that would happen in television." Everything he wore, right down to his glasses, had to be approved by Disney executives in Burbank. He wanted to wear a jacket and tie on the show, but that idea was vetoed by someone high up the corporate ladder who believed that no one would ever wear a tie at the movies.

When Phillips and Scott took over the show from Lyons and Mankiewicz, they inherited a simplified version of their "updated" set—which Phillips says was "one of the funniest failures of visual imagination ever. It's like, 'Okay, let's get something with zero sense of film or cinema and really is more like the waiting room at your podiatrist.' That's what it looked like." The fact that Disney didn't care enough to change the set suggested to some on the staff that the show was already on its last legs and their job was to carry on until the company had fulfilled whatever existing syndication contracts were still on the books.

"When [A. O. Scott] and I got on the show, it was already on the fade, and it felt like the beginning of the end," Phillips says.

"And then when we were on the show, it felt like the middle of the end. And then at some point just past the middle of the year it felt like, 'Okay, the end isn't near, it's coming.' And that's actually when we started screwing around with the format a little bit and the show got pretty good by the end, because there was literally nothing to lose."

Both men's number one gripe with the show was its pacing, which Phillips says he outright hated. "They were determined to cover five movies no matter how stupid and minor," he explains. "Tony [Scott] and I were in agreement on that—can we *not* do that?"

Scott confirms that he found the pace to be an enormous technical challenge. "We had like forty-five seconds for crosstalk. That's something that in the podcast world or the streaming world or the cable world or the radio world doesn't exist in quite the same way. The absurdity of trying to say, 'Okay, we're going to do five segments in twenty-two minutes, everything timed to the second—but it's going to be spontaneous and it's going to be lively and it's going to be smart.' And it's just like, 'Well, okay.'"

The turning point, at least in their minds, came in an episode dedicated to Martin Scorsese's *Shutter Island*. Rather than discuss the film for a couple of minutes and then move on to the next new release, they lingered over the film and Scorsese, debating his work and picking their favorite movies.

"It was hardly original," says Phillips, "but it was an easy way to get some contrasting viewpoints on a director who was in the news that week. We got a lot of good mail about that, saying you guys seem very comfortable, you had good disagreements, and it was less that kind of rabbity frantic rushing through it to get to film number four, which nobody cared about. . . . It took us too long to come to that realization."

Ebert was a fan of both Scott's and Phillips's work in print, and he watched their *At the Movies* and offered occasional advice. While Scott and Phillips were both opinionated men, they liked each other and got along well; like so many other teams created to emulate Siskel and Ebert, they didn't share their forebears' prickly relationship. Ebert told Scott, "You need more conflict, you need more drama, there has to be *something* happening, *something* at stake." But Phillips and Scott, stellar critics as they were, couldn't fake the oil-and-water chemistry that Siskel and Ebert had for real.

Phillips believes even if they had tried to introduce more conflict it wouldn't have saved the show. "I think the problem that the show had in its later iterations honestly is that it was just blatantly trying to replicate the formula that worked in other eras—not that many years earlier, but these eras happen quickly. Every ten years in movies and movie criticism spell enormous change." The entire world of movies had reinvented itself multiple times since Gene and Roger first signed on at WTTW in 1975. The hosts had changed, and the set looked different, but the *At the Movies* of 2009 was otherwise essentially the same as it had been in 1999, or 1989, or 1979.

The show had run its course, or at least Disney thought so. In March of 2010, they announced that *At the Movies* would come to an end on the weekend of August 14, 2010. Calling it "a very difficult decision," Disney said in a statement that "from a business perspective it became clear this weekly, half-hour, broadcast syndication series was no longer sustainable." David Plummer, who had joined *Siskel & Ebert* during Gene's final year and gradually worked his way up to executive producer during its run with Lyons, Mankiewicz, Scott, and Phillips, says it was "devastating" to see the show slip away and to oversee its final years, adding, "I loved the show. I loved what it stood for. It took me a long time to get over it."

Roger Ebert could relate to that feeling. When he ended his affiliation with Disney in 2008, he wrote that he was "surprised how depressed [he] felt" at the realization of what a "large empty space it left behind" in his life. When Disney canceled the show for good in 2010 he wrote again: "Was I sad today? You bet I was." He attributed the show's end not to A. O. Scott, Michael Phillips, Ben Mankiewicz, or even Ben Lyons, but to the proliferation of criticism on the internet, cable television's shrinking and fragmenting audience, and to a sluggish economy for local TV stations, who could make more money airing infomercials than expensive syndicated programming, especially the kind that only aired once a week like *At the Movies* always had.

But while the internet may have helped doom Disney's *At the Movies*, it had helped reenergize Roger Ebert's own work. Deprived of his ability to speak, he found a new voice online. At RogerEbert .com, he expanded his writing beyond the boundaries of movie reviews. He began blogging about everything from politics to cooking—even though he could no longer eat. (A blog post titled "The Pot and How to Use It" later became its own cookbook with the subtitle *The Mystery and Romance of the Rice Cooker.*) He reached new readers, and then interacted with them in his blog's comments, and on Facebook and Twitter, where he quickly amassed one of the largest followings of any of the new social media site's users. "My web site and blog at the *Sun-Times* site have changed the way I work, and even the way I think," he wrote. "When I lost my speech, I speeded up instead of slowing down."

And with that, he and Chaz set off to make their own version of *At the Movies.* Ebert continued to believe that the show provided an important public service, and Disney's final cancellation of their *At the Movies* did nothing to change his mind. "I can't prove it, but I have the feeling that more different people are seeing more different movies than ever before," he wrote the week Disney announced the final curtain for *At the Movies*. He promised his version of the show would go "full-tilt New Media: Television, net streaming, cell phone apps, Facebook, Twitter, iPad, the whole enchilada. The disintegration of the old model creates an opening for us. I'm more excited than I would be if we were trying to do the same old same old."

Ironically, the show wound up back at the same old place where it all began. What became known as *Ebert Presents: At the Movies* was shot at WTTW, in the same studio where *Opening Soon . . . at a Theater Near You* had begun some thirty-five years earlier. The new hosts—Associated Press film critic Christy Lemire and Chicago-based film writer Ignatiy Vishnevetsky—even sat on Gene's and Roger's old theater seats, which WTTW had saved from Michael Loewenstein's original Balcony set. When the station heard that Roger and Chaz were trying to bring the show back, they offered up their facilities. Chaz Ebert, who served as executive producer on the show, says the move back to PBS and WTTW just made sense. "It was so easy. When people heard about it, they got clearances for like ninety-eight percent of the country. Everybody wanted it back. People were eager."

As a kid growing up in 1980s Los Angeles, Christy Lemire watched *Siskel & Ebert* every weekend. She still harbors fond memories of the theme song—and she credits Gene Siskel with inspiring her career in film criticism. She was working at the Associated Press in Dallas when Siskel passed away. His death gave her an epiphany: "He did what he loved for a living. He wrote about and talked about movies, and what a privilege that is. So he was one of the inspirations for me to pester the arts editor in New York to give me a shot to be a film critic," she says. A few years later, she became the Associated Press's lead critic.

When Ebert had to leave *Ebert & Roeper* to treat his cancer, Lemire was one of the guest hosts who filled in for him. Ebert was impressed with her appearances, and when he and Chaz began thinking about producing their own version of the series, they asked her to be one of the hosts. At one point, they tried shopping around a version starring her and Richard Roeper. Later, they considered a version with Lemire and former *New York Times* critic Elvis Mitchell. But when the show premiered on WTTW, Lemire sat across the aisle from Ignatiy Vishnevetsky, a writer for the website Mubi.com and a contributor to the *Chicago Reader*.

Vishnevetsky, who was just twenty-four years old at the time and hadn't grown up a *Siskel & Ebert* viewer, had never even had a conversation with Ebert when he was first invited to audition for the show. Roger simply heard him talking with friends at the Chicago screening room and thought he had smart things to say about movies. "He googled my writing, and he liked it. That's why they approached me," Vishnevetsky says.

That set off a wild flurry of events. Suddenly, Vishnevetsky was summoned to the Eberts' townhouse in Chicago for a meeting, then flown to a PBS conference in Palm Springs for a series of auditions a few days later, followed by on-camera coaching along with private screenings of recent movies Vishnevetsky had missed. In Vishnevetsky, Ebert had found someone who resembled himself at the start of his own TV career: a young writer with a great eye for film and enormous potential who had essentially never been on camera before. He and Lemire had good chemistry in his auditions. In December of 2010, the Eberts offered him the job cohosting *Ebert Presents*.

Today, Vishnevetsky is blunt about his performance on the show: "I don't think I was a very good choice," he says. "Were I a few years older and more experienced, I probably would have said no when they offered it to me and been like, 'I think these other people are better.'" He recalls being so nervous at times that he "couldn't wait for the segments to end. I knew I wasn't doing as good of a job as someone else could . . . because up to that point, I had basically just written about things I found interesting. And most of what I got paid for were 'foreign' films. Sure, I can write two thousand words on Raúl Ruiz and his latest film, but then how do I come up with three minutes of something to say about *Mr. Popper's Penguins*?" Lemire remembers Vishnevetsky was so anxious at the first taping that she reached across the aisle, grabbed his hand, and told him, "We're gonna be okay. We're gonna do this and we need to look out for each other."

"And I feel like we did," Lemire adds, "but the result was perhaps not the exhilarating fireworks that you came to expect from *Siskel & Ebert*. We're just not them." Vishnevetsky agrees, noting that he and Lemire had "the complete opposite dynamic" from Gene and Roger, who were "fundamentally the same kind of guys; guys with very similar backgrounds, kind of the same generation, who butted heads. Whereas Christy and I were completely different people with completely different interests who happened to get along really well."

Even with Vishnevetsky's nerves, and without Gene and Roger's unique rivalry, *Ebert Presents* got off to a solid start in January 2011. As Ebert had promised, the show recruited contributors from around the internet to produce segments about classic films and notable developments in cinema technology. Ebert himself appeared as well, with Siskel's old colleague from WBBM, Bill Kurtis, voicing his reviews. The show's ratings were good for a PBS series, and the Eberts had interest from stations all across the country. But there was another problem. While WTTW provided a home for the series, they did not actually pay for it; the Eberts had to do that themselves. Which they did, under the assumption that they could find sponsors and financial supporters along the way. In hindsight, Chaz says, they "probably should have taken more time to get the financing first."

Between the sets, the hosts' salaries and travel, and the rent on the offices and equipment, the costs ballooned in a matter of months. When PBS came to the Eberts to ask if the show would continue into 2012, they had to say no. The final episode of the final iteration of *At the Movies* aired in late December 2011. After Christy, Ignatiy, and Roger all revealed their picks for the best movies of the year, Roger returned to the Balcony one last time, seated across the aisle from Chaz.

Roger still couldn't speak, so his words were read off his Mac-Book by a computerized voice. He called the show "a wonderful adventure" and "a great success in proving there is a national television audience for serious film criticism." Then a forlorn Chaz promised updates on the show at their website before the lights dimmed and the credits rolled. But updates never came; although Chaz and Roger explored alternative options to revive the series— at one point, Mark Cuban was interested in the show for one of his cable channels—*Ebert Presents* never returned.

After thirty-six years, the Balcony was closed for good. It was a remarkable run for a man who originally planned on writing film criticism at the *Sun-Times* for five years before moving on to greener pastures. And he still wasn't done.

UNTIL NEXT TIME, WE'LL SEE YOU AT THE MOVIES

The other thing that I felt about watching this show again was how great our jobs are. . . . It's a fabulous job.

—GENE SISKEL

That's it for this special edition of *Sneak Previews*. Join us again next week when Gene and I once again will be laboring away at our favorite job: going to the movies.

—ROGER EBERT

Roger Ebert wrote more reviews in 2012 than he had in any other year in his near half century as a film critic: 306. In the fall of 2011, he also published his memoir, *Life Itself,* much of it drawn from the autobiographical blog posts and columns he had begun writing after his illnesses. Filmmaker Steven Zaillian, the Academy Award–winning screenwriter of *Schindler's List,* loved the book and thought it would make a good documentary. He asked Steve James, whose *Hoop Dreams* Ebert named the single best film of the 1990s, if he would direct it. The world's foremost movie critic would now become the subject of a movie himself.

"I knew he had a memoir out. I had not read it," says James. "I was approached by Garrett Basch, who worked with Steve Zaillian running his company. They asked, 'Would you have an interest in this?' And I said, 'Well, I need to read the memoir. Maybe.' And so I started reading the memoir and, to be honest, about a hundred and thirty pages into it, I wasn't sure I wanted to do it because the first one hundred and thirty pages are about growing up in Champaign, and it's kind of interesting, but I remember thinking, 'My God, this guy remembers his youth too much.' I remember saying to my wife, 'I hope it gets more interesting when he gets to Chicago.' And it did, of course. As soon as it gets to Chicago, it's a great memoir."

James agreed to make *Life Itself* for several interconnected reasons. After falling in love with (the rest of) Ebert's memoir, he realized the man defied the stereotypes of most critics he had met in his career, guys "who seem to spend way too much time in the dark and are kind of nerdy and very intellectual—not the kind of guys you'd necessarily hang out with. Reading his memoir, I was like, 'This is a guy who led an incredibly full life *and* was one of the most prolific and well-respected and powerful critics.' So I liked the idea of telling that story."

James also felt that on some level he owed Roger for all his support of his movies through the years, and not just with *Hoop Dreams*. "He continued to be a champion of my films, which I greatly appreciated because he certainly didn't need to do that. And so there was a part of me that thought if I really like this guy, and I feel like I can tell his story in a sympathetic and interesting way, then I should do this."

His initial plan for the documentary was to film Roger as he went about his still-active life despite all the challenges to his health, and then to use those scenes in the present to springboard back into Ebert's past. But life itself had other plans. At a preproduction meeting in December 2012, Ebert complained in passing about some pain in his hip. The following day, Ebert was back in the hospital, where doctors discovered a hairline fracture. For the next four months, instead of following Roger to screenings and events, James and his crew trailed Ebert from the hospital to physical therapy and back. In all of that time, Ebert spent just two days at home. Instead of an uplifting story of a man who had triumphed over incredible physical adversity, the movie version of *Life Itself* became a deeply moving account of perseverance in the face of illness and death.

For longtime *Siskel & Ebert* fans, it was impossible not to notice the stark contrast in the ways Gene and Roger lived out their final days. Gene kept the extent of his illness a secret even from his friends and coworkers. Roger had James's film crew document his struggle to walk on a treadmill and his wincing in pain as the G-tube used to feed him his liquid diet was suctioned. Even as Ebert's health deteriorated, he refused to allow James to stop filming.

"He never once shied away from showing what he was going through," James says. "In fact when [he and Chaz] went home that one day, you see that in the film they kind of get in an argument. I fully expected Chaz to turn around and say, 'Stop.' But they didn't. And they never came back to me and said, 'Hey, does that need to be in there?' He was a perfect subject because he was knowledgeable, but he didn't use that knowledge against me in any way. And he was famous and he didn't leverage his fame in terms of wanting any kind of control over any of it. He never even attempted in any way to influence that while we were filming."

While examining him for his broken hip, doctors made an

alarming discovery: Ebert's cancer had returned and had spread through his head and neck. He began radiation treatments knowing they would, at best, prolong his life for a few more years. Attending to his cancer would mean less time and energy to devote to his writing, and so on April 2, 2013, Ebert announced he would be stepping back from his job as the film critic at the *Chicago Sun-Times*. On his website, he wrote that he would take a "leave of presence"—he would slow down, but, as he put it, "I am not going away." The last words of his announcement—and the very last words Roger Ebert published out of the millions he wrote in his lifetime—were "I'll see you at the movies."

The very next day, Chaz and her daughter, Sonia, were preparing to take Roger home from the hospital, when he suddenly put his head down. "We thought he was meditating, maybe reflecting on his experiences, grateful to be going home," Chaz recalled in 2013. "As we realized he was transitioning out of this world and into the next, everything, all of us, just went calm. They turned off the machines, and that room was so peaceful. I put on his music that he liked, Dave Brubeck. We just sat there on the bed together, and I whispered in his ear. I didn't want to leave him. I sat there with him for hours, just holding his hand."

In 2009, Ebert wrote one of his most famous blog posts; later, he expanded it into the final chapter of *Life Itself*. Both began the same way: "I know it is coming, and I do not fear it, because I believe there is nothing on the other side of death to fear." Near the piece's end, he mused, "Someday I will no longer call out, and there will be no heartbeat. What happens then? From my point of view, nothing. Absolutely nothing. Still, as I wrote today to a woman I have known since she was six: 'You'd better cry at my memorial service.'"

Ebert was a staunch atheist, although he rejected that and all labels about his beliefs. Raised Catholic, he said he ultimately internalized the religion's social values and discarded the rest, including its theology—although Chaz Ebert has said that in his last days he wrote her a note that read "This is all an elaborate hoax" and described another place he was beginning to visit, a "vastness that you can't even imagine . . . where the past, present, and future were happening all at once." (Ebert's description sounds a bit like the climax of one of his favorite films, *2001: A Space Odyssey*.) In Roger's blog post about why he was unafraid of his impending death, he wrote that despite his lack of faith in an afterlife, he was "comforted" by the idea of memes—those little mental units of thoughts, ideas, images, and phrases that move "from mind to mind as genes move from body to body. After a lifetime of writing, teaching, broadcasting and happily torturing people with my jokes, I will leave behind more memes than many."

He did. Now a decade after Roger Ebert's death—and almost twenty-five years since Gene Siskel's passing—they are still the most famous film critics on the planet. Chaz Ebert continues to oversee RogerEbert.com, which lives on not only as an archive of Roger's writing, but as one of the most comprehensive sources of criticism on new movies, with reviews provided by a fleet of talented critics, including former *Ebert Presents* host Christy Lemire. And every year or two, someone rediscovers one of Gene and Roger's best clips—jousting while trying to record promos, yelling at each other about *Cop and a Half*—and *Siskel & Ebert* goes viral all over again. (Just wait until someone discovers the episode of their annual "Holiday Gift Guide," where they sang karaoke together. It is . . . quite something.)

But Roger *and* Gene left behind far more than just memes. There were times, like when Richard Corliss launched his attack against the show in *Film Comment*, that *Siskel & Ebert* was treated as a punching bag, a symbol of the "death" of "legitimate" film criticism. In fact, *Siskel & Ebert* gave birth to hundreds of professional critics (including the author of this book) and thousands of amateur ones. They might have initially watched the show for Gene and Roger's arguments, but their bickering served as a gateway drug to the movies themselves, and they introduced viewers to all kinds of obscure films they never would have discovered otherwise. As *At the Movies* host Michael Phillips puts it, "Those two and that show steered a hell of a lot of people to their first foreign language film. I know because I worked with some guys at the factory who'd say, 'I saw them talk about it on the show and I thought, "Eh, what the hell?"'" If Gene and Roger argued sometimes, they taught viewers that the movies, like all great art, is subjective. Beautiful and transformative though films might be, they are nothing without the discussions they inspire. Watching was only one part of the equation; talking was the other. (As Thea Flaum puts it, *Sneak Previews* and its descendants "changed, and to some extent created, the American dialogue about the movies.")

Gene and Roger also inspired a new generation of filmmakers, like Ramin Bahrani, the director of acclaimed films like *Man Push Cart* and *Goodbye Solo*, who watched *Siskel & Ebert* growing up in his little hometown in North Carolina. Initially, Bahrani tuned in just to see Gene and Roger fight. "But then," he says, "little by little you become so interested in the movies that they're actually so passionately discussing. As you start to get older, your interest shifts, and you're interested in other kinds of movies—Spike Lee, Martin Scorsese, all these other directors. Seeing them talk and reading their writing made me think, 'Wow, maybe this is something that has value.'"

There have been a few attempts to re-create the *Siskel & Ebert* formula since the end of *Ebert Presents: At the Movies*, but as of this writing, no show like it airs in national distribution. When Gene Shalit retired from the *Today* show in 2010, he was not replaced. Film critics on scattered local TV stations in a few major markets are all that remain of what was once a burgeoning subgenre: talking about movies on television.

That doesn't mean Roger and Gene's influence is gone from TV, though. While no one else has successfully re-created their formula in the realm of movie criticism—where they would inevitably suffer in comparison to Siskel and Ebert—networks have found great success applying it to other fields. Siskel and Ebert's original TV home, WTTW, later distributed *The McLaughlin Group*, a show where political journalists and pundits from across the political aisle debated the issues of the day. Around that time, CNN launched *Crossfire*, which became one of the channel's signature programs for the next twenty years. Today, the concept of opposed talking heads passionately defending their opinions seems to make up most of the prime-time lineups on every cable news channel— and almost as much of the daytime programming on sports networks like ESPN, where series like *First Take* and *Pardon the Interruption* are clearly cut from the *Siskel & Ebert* cloth. Perhaps some of the people who gravitated toward *Siskel & Ebert* less for the film criticism and more for the lively discussion have found some of these programs.

"They really were pioneers of that genre," says *At the Movies* production assistant Marilyn Gill, who went on to a long career in television production. "That was the beginning of people on television disagreeing with each other over common cultural things. And they did it so well. And then you saw on television, that was authentically who they were. They pretty much agreed to disagree. They weren't afraid to show up and be who they were: two competitive journalists."

Disney created a website for *Siskel & Ebert* in the mid-'90s—one of the earliest official sites for a TV show—and they maintained it all through the end of *Ebert & Roeper*. You could see Gene's and Roger's votes, listen to reviews, and, once broadband internet got fast enough, watch clips from the show online. But after Buena Vista ended their relationship with Ebert, the archive disappeared. Chaz Ebert has talked about reviving it in a more official and comprehensive way, but right now the only way to watch clips from the show is to find whatever is available on YouTube or diligently maintained fan websites like SiskelEbert.org. Gene and Roger never wrote their own history of the show, a fact that Chaz Ebert says Roger came to regret. ("After Gene died, Roger would say, 'Why was I so insistent that I had to go it alone?'")

The old *Sneak Previews* and *At the Movies* episodes are not timeless. But the show's archive is valuable for that very reason. Roger Ebert once said that when he watched silent movies he didn't feel like he was looking at old films; he felt he was "looking at a Now that has been captured. Time in a bottle." That's exactly the sensation one gets looking at *Siskel & Ebert* today. The series offers hundreds of snapshots of the movie world during a period of enormous upheaval. From the rise of the blockbuster to the rise of Blockbuster Video; from the battles over the MPAA ratings system to the earliest days of streaming. If journalism is the first draft of history, then *Siskel & Ebert* is the first draft of film history from 1975 to 1999.

Now that Gene and Roger are gone, the task of providing that first draft is left to websites like Rotten Tomatoes, which aggregates hundreds of movie reviews from newspapers, television, and the internet, divides them into "fresh" (the equivalent of thumbs up) and "rotten" (i.e., thumbs down) reviews, determines the percentage of fresh versus rotten, and then displays that information as a number. Over 60 percent and the movie is deemed fresh; under 60, the movie is rotten. "Certified Fresh"—meaning movies with a score of 75 percent or higher—has become the new "Two Thumbs Up!" in movie ads; marketing shorthand meant to indicate critical acclaim.

As a survey of what the overall general consensus looks like on a movie, Rotten Tomatoes has its purpose. But a lot of readers see that number and take it as some kind of objective measurement of quality, not what it really is: a calculation of the overall number of critics who recommended something. And everywhere you look online, you can see numbers that supposedly represent reader reviews and customer grades. People rate the toothpaste they buy on Amazon and pan the restaurant that served them cold soup on Yelp. Netflix users can rate the films they watch with a thumbs down, a thumbs up, or two thumbs up for something they absolutely love. All of this bears Gene and Roger's influence: they democratized criticism, turned it into mass entertainment, and brought it to millions of people all over the country for decades. And now the internet has given everyone an outlet to practice it in public, for better or for worse.

Around the time of *Siskel & Ebert*'s five hundredth episode—or at least when they *estimated* they were around five hundred episodes and made an hour-long special celebrating the show's history; no one ever actually kept track of the precise number of shows they had produced—Roger described what *he* felt the show's legacy would be. He believed it wouldn't be the thumbs or the fighting but rather the fact that the audiences heard "week after week, two guys talking to each other who took the movies seriously, and loved them, and were sometimes thrilled and sometimes disappointed by them, and tried to say why. The underlying assumption is that movies are not simply an entertainment product to be hyped, but an experience that must be evaluated, lest we become merely passive consumers of escapism."

If Gene and Roger were alive today, they would surely be pleased by this part of their legacy. While there may not be a show like *Siskel & Ebert* on television, there are hundreds—maybe thousands—of websites, podcasts, YouTube channels, message boards, and social media threads dedicated to exactly this: to discussions of movies not as objects of commerce but as works of art. The constraints of commercial television meant even when Gene and Roger wanted to go long on a film, they could never discuss it for more than eight minutes. A good podcast or YouTube video essay might debate a single film for two hours or more.

It's not the same thing as *Siskel & Ebert*; most podcasts are hosted by friends who want to be talking to one another, not business rivals who can't stand each other's company. But in some ways, these outlets offer a more evolved version of what *Siskel & Ebert* created: more focus on the movies, less focus on the arguing and the snappy insults. Just as *Sneak Previews* broke ground on television in the 1970s by presenting honest and unfiltered discussion in a world of canned debate, these internet critics have evolved the notion of critical discussion for a new era and new mediums. But they all share common roots in *Siskel & Ebert*. There aren't enough thumbs in the world to measure Roger and Gene's influence on these critics.

The Chicago of today looks less and less like the one Gene and Roger knew—although Gene's favorite popcorn shop, the Garrett on Randolph Street around the corner from the Chicago Theatre, where press screenings used to be held, still sells CaramelCrisp and CheeseCorn to hungry tourists. The *Chicago Tribune*'s gorgeous neo-Gothic headquarters remains on North Michigan Avenue, but the company that gave the building its name moved out in 2018. While the exterior and its famous fragments of world icons like the Alamo and the Great Wall of China looks much the same, the interior floors are in the process of being turned into "luxury residences," while the ground level now houses a Museum of Ice Cream. The old *Sun-Times* office at 401 North Wabash, where Ebert worked, is long gone; today that site houses the enormous Trump International Hotel & Tower. The *Sun-Times* itself endures; it's now headquartered on Racine Avenue in the West Loop and owned by the nonprofit Chicago Public Media. Richard Roeper is its film critic.

For years, people tried to create the successors to *Siskel & Ebert*. A. O. Scott says that after his version of *At the Movies* with Michael Phillips was canceled, they tried to sell the show to other distributors and "failed miserably. Part of it might just have been that the era of the two white guys in the chairs was over." Ignatiy Vishnevetsky thinks *Ebert Presents* failed because it came along at the worst possible moment—at a time when the idea of two people fighting in a movie theater balcony "felt like an anachronism, but a new paradigm had not yet emerged" online. (For one thing, most movie theaters were so small they no longer even had balconies.) As *Ebert Presents* cohost Christy Lemire puts it, "Many of us tried to re-create that magic and no one's done it. People who are good on television, people who are smart about movies—no one can do it."

They can't do it because they have all approached the notion the wrong way. All these attempts to replace Siskel and Ebert have done so from the mindset of re-creating them as an act. But that's not what Gene and Roger were—at least not in their minds. In 1998, they were asked to explain the secret of their success as a team.

"As a team?" Ebert replied. "Our success is the fact that we are two individuals. If we were a team, the show wouldn't be any good and we wouldn't be very good as critics."

"Well, that's interesting. That's very well expressed," Siskel concurred.

Those sentiments may be best understood by comparing Gene and Roger to yet another comedy team from Hollywood's golden age. The Three Stooges were a trio of extremely unique individuals. When Moe's, Larry's, and Curly's distinct personalities came into conflict on-screen, sparks flew. And after Curly had a stroke and was replaced by Joe Besser or Curly Joe DeRita, the act was never the same. Even with some of the same cast and the same basic formula, the innate magic was lost. And it could never be re-created by anyone else.

"I used to say there are two shows that are really just all about the talent and who they are and the fact that what they do and how they do it is perfect TV. Gene and Roger was one and Julia Child was the other one," says Jamie Bennett, the former TV executive who brought *Siskel & Ebert* to Disney syndication. "These are essential talents who just do what they do naturally. They make it all look like there's no work to it and the format's been designed for them and they just do what they do. And it's as natural as breathing. The format got spoiled afterwards because you see all these mediocre television performers trying to do Gene and Roger, and it just didn't look as good. You'd watch it for five minutes and you'd say, 'The original is great. This is not.'"

Gene Siskel felt there was more to it than that. Like so many other things in life, in his mind it all came down to the importance and benefits of competition. In the Chicago newspaper world, after the staffs of the *Tribune* and the *Sun-Times* had finished their respective editions of the paper, they would traditionally retire to their respective bars for an evening of drinking; the Corona for the *Tribune* staff and Ricardo's for the *Sun-Times*. There, each group of reporters and editors would look at the competition's work and trash it behind their backs.

"What happened with Roger and I is our back-biting is front-biting," Siskel said in 1998. "And I think there's a lesson there, which is that you should be encouraged to meet your competitors, to engage them, because you can learn from them, be stimulated from them. I enjoy these discussions. It sharpens both of us." Engaging your competition, Siskel added, "makes business better, we know that. It even makes film criticism better."

Roger could even pinpoint the precise way that Gene made him better. "Gene is very sharp and he challenges me," he said. "If you read reviews from around the country, people deal only in emotions. 'I liked it, I didn't like it.' That's not a review. That's simply a poll answer. A review explains." In the environment of *Siskel & Ebert*, Gene and Roger couldn't rely on their feelings, because "the other guy has to defend his feelings in words and in ideas. And that's where the growth comes." *Siskel & Ebert* wasn't just a show that starred rivals; it was a showcase for the way rivalries could make both sides better than they were without each other. And in making each other better, they made their viewers better filmgoers and debaters as well.

That's a particularly sad sentiment to ponder because Roger and Gene's time together was cut so short. They did appear together (as individuals) for twenty-three years. But Gene died when he was only fifty-three years old, and Roger passed away when he was seventy. With better luck and better health, they could have worked together for several more decades. And if they had experienced better fortune, it's interesting to ponder what they would have been doing now. Would *Siskel & Ebert* still be on the air, despite the fractured media landscape, if Siskel and Ebert were still alive?

True to form, the people I spoke to for this book had very different opinions about what Gene and Roger would be up to if they were alive today. Some believed Gene and Roger would still have their show. If Disney had canceled it at some point, they argued, they might have found somewhere else that wanted it. Given Siskel's fantasy from 1995 that they'd be pushed around in wheelchairs by nurses forty years down the road, it doesn't seem that far-fetched.

Thea Flaum believes they would have responded to the cable and streaming TV boom of recent years by expanding their beat to include television reviews.

Richard Roeper thinks they would have become the "kings of podcasts."

Al Berman, Siskel's old producer at *CBS This Morning*, thinks they could have made a fortune off "Two Thumbs Up!" merchandise.

Siskel & Ebert director/producer Jim Murphy thinks they would have found their way to Turner Classic Movies, one of television's few remaining bastions of cinephilia.

At the Movies' final executive producer, David Plummer, says he could envision Roger and Gene launching a "web movie review empire" to rival Rotten Tomatoes.

Chaz Ebert believes they both loved watching and talking about the movies so much that there's a good chance they might still be working together—although she says she also could see Gene "migrating to one of the sports channels" to cover the Bulls full-time. As for Roger, whatever else he was doing, she thinks he would still be teaching classes about film at the University of Chicago, as he had since 1968. "If he hadn't lost his ability to speak," she says, "he'd still be talking about movies for sure."

To me, the answer to the question of where Gene and Roger would have wound up is obvious. Whatever projects they did separately, Gene and Roger would have remained Siskel and Ebert as long as they lived: two individuals who were better at arguing about movies together than anyone else in history. Besides, you really think one would quit and give the other the chance to gloat about how they had stayed on the job longer? No chance.

BURIED TREASURES THAT SISKEL AND EBERT LOVED

From the fall of 1978 to the winter of 1999, Roger Ebert and Gene Siskel discussed four to six movies per week, forty or more weeks a year. During their run on *Sneak Previews*, *At the Movies*, and *Siskel & Ebert*, the pair jointly reviewed over three thousand films, along with hundreds of Dogs and Stinkers of the Week and video recommendations.

A fair number of the titles they reviewed came to be considered classics, with a rave from Siskel and Ebert serving as a key early step toward canonical status. But not all of their favorites are considered iconic works of their era. In fact, as I rewatched two decades of the show, it's surprising how often a title Roger and Gene gave two enthusiastic yes votes or thumbs up to wound up falling through the cracks of film history. For every *My Dinner with Andre* or *Hoop Dreams*, there are ten other movies they championed that, for one reason or another, never quite achieved that same level of widespread acclaim and recognition.

At least not yet.

In their PBS days, Gene and Roger occasionally hosted special episodes on what they called "Buried Treasures." Rather than devote more time to covering the latest undeserving Hollywood blockbusters, they would direct viewers' attention toward valuable little movies that hadn't done much business in theaters. They continued these kinds of shows under different names at Tribune and Buena Vista. As the home video market exploded, Gene and Roger began to use them as opportunities to recommend films on VHS or DVD that viewers missed in multiplexes.

This book about the twentieth century's most widely seen film critics felt incomplete without a little film criticism—or at least film advocacy—of its own. So this appendix is designed to serve as a print version of one of those "Buried Treasures" episodes; one more chance for some of Gene and Roger's favorites to find a new audience.

Each of the following twenty-five titles received two thumbs up from Roger and Gene. You may not have seen some of them—you may not have even heard of a couple. But it's never too late to change that.

The Silent Partner (1978)
Directed by Daryl Duke

Decades before he became one of Hollywood's most acclaimed directors with *L.A. Confidential, Wonder Boys,* and *8 Mile,* Curtis Hanson wrote the screenplay for this obscure but wonderfully suspenseful Canadian crime drama. Elliott Gould plays a meek bank teller who squares off with a cunning criminal disguised as a mall Santa Claus, played by a menacing Christopher Plummer. Gould's character discovers the thief's plan, then tries to steal from *him,* setting off a series of shocking plot twists. One of Siskel's perpetual complaints during his career as a critic was the lack of movies "in which the people are at least as intelligent as the ordinary person watching the movie. Most movie characters are not that smart." No wonder he called *The Silent Partner* "a real jewel." Everyone in this movie is smart, and so is Hanson's clever screenplay.

One-Trick Pony (1980)
Directed by Robert M. Young

Paul Simon's biggest cinematic legacy will always be his contributions to *The Graduate* soundtrack. But thirteen years later, he wrote and starred in this lovely little drama as Jonah Levin, a washed-up folk singer struggling to eke out a living playing tiny Midwestern clubs while his marriage implodes back in New York. A record company executive (Rip Torn) offers Jonah a chance to reinvent himself—but that second chance at stardom comes at a heavy cost, namely what little he has left of his artistic integrity and political convictions. Gene and Roger were particularly taken with Simon's intelligent portrayal of an idealistic baby boomer coming to grips with middle-aged disappointments. Today, *One-Trick Pony*'s details of Jonah's disintegrating life on the road play like a minor-key variation of *This Is Spinal Tap*, another carefully observed film about musicians who refuse to recognize that time has passed them by.

Diva (1981)
Directed by Jean-Jacques Beineix

The wild French thriller *Diva* could have been made expressly to delight Gene and Roger. It threw together many of their favorite cinematic elements into a single, intoxicating brew. Its plot was utterly unique and unpredictable, with a Parisian courier (Frédéric Andréi) drawn into a web of intrigue involving two illicit audio recordings—one he makes of a brilliant opera singer and another containing evidence of police corruption that a dying prostitute slips into his bag. Multiple groups begin hunting for the two tapes, leading to a rousing chase through the Paris Metro that Siskel giddily compared to similar sequences in *Bullitt* and *The French Connection*. And yet even with all the excitement, the film still found time to explore its eccentric characters and their complicated relationships. Roger and Gene sang the film's praises in multiple duets, reviewing it rhapsodically on *Sneak Previews*, and then including it in their list of the year's best films after they jumped to syndication with Tribune. *Diva* is now regarded as a key entry in the French film movement known as *cinéma du look*, but the movie's recognition in America has never quite passed from the fringes to the mainstream.

Personal Best (1982)
Directed by Robert Towne

"Winning is like sex. Sometimes you think there's just got to be more," one character says early in the sports drama *Personal Best*. And for the next two hours, winning and sex intermingle in riveting ways, as two pentathletes played by Mariel Hemingway and real-life track-and-field star Patrice Donnelly fall in love as they train and compete for a spot on the US Olympic team. *Personal Best*, which wound up on both Ebert's and Siskel's lists of the best movies of 1982, was a prime example of what Siskel called a "how-to movie"—a detail-rich drama that took audiences into a subculture it did not previously know and explained how it worked with insider knowledge. *Personal Best* also displayed a casual frankness about nudity and sexuality that became increasingly rare during the twenty years that *Siskel & Ebert* was on the air. Those who find modern movie dramas stale and bland and believe there's just got to be more would be wise to seek out this overlooked winner.

Evil Under the Sun (1982)
Directed by Guy Hamilton

Here is another of Gene Siskel's movie tests: with murder mysteries he liked to ask, "When the climactic scene arrives, and the killer is revealed, am I interested enough to try to guess along?" In the case of *Evil Under the Sun*, the answer was a resounding yes. Peter Ustinov stars as Agatha Christie's eccentric detective Hercule Poirot, this time investigating a slaying at a posh island resort inhabited by the likes of Maggie Smith, Roddy McDowall, James Mason, and Diana Rigg. Siskel got so wrapped up in the solution to the mystery that he snuck over to Ebert's seat in the theater in the middle of the screening and whispered, "Do you know who did it?" Ebert replied with a name, and Siskel agreed with his guess—which turned out to be the correct solution. That meant the film played fair with its audience, which, in their estimation, was another mark of a solid puzzle picture. *Evil Under the Sun* has never been one of the more famous Poirot films, but it got a slight boost in profile when writer/director Rian Johnson cited it as an influence on his second Benoit Blanc mystery, *Glass Onion*.

Love Letters (1984)
Directed by Amy Jones

A daughter's discovery of a stash of love letters to her late mother from a man who isn't her father rocks her world, and then sets her on a path to her own affair with a married man in *Love Letters*. (Appropriately, the return address on the all-important letters is "Eureka, California.") The daughter, played by Jamie Lee Curtis, works as a disc jockey at a public radio station. That's where she meets a photographer named Oliver (James Keach). He's married with kids, but he makes no attempt to hide his interest in her, and she reciprocates—perhaps spurred on by the swooningly romantic letters from the stranger in Eureka to her dead mother. This unusually thoughtful production from B-movie producer Roger Corman benefits greatly from the perspective of its female writer/ director, Amy Jones, who takes material that a lesser filmmaker would turn into a tawdry stalker thriller and treats it with sensitivity and empathy. Siskel and Ebert waved their upturned thumbs at Curtis, then known primarily as a scream queen, for a performance of impressive range and depth as a woman so haunted by her mother's choices that she can't help but repeat them.

Wetherby (1985)
Directed by David Hare

There is a mystery at the center of *Wetherby*, but it's less of a whodunit than a *why*dunit. After an acquaintance kills himself in her house, a lonely schoolteacher (Vanessa Redgrave) finds it impossible to move on, as the incident dredges up memories from another sad chapter of her life. That sends the film pinballing back and forth between past and present, while an equally lonely policeman (Stuart Wilson) tries to get to the bottom of this peculiar suicide. The results add up to a bleak but powerful contemplation of middle-class dissatisfaction in 1980s England, with an absolutely first-rate cast that also includes Judi Dench, Ian Holm, and Tom Wilkinson. Both hosts admired the movie's naturalistic, character-driven approach to the tired crime genre; Gene said *Wetherby* played "as unexpectedly as life itself," as it exposed the "maelstrom of discontent" hidden behind Britain's stiff upper lip.

The Official Story (1985)
Directed by Luis Puenzo

"By understanding history, we learn to understand the world. No people can survive without memory. History is the memory of people." Those are the prophetic words of a high school teacher named Alicia, the central figure in this heartbreaking Argentinian drama set during the final years of the country's military dictatorship of the late '70s and early '80s. Alicia (Norma Aleandro, who won a prize at Cannes for the role) lives in blissful ignorance of her government's repression; outside the classroom, she spends most of her time enjoying lavish parties with her bureaucrat husband (Héctor Alterio) and adopted daughter (Analía Castro, a child actress of astonishing naturalism). But when one of Alicia's old friends returns from exile in Europe and reveals the horrific circumstances of her disappearance years earlier, she opens Alicia's eyes to the possibility that her beloved little girl may have been stolen from political dissidents. Once the possibility enters her mind, Alicia can't ignore it, and she becomes consumed with uncovering the truth behind her distant husband's empty reassurances. Director Luis Puenzo never allows *The Official Story* to turn into a dry or simplistic history lesson; instead, the film, which won a Best Foreign Language Academy Award and landed on Gene's top ten list for 1985, roots its political intrigue in a haunting character drama about a deeply conflicted woman who learns the true importance of memory.

Back to the Beach (1987)
Directed by Lyndall Hobbs

When reviewing "dead teenager movies" of the 1980s like *Friday the 13th,* Siskel and Ebert often bemoaned the lack of upbeat, up-lifting motion pictures for high schoolers, occasionally citing the beach films of Frankie Avalon and Annette Funicello as examples of the sort of wholesome entertainment for young adults missing during the period. Not surprisingly, then, they were a very recep-tive audience for *Back to the Beach,* which reunited Frankie and Annette twenty years after their glory days for a likable piece of winking self-parody. This time the former beach blanket bingoers play a grumpy middled-aged couple who rediscover their zest for life when they return to their old stomping grounds on the Califor-nia coast. Back on the beach, they get dragged into a rivalry with a new generation of surfers. Gene loved Frankie's and Annette's willingness to "make fun of themselves and their squeaky-clean images," while Roger giddily praised Pee-wee Herman's energetic cameo singing "Surfin' Bird." (And with good reason; it's an unfor-gettable musical number.) Appearances by Jerry Mathers and Tony Dow as judges who give thumbs up and thumbs down to the cli-mactic surfing competition while playfully bickering probably didn't hurt the film's case with Gene and Roger, either.

Happy New Year (1987)
Directed by John G. Avildsen

Gene and Roger could get downright indignant when they be-lieved a studio had unfairly discarded a worthwhile movie. The 1987 comedy *Happy New Year* got such a tiny theatrical release from Columbia Pictures that *Siskel & Ebert* didn't even cover the film until it came out on home video. When it did, both men raved about Peter Falk's performance and razzed Columbia for burying what Siskel called a "joyful, wonderful film." In this remake of a Claude Lelouch crime flick, Falk plays a resourceful thief who employs a variety of disguises to pull off a cunning jewel heist while romancing a beautiful dealer of antiques (Wendy Hughes). Cramming an endless array of twists into its eighty-five-minute run time, *Happy New Year* is a lovely bauble to rival the ones that Falk tries to steal from Harry Winston. Columbia had a tiny gem on their hands, but it took critics like Gene and Roger to recognize it.

The Plot Against Harry (1970/1989)
Directed by Michael Roemer

This one had already been forgotten once by the time Roger and Gene watched it. In 1970, Yale film professor Michael Roemer made *The Plot Against Harry,* an oddball independent comedy about a low-level Jewish gangster who gets out of prison only to find his business in shambles and his personal life a mess. No matter what he tries to do to go straight, make amends, and repair his relationships with his ex-wife or his children, he only seems to make things worse. (The "plot" against Harry, if there is one, appears to be divine in nature.) Roemer tried to release the film in the 1970s, but its black-and-white photography and observational humor about middle-class Jewish life didn't strike potential distributors as blockbuster material. So Roemer put it on a shelf for almost twenty years, until he decided to transfer his print to VHS to show his children. On a lark, he also submitted it to film festivals, and landed spots in several major ones. That finally got the movie distributed, at which point Siskel and Ebert gave it two enthusiastic thumbs up. Gene said its quirky story rhythms and droll jokes ran "counter to everything that seems so forced and artificial in American movies."

The Mighty Quinn (1989)
Directed by Carl Schenkel

In 1989, both Siskel and Ebert went to bat for *The Mighty Quinn*, a charmingly low-key cop movie about a Jamaican police chief whose buddy becomes the prime suspect in an island murder. The policeman was played by a young actor named Denzel Washington, fresh off his stint on TV's *St. Elsewhere* and his breakthrough film role in *Cry Freedom*. Ebert called Washington a "real discovery" whose "charm, humor, and sex appeal" suggested he was a "major star" in the making. ("When the camera hits him, the screen lights up," Siskel agreed.) The following spring, Washington won his first Oscar for his supporting performance in the Civil War drama *Glory*, and he was well on his way to fulfilling Gene and Roger's prediction for his career. Even after Denzel's movie career took off, they kept on plugging *The Mighty Quinn* anyway; it later appeared as an overlooked movie on *Siskel & Ebert*'s annual "Holiday Gift Guide" and again when Gene selected it as a Video Pick of the Week in 1993.

Monsieur Hire (1989)
Directed by Patrice Leconte

"The movies were built for eavesdropping. That is one of the most compelling, indigenous subjects to film: somebody looking at somebody else, and we're watching them," said Gene Siskel, describing the core appeal of this outstanding entry in the durable subgenre of psychological thrillers about people staring out apartment windows and spying on their neighbors while they do violent and/or kinky stuff. In the case of *Monsieur Hire*, a fastidious bachelor named Hire (Michel Blanc) is the Peeping Tom, and the none-too-obscure object of his desire is Alice (Sandrine Bonnaire), who soon realizes Hire is watching her . . . and then begins watching him back. While both critics loved this moody French drama, Siskel had the more trenchant insights in his review, noting that the core tension between Hire and Alice is merely a heightened version of the drama central to all couple's relationships: "We're staring at each other and we *think* we know what we want, but we're not sure. And we certainly have no idea whether we're going to get it." "That's a very interesting point," Ebert replied, before catching himself and adding a sarcastic "Congratulations." He just couldn't bear to give his partner too much credit.

Mr. & Mrs. Bridge (1990)
Directed by James Ivory

Siskel and Ebert were reliable supporters of Merchant Ivory Productions, including this little-seen 1990 drama based on two novels by author Evan S. Connell about a married couple (played by real-life husband and wife Paul Newman and Joanne Woodward) struggling to connect to their children and each other. Gene often praised fictional movies that lacked a predictable three-act structure and contained what he saw as "documentary-like" depictions about human behavior, and that's precisely what he responded to here as he hailed its tale of "people who find it easier to follow rules than follow their hearts." Roger felt the two lead performances were so "perfectly observed" that *Mr. & Mrs. Bridge* became less about the events of the movie's minimalist story than about recognizing the universality of the characters' plight as they struggle against mid-century American society's expectations.

The Man in the Moon (1991)
Directed by Robert Mulligan

Today, 1999's *Election* and 2001's *Legally Blonde* are considered actress Reese Witherspoon's breakthrough performances. But Gene and Roger recognized Witherspoon's talents eight years earlier in the moving coming-of-age drama *The Man in the Moon*. She plays Dani, a wide-eyed tomboy who learns some tough lessons about love after a handsome older boy (Jason London) moves in next door to her family's Louisiana homestead. Roger and Gene praised the movie and its refusal to submit to Hollywood teen movie clichés, but they *loved* Witherspoon, who more than held her own opposite experienced pros like Sam Waterston as Dani's stern but loving father. Siskel went so far as to compare Witherspoon, in her very first on-screen performance, to the naturalistic work of a young Jodie Foster. Through the years, both Siskel and Ebert had an eye for spotting up-and-coming talent, but comparing a novice in her debut to one of the era's biggest stars turned out to be one of their smartest calls.

Bright Angel (1991)
Directed by Michael Fields

In this hybrid of Westerns, road movies, and coming-of-age dramas, an aimless young man named George (Dermot Mulroney) meets an alluring hitchhiker named Lucy (Lili Taylor) on her way to spring her brother from jail. After George's mother walks out on him and his stern father (Sam Shepard), George agrees to leave his tiny hometown in Montana and become Lucy's driver. Their journey takes them through dive bars and into encounters with all kinds of offbeat characters, including a couple of crooks played by Burt Young and Bill Pullman. Although he didn't ultimately include it on his best movies of 1991 list, Gene called *Bright Angels* "one of my favorite films I've seen in a long time" and Roger dubbed it a "very special new movie" worthy of comparison to Gus Van Sant's *Drugstore Cowboy* and Terrence Malick's *Days of Heaven*.

Brother's Keeper (1992)
Directed by Joe Berlinger and Bruce Sinofsky

Roger and Gene always compared their relationship to that of loving but highly competitive siblings. That adds an interesting dimension to their review of *Brother's Keeper*, the first documentary from Joe Berlinger and Bruce Sinofsky, the team that would go on to create the famous *Paradise Lost* trilogy about the West Memphis 3. *Brother's Keeper* explores a similarly murky murder case, this one about an illiterate dairy farmer named Delbert Ward accused of killing his own brother, and the neighbors who rallied to defend him from what they perceived as an overzealous justice system. Throughout their time together, Siskel and Ebert saw documentaries as the antidote to the superficiality of formulaic Hollywood pictures. Ironically, Berlinger and Sinofsky's portrait of a fiercely loyal and protective upstate New York town recalls nothing less than Bedford Falls, the setting of Frank Capra's *It's a Wonderful Life*. Like George Bailey, Delbert Ward ultimately learns that no man is a failure who has friends.

Matinee (1993)
Directed by Joe Dante

This perceptive comedy hides a clear-eyed message about the world beneath its amusing tale of a schlock film director (John Goodman) showing his latest horror picture in Key West right as the Cuban Missile Crisis touches off to the south. Rather than mocking cheesy old sci-fi movies—the director's latest is about a man who turns into a giant ant—*Matinee* celebrates their showmanship and low-budget ingenuity, and it smartly contrasts old movies' escapist scares with the true terror of nuclear power. Goodman's Lawrence Woolsey may be a huckster, but he clearly believes in the power of cinema, and so does director Joe Dante, who re-creates the joys of 1960s moviegoing in painstaking detail. *Matinee* leaves the audience with a big idea, provided by Woolsey to one of his patrons at the climax: "You think grown-ups have it all figured out? That's just a hustle, kid! Grown-ups are making it up as they go along, just like you." The Cuban Missile Crisis is a lot more serious than a giant ant, but they're both caused by the same thing: grown-ups who have no idea what they're doing.

Household Saints (1993)
Directed by Nancy Savoca

In praising this saga about several generations of one Italian-American family, Gene Siskel said, "It's going to take a lot of good pictures to knock this off my best of the year list." But when the end of 1993 rolled around, *Household Saints* didn't make the cut; there *were* a lot of good pictures that year, including *Schindler's List*, *The Piano*, *The Age of Innocence*, and *Short Cuts*, all of which appeared on both of Roger's and Gene's top tens. *Household Saints* is smaller in its ambitions, but its insights about spirituality and assimilation are truly profound. The first half follows a Little Italy butcher (Vincent D'Onofrio) who wins the right to marry the shy woman (Tracey Ullman) he desires in a pinochle game. The butcher's immigrant mother (Judith Malina) dislikes her secular-minded daughter-in-law, and makes her pregnancy miserable by threatening her with old wives' tales and forcing her to pray to St. Teresa to protect her unborn baby. Years later, the couple's daughter, Teresa (a remarkable Lili Taylor), finds herself consumed by a more intense version of her grandmother's religious fervor, even experiencing a vision of Jesus in her home at one point. Has she had a psychotic break or been touched by something divine? This unique film is impossible to categorize; it's a hilarious comedy and a devastating tragedy, and it treats religion seriously and skeptically at the same time. Roger and Gene both adored *Household Saints*, and heaped praise on D'Onofrio, Taylor, and Savoca, but after they left it off their best-of lists, the film faded into semi-obscurity.

Who's the Man? (1993)
Directed by Ted Demme

Throughout the 1980s and '90s, Siskel and Ebert frequently championed movies about African American life that eschewed clichés about gangs and violence. That might explain some of their affection for *Who's the Man?* despite their professed ignorance of its two stars, MTV VJs Doctor Dre and Ed Lover, in their big-screen debuts. They play a pair of out-of-work Harlem barbers so desperate for jobs they reluctantly join the NYPD. After their old boss at the local barbershop gets murdered, they take it upon themselves to solve the case. This comic caper features some pointed commentary about gentrification and urban policing, and it boasts an all-star cast of '90s hip-hop artists including Naughty by Nature, House of Pain, and Ice-T. Ebert favorably compared Dré and Lover to comedy teams like Abbott and Costello and Cheech and Chong; Siskel liked it so much he said he hoped they'd make a sequel. Neither pointed out the film's early roles for future stars Bernie Mac, Terrence Howard, and Denis Leary.

Once Upon a Time . . . When We Were Colored (1996)
Directed by Tim Reid

This sprawling drama—which features eighty-three different speaking roles—charts the evolution of a small Mississippi town through the middle of the twentieth century. Based on Clifton Taulbert's memoir of his own childhood, Tim Reid's film version features an outstanding cast including Phylicia Rashad, Richard Roundtree, and Al Freeman Jr., as the Poppa of Taulbert's stand-in, Cliff. In *Once Upon a Time . . . When We Were Colored*'s most gut-wrenching sequence, Poppa must teach his young great-grandson to read the letters *W* and *C* so that he can tell the difference between their town's segregated bathrooms. Roger and Gene loved the way scenes like that one laid bare racism's generational legacy, and they also commended Reid for his skill at balancing all-too-real tales of segregation's insidious impact with uplifting human stories, as the Black residents of this community work together to persevere through endless adversity.

Family Name (1997)
Directed by Macky Alston

As a boy, Macky Alston attended public school with African American children who shared his last name—which they all inherited from Macky's ancestors in a prominent clan of North Carolina plantation owners. After Alston grew up to become a documentarian, he explored his family's history in *Family Name*, in which he not only traces his personal roots but also contemplates his genealogical role in the slave trade. His travels introduce viewers to a fascinating mix of people, both Black and white, who share a common last name but come from wildly divergent backgrounds and have received vastly different opportunities as a result. Until Alston came along, it seems like many of them never discussed that subject, leading him to wonder: "Is something a secret if everybody knows it and nobody talks about it?" Gene and Roger praised Alston's methodical and sensitive approach to topics like race and privilege that are sadly still relevant a quarter century after this film's release. Amid this exploration of a deeply painful chapter in our nation's history, *Family Name* suggests reasons for hope, as Macky's film helps unite Alstons of all colors and classes in a greater understanding of each other's joy and pain.

Love and Death on Long Island (1997)
Directed by Richard Kwietniowski

As film critics, Gene and Roger knew a thing or two about finding beauty in the most unexpected places. That also happens to be the theme of *Love and Death on Long Island*, a beguiling and humane comedy about a reclusive British writer named Giles De'Ath (John Hurt), who has absolutely no concept of the modern world. One day, De'Ath gets locked out of his apartment and decides to kill a few hours at a movie theater. He wanders into the wrong auditorium and accidentally encounters a trashy teen comedy called *Hotpants College II*, where a handsome teen actor (played by '90s TV heartthrob Jason Priestley) catches his eye. De'Ath instantly becomes obsessed, and soon he abandons his work to travel across the Atlantic to find and meet the subject of his fixation. Gene and Roger both appreciated the unusual premise, the film's sweetness about its protagonist, and his fervent admiration for the Priestley character. "Any passion so well expressed, as in this film, is simply captivating," said Siskel. He also warned viewers that *Love and Death on Long Island* was "the kind of small picture that plays a couple weeks in one theater in most cities and then disappears and people wonder later how they missed it." Decades later, it's still a hard film to see—and still one worth seeking out.

Simon Birch (1998)
Directed by Mark Steven Johnson

Never ones to concern themselves with critical consensus, Roger and Gene were enthusiastic supporters of this commercial and critical flop suggested by the John Irving novel *A Prayer for Owen Meany*. While many other reviewers faulted *Simon Birch* for what they perceived as its maudlin preachiness, Gene, in his last year hosting *Siskel & Ebert* before his death, was moved by its unabashed spirituality, which he argued was otherwise "absent from so much of today's popular entertainment." The film concerns the childhood friendship between two outsiders in a little town in Maine: Joe (Joseph Mazzello) and a dwarf named Simon (Ian Michael Smith, about as charismatic and unassuming a child actor as you'll ever see). Simon, a devout believer in God and a skeptic in the local church, loudly proclaims that all of his actions are part of a divine plan; his pronouncements bring him into conflict with the town's oppressive reverend, played by David Strathairn. During their crosstalk, Gene asked Roger whether the film's message about faith and destiny inspired Roger to think about his own purpose in life. "I've been thinking about that for a long time," Roger replied. "My purpose is to give good reviews to movies like *Simon Birch*. That's what I'm on Earth for."

Living Out Loud (1998)
Directed by Richard LaGravenese

In one of their final episodes together, Siskel and Ebert strongly recommended this dramedy about a pair of lonely New Yorkers who make an unlikely connection when they meet in an elevator. Holly Hunter plays a newly divorced nurse; Danny DeVito, a perennial *Siskel & Ebert* favorite as both an actor and a director, is a building super who just lost his daughter. They start talking, she helps him pay off a debt, and a surprising relationship blossoms. Roger and Gene responded to *Living Out Loud*'s sharp screenplay, which avoids conventional story beats, and provides Hunter and DeVito with tons of witty dialogue to volley back and forth. (They also loved Queen Latifah as the vivacious lounge singer at a local nightclub.) It adds up to the sort of personal, intimate movie for and about adults that Siskel and Ebert supported and promoted throughout their careers, and have all but vanished from the big Hollywood studios since their passing. That may not be a coincidence. It also may not be a coincidence that *Living Out Loud*'s central theme about the importance of improbable friendships mirrored Gene and Roger's own relationship. They never intended to come into each other's lives, and then found themselves transformed by a partnership that changed the course of film, television, and film criticism in America.

ACKNOWLEDGMENTS

Some teenagers sneak around behind their parents' backs to do drugs. I did it to watch *Siskel & Ebert.*

I don't remember how I discovered the show, or the first episode I watched. But I do know that by the age of thirteen, *Siskel & Ebert* was appointment television for me—and not an easy appointment to keep, since the show bounced around the dial and, at least in the New York market in the early 1990s, was often on late at night, far after a middle school kid's bedtime. I was so obsessed with the show in those days that I would pretend to go to sleep, lie quietly in the dark until the rest of my family went to bed, then turn on the tiny thirteen-inch Sanyo TV in my room at the lowest possible volume to watch Roger and Gene mix it up.

So first and foremost I have to thank my parents, not only for nurturing my love of film from a very early age, but also for being such deep sleepers. This book, and really anything else I have done or will ever do, is a testament to their constant support. My thanks also to the rest of my family, especially my brother, Doug, who's never doubted I could pull this off—even when I sometimes did. And I can't forget to thank my daughters, Riley and Eloise, for all of their love and inspiration. They're already just as feisty as Gene and Roger (but much cuter).

There are many other people who made this book possible. My

agent, Peter Steinberg, was the one who singled out *Siskel & Ebert* from a list of topics I was interested in writing about—and then was even more convinced after he heard about my passion for the subject. I'm also deeply grateful to Keith Phipps, my old boss at the late, lamented film website the Dissolve, who took the hint when I asked him if he had any advice on how to find a literary agent and introduced me to his. Thank you also to my editor, Michelle Howry, and everyone at Putnam, who've been so wonderful to work with throughout this project.

The phrase "Never meet your heroes" is such a cliché at this point it could have been featured on one of *Siskel & Ebert*'s "They'll Do It Every Time" episodes, where Roger and Gene would lash out at the most hackneyed tropes in cinema. But in the world of *Siskel & Ebert,* "Never meet your heroes" is simply not true. Gene Siskel died while I was still in college, but I got to meet and collaborate with Roger Ebert on *Ebert Presents: At the Movies* as one of the show's contributing critics. Despite my inexperience (and occasional awkwardness trying to play it cool around the man I had looked up to since I watched him on that tiny TV as a kid), he was funny and endlessly supportive. I still have every email he sent me and every book he signed to me. I hope I did him and Gene proud.

Gene and Roger clearly led by example, because I have nothing but good things to say about the dozens of people I met who were associated with every iteration of *Sneak Previews, At the Movies,* and *Siskel & Ebert.* I thank each and every one of them for their time and their stories.

A few names must be singled out for additional praise. Roger's and Gene's widows, Chaz Ebert and Marlene Iglitzen, respectively, have both been extremely kind and encouraging, even in the face of many pestering emails. I'm also indebted to Valerie Kyriakopoulos, the archivist at Chicago's Museum of Broadcast Communications, who dug up the original VHS tape of *Siskel & Ebert's* twenty-third-anniversary benefit dinner, which is eighty-five extremely rare minutes of Gene and Roger telling wonderful stories and trading fascinating insights about their careers.

For more than forty years, Robert Feder covered the world of Chicago media, first as a columnist for the *Chicago Sun-Times*, and later at *Time Out Chicago* and his own website, RobertFeder .com. During that time, he maintained an exhaustive archive of material on many of the key members of the Chicago TV and radio landscape—including Gene Siskel and Roger Ebert, who Feder also knew personally. Over the course of a very long summer day, he allowed me to examine his files, which included articles, rare artifacts, and even personal correspondences from Gene and Roger. His generosity with his time, insights, and collection of clippings cannot be overstated and were deeply appreciated.

Back when I was watching *Siskel & Ebert* in my darkened childhood bedroom, Roger and Gene were my first film teachers. Through their show, I learned about camerawork, editing, acting, writing, and the movie industry, and their enthusiasm inspired me to study cinema more directly. Throughout my education I was lucky enough to learn from several teachers who imparted not only their knowledge but also their own passion for film. At Syracuse University, a class on Alfred Hitchcock taught by critic and author Douglas Brode was almost as impactful as all those hours watching Roger and Gene and led to my decision to go to grad school at New York University, where I was incredibly fortunate to study with more brilliant critics and scholars, including J. Hoberman and the late Robert Sklar. If you've enjoyed this book, you owe them almost as much as I do.

Watching movies, especially as a working critic or journalist, can feel like a very solitary act. But as Siskel and Ebert proved, film is best enjoyed and most appreciated with someone to talk to about the experience. Everywhere I have studied or written about movies, I have found wonderful communities of friends and colleagues whose companionship have made the movies seem like something bigger than mere strips of celluloid or masses of data on hard drives. From my comrades who helped me run Syracuse University's on-campus UU Cinemas to my colleagues in the Cinema Studies Department at NYU, this book would not have been possible without you. To those I have shared screening rooms, podcast microphones, red carpets, website offices, and television studios with: thank you, thank you, thank you.

Before I sent my book ideas to Peter Steinberg, there was someone else I showed them to first. That was my wife, Melissa, who took one look at the first version of the list and said, "Why isn't *Siskel & Ebert* on here?" I'll tell you what I told her: I was scared. How do I write the story of two writers whose work I revere? What if I can't measure up to Siskel and Ebert?

"You can," she replied. "Plus, no one loves that show more than you. And if someone else ever wrote this book and you didn't, you would be furious."

As usual, she was right. In the twenty years leading up to that conversation, and in every moment since, she has been my biggest supporter, not to mention the first reader of everything in this book. Thank you, Melissa. This book literally would not exist without you. I hope it was worth all those nights I ditched you to watch Gene and Roger debate the merits of *Speed 2: Cruise Control*.

(I still can't believe they gave that one two thumbs up.)

NOTES

INTRODUCTION: COMING ATTRACTIONS

1 **"get more detailed":** *Siskel & Ebert*, episode 305, YouTube video, October 9, 1993, https://www.youtube.com/watch?v=apGNWEVqR14.

1 **"is the truth":** Roger Ebert, "Nothing Simple about the Truth," *Chicago Sun-Times*, May 26, 2005, https://www.rogerebert.com/reviews/kings-and-queen-2005.

2 **"and Hillary Clinton":** Marcia Froelke Coburn, "The Last Reel," *Chicago*, December 1999, 134.

4 **"a show about movies":** Thea Flaum, author interview, Brooklyn, NY, October 19, 2022.

6 **"and very smart":** Flaum, author interview.

7 **"Anyone else":** Roger Ebert, "Farewell, My Friend," *Chicago Sun-Times*, February 21, 1999, https://www.rogerebert.com/interviews/farewell-my-friend.

10 **"*anyone* on television":** Ty Burr, "From New Hollywood to New Media, He's Seen It All," *Boston Globe*, October 9, 2011, http://archive.boston.com/ae/movies/articles/2011/10/09/from_new_hollywood_to_new_media_roger_ebert_has_seen_it_all/?page=2.

10 **hated it so much:** Stuart Cleland, author interview, Brooklyn, NY, September 21, 2022.

10 **"relationship on television":** *The Museum of Television & Radio Seminar Series: Siskel & Ebert: Thumbs Up*, VHS, Paley Center for Media Archive, November 12, 1992.

12 **"a big deal":** Thea Flaum, author interview, Brooklyn, NY, January 14, 2022.

12 **"wait and see":** Roger Ebert, "The Balcony Is Closed," RogerEbert.com, July 24, 2008, https://www.rogerebert.com/roger-ebert/the-balcony-is-closed.

CHAPTER ONE: EBERT BEFORE SISKEL

15 *"Chicago Sun-Times"*: Roger Ebert, *Life Itself: A Memoir* (New York: Grand Central, 2011), 144–45.

15 **at his college:** Roger Ebert, "The Original, or Maybe the Third Guy Who Has Seen Every Movie of Any Consequence," in *Citizen Sarris: American Film Critic*, ed. Emanuel Levy (Landham, MD: Scarecrow Press, 2001), 31–36.

16 **the Great American novel:** Chaz Ebert, author interview, Chicago, IL, August 15, 2022.

16 **"any conscious plan":** Ebert, *Life Itself*, 5.

16 **"becomes your life":** Ebert, *Life Itself*, 98.

16 **"not a planned move":** Chaz Ebert, author interview.

17 **"as a result":** *Later with Bob Costas*, episode 1-114, SiskelEbert.org video, April 19, 1989, https://siskelebert.org/?p=5996.

18 **"everybody entertained":** Ramin Bahrani, author interview, Brooklyn, NY, August 8, 2022.

18 **"his own jokes":** Robert Feder, author interview, Brooklyn, NY, July 6, 2022.

18 **"just a cover-up":** Brooks Egerton, "Citizen Ebert," *Capital Times*, November 14, 1987, 33.

18 **"studying the students":** Ebert, *Life Itself*, 91.

19 **"cup of coffee":** Chaz Ebert, author interview.

19 **"from another world":** Roger Ebert, *Two Weeks in the Midday Sun: A Cannes Notebook* (Kansas City, MO: Andrews McMeel, 1987), 106.

19 **"a prudent reserve":** Ebert, *Life Itself*, 98.

20 **"good at that":** Ignatiy Vishnevetsky, author interview, Brooklyn, NY, September 23, 2022.

20 **"directly to me":** *Siskel & Ebert*, "The Movies That Made Us Critics," YouTube video, November 12, 1988, https://www.youtube.com/watch?v=myY587VgNw4.

21 **"the same knowledge":** *Siskel & Ebert*, "The Movies We Loved as Kids," YouTube video, May 4, 1991, https://www.youtube.com/watch?v=Swto-AtTGVo.

22 **"a movie critic":** *Siskel & Ebert*, "The Movies We Loved as Kids."

22 **"formative acts":** Roger Ebert, "Thought Experiments: How Propeller-Heads, BNFs, Sercon Geeks, Newbies, Recovering GAFIAtors, and Kids in the Basements Invented the World Wide Web, All Except for the Delivery System," Asimovs.com, January 2005, http://web.archive.org/web

/20050101021525/http://www.asimovs.com/_issue_0501/thought experiments.shtml.

22 **"book I've read"**: John Schoenherr, "Amazing Bedfellows," *John Schoenherr* blog, June 12, 2013, https://johnschoenherr.blogspot.com /2013/06/amazing-bedfellows.html.

23 **"outsider world view"**: Ebert, "Thought Experiments."

23 **"from the country"**: Roger Ebert, "Room," *Stymie* no. 1 (June 1960): 4.

23 **"fumbled and fell"**: Ebert, *Life Itself*, 77.

24 **"An important one"**: *Life Itself*, directed by Steve James (Magnolia Pictures, 2014).

25 **"to shield us"**: Roger Ebert, "The Loud Silence," *Daily Illini*, November 26, 1963, https://archives.library.illinois.edu/ebert/files/2017/02 /1963-11-26-Ars-Gratia-Loud-Silence-resizeconvertedPDF.pdf.

26 **"lacking in taste"**: Bosley Crowther, "Screen: *Bonnie and Clyde* Arrives," *New York Times*, August 14, 1967, 36.

26 **"the moron trade"**: Louis Menand, "*Bonnie and Clyde*, Fifty Years Later," *New Yorker*, August 14, 2017, https://www.newyorker.com/culture /cultural-comment/bonnie-and-clyde-fifty-years-after.

27 **"it's about us"**: Roger Ebert, "*Bonnie and Clyde*," *Chicago Sun-Times*, September 25, 1967, https://www.rogerebert.com/reviews/bonnie-and -clyde-1967.

27 **restaurant next door**: Ebert, "The Original, or Maybe the Third Guy."

27 **"is that man"**: Ebert, *Life Itself*, 154.

28 **"a moron"**: Carol Felsenthal, "A Life in Movies," *Chicago*, December 2005, 106.

28 **"community critic"**: "The Press: Populist at the Movies," *Time*, March 30, 1970, https://content.time.com/time/subscriber/article/0,33009,942232 -2,00.html.

28 **"go anywhere else"**: Chaz Ebert, author interview.

29 **"cheap, dreary productions"**: Roger Ebert, "*Vixen!*," *Chicago Sun-Times*, February 24, 1969, https://www.rogerebert.com/reviews/vixen-1969.

29 **"the human anatomy"**: Ebert, *Life Itself*, 208.

32 **was never finished**: Ebert, *Life Itself*, 213–14.

33 **"screenwriting neophyte"**: Gene Siskel, "*Beyond the Valley*," *Chicago Tribune*, July 14, 1970, https://www.newspapers.com/clip/43386008 /gene-siskel-movie-reviewsbeyond-the.

CHAPTER TWO: SISKEL BEFORE EBERT

35 **"a lot of fun":** James L. Coppens, "Portrait of a Film Critic: 'What's Gene Gonna Do?'" *Culver Alumni Magazine*, Summer 1980, 17–18.

35 **size 28 waist:** Rose Etherington, "John Travolta's *Saturday Night Fever* Suit Rediscovered," *Dezeen*, August 24, 2012, https://www.dezeen.com /2012/08/24/john-travoltas-saturday-night-fever-suit-rediscovered.

36 **"*Rocky* and *Mean Streets*":** Gene Siskel, "*Saturday Night Fever*," *Chicago Tribune*, December 16, 1977, https://www.chicagotribune.com/history /ct-gene-siskel-chicago-tribune-movie-review-saturday-night-fever-1977 -20220520-ev36xnwjx5glhnamuupn7353ti-story.html.

37 **visible on-screen:** "Hollywoodland Tribute: Gene Siskel," *Premiere*, April 1999.

37 **start the movie:** Richard Roeper, author interview, Brooklyn, NY, August 30, 2022.

37 **"realities of time":** Bret Watson, "They Still Like to Watch," *Entertainment Weekly*, May 17, 1996, 48.

38 **"no longer required":** Stuart Cleland, author interview, Brooklyn, NY, September 21, 2022.

38 **"get away with":** Carie Lovstad, author interview, Brooklyn, NY, May 23, 2022.

38 ***Wizard of Oz:*** Roger Ebert, "Movie Answer Man," *Chicago Sun-Times*, December 27, 1998, https://www.rogerebert.com/answer-man/movie -answer-man-12271998.

38 **"vicariously on film":** Coppens, "Portrait of a Film Critic," 23.

39 **"of a society":** Tom Shales, "Tom Shales Lunches with Siskel & Ebert," *Washington Post*, September 4, 1983, https://www.rogerebert.com /features/tom-shales-lunches-with-siskel-and-ebert.

39 **and political turmoil:** Coppens, "Portrait of a Film Critic," 21.

39 **"a basic question":** Coppens, "Portrait of a Film Critic," 23.

40 **both of illnesses:** Marlene Iglitzen, author interview, Brooklyn, NY, September 18, 2022.

40 **"she was dead":** Rick Kogan, "He Changed the Way We Look at Movies," *Chicago Tribune*, February 21, 1999, 16.

40 **"terrifying to me":** Lawrence Grobel, "Playboy Interview: Siskel & Ebert," *Playboy*, February 1991, 70.

40 **"I think I can!":** *Siskel & Ebert*, "The Movies That Made Us Critics," YouTube video, November 12, 1988, https://www.youtube.com/watch ?v=myY587VgNw4.

41 **into their seats:** Gene Siskel, ". . . But Why on a Dingus Like This?," *Chicago Tribune*, November 22, 1970, E-5.

41 **their sour pickles:** George Castle, "Movie Maven: An Interview with Film Critic Gene Siskel," *JUF News*, December 1988, 16.

41 **"the unhappiness underneath":** *Siskel & Ebert,* "The Movies We Loved as Kids," YouTube video, May 4, 1991, https://www.youtube.com/watch?v=Swto-AtTGVo.

41 **"the big screen":** *Siskel & Ebert,* "The Movies We Loved as Kids."

41 **"about those issues":** Jamie Bennett, author interview, Brooklyn, NY, August 30, 2022.

42 **"mankind's greatest achievements?":** *Siskel & Ebert,* "The Movies We Loved as Kids."

42 **"than standard stories":** *Siskel & Ebert,* episode 1305, YouTube video, October 10, 1998, https://www.youtube.com/watch?v=P2y-Fc9ewVk.

42 **"hit the ball back":** "Tribute: A Life at the Movies," *TV Guide,* March 20, 1999, 46.

43 **"pick it up":** Bennett, author interview.

43 **$10,000 in prizes:** Judy Hevrdejs, "The Rise of 'Beat Siskel': From Dinner for 2 to $10,000 in Prizes," *Chicago Tribune,* October 15, 1999, 9–18.

44 **"actors having lunch":** Roger Ebert, "*Monster* of a Mistake," *Chicago Sun-Times,* May 12, 2005, https://www.rogerebert.com/reviews/monster-in-law-2005.

44 **"that much sweeter":** Iglitzen, author interview.

44 **the Army Reserve:** Coppens, "Portrait of a Film Critic," 18.

45 **"pick a journalist":** Robert Feder, "Famed Film Critic," *Chicago Sun-Times,* February 21, 1999, 2A.

45 **twentieth-century journalism:** Coppens, "Portrait of a Film Critic," 18.

45 **neighborhood news section:** Kogan, "He Changed the Way We Look at Movies," 16.

45 **$150 a week:** Robert Feder, "Chicago's TV Millionaires—Some Facts and Fantasies," *Chicago Sun-Times,* December 13, 1987, 5.

45 **days of Abraham Lincoln:** Owen Youngman, "How Siskel Became Our Critic: A Legend in the Making," *Chicago Tribune,* February 22, 1999, 5-5.

46 **"got the guts":** Michael Sneed, "Michael Sneed," *Chicago Sun-Times,* February 23, 1999, 4.

47 **"should be me":** Youngman, "How Siskel Became Our Critic."

47 **"this proves it":** Youngman, "How Siskel Became Our Critic."

47 **"and self-assurance":** Iglitzen, author interview.

47 **"before his time":** Toni Schlesinger, "Best Enemies," *Chicago,* May 1987, 124.

48 **"himself soon after":** Iglitzen, author interview.

48 **"trying to accomplish":** Gene Siskel, "Siskel's 10 Years of Movie Memories," *Chicago Tribune,* October 8, 1979, 6-3.

48 **"on that basis":** *The Museum of Television & Radio Seminar Series: Siskel & Ebert: Thumbs Up,* VHS, Paley Center for Media Archive, November 12, 1992.

48 **"trying to be accurate":** Grobel, "Playboy Interview," 54.

48 **"no-bad-scenes concept":** Castle, "Movie Maven," 17.

49 **"really going on":** Coppens, "Portrait of a Film Critic," 19.

49 **"success in movies?":** *Siskel & Ebert,* episode 719, YouTube video, January 23, 1993, https://www.youtube.com/watch?v=vIQ2bxPZRGU.

49 **"not to great success":** *Siskel & Ebert,* episode 839, YouTube video, June 11, 1994, https://www.youtube.com/watch?v=gsWsTiYVMBs.

49 **more or less:** *Siskel & Ebert,* episode 710, YouTube video, November 21, 1992, https://www.youtube.com/watch?v=-oiph_WQjyU.

49 **which she did:** Bill Zwecker and Brenda Warner Rotzoll, "Legendary Critic Was Family Man First," *Chicago Sun-Times,* February 23, 1999, 2.

50 **"movie next time":** Paul McCartney interview, *CBS News,* YouTube video, October 18, 1984, https://www.youtube.com/watch?v=RtTzVwXaCb0.

50 **"a terrible idea":** Ray Solley, author interview, Brooklyn, NY, August 31, 2022.

50 **"that's a good thing":** *Later with Bob Costas,* April 19, 1989.

50 **"I believed him":** Al Berman, author interview, Brooklyn, NY, August 25, 2022.

51 **"to his daughter":** Gene Siskel, "Siskel Meets 2 of His Toughest Tests, Finds Them Easier to Take," *Chicago Tribune,* February 9, 1986, https://www.chicagotribune.com/news/ct-xpm-1986-02-09-8601100771-story.html.

51 **"gracious, and giving":** Berman, author interview.

52 **"'a good investment'":** John Davies, author interview, Brooklyn, NY, January 19, 2022.

52 **"for the glasses":** Janet LaMonica, author interview, Brooklyn, NY, June 2, 2022.

53 **"to this day":** Lovstad, author interview.

54 **"the fucking book!":** Lovstad, author interview.

54 **right from wrong:** Brigitte Dayan, "Gene Siskel, Movie Critic and Devoted Jew," *JUF News,* April 1999, 105.

54 **"family to come home":** *Siskel & Ebert*, episode 721, YouTube video, February 6, 1993, https://www.youtube.com/watch?v=WUE17 tTa3Kw.

54 **smeared in jelly:** *Siskel & Ebert*, episode 702, YouTube video, September 19, 1992, https://www.youtube.com/watch?v=dA2SPqBkENg.

54 **up to fifty cents:** Gene Siskel, "Ushers Are Ignoring the Pleas for Silence," *Chicago Tribune*, May 15, 1977, 8-6.

55 **"that reflected light":** Coppens, "Portrait of a Film Critic," 23.

55 **into the *Tribune*:** Lewis Beale, "Siskel and Ebert: Windy Critics," *Los Angeles Times*, January 5, 1986, https://www.latimes.com/archives/la-xpm-1986-01-05-ca-24440-story.html.

55 **"I got him again":** Beale, "Siskel and Ebert."

CHAPTER THREE: OPENING SOON AT A THEATER NEAR YOU

57 **"on being truthful":** *Sneak Previews*, episode 103, SiskelEbert.org video, November 3, 1978, https://siskelebert.org/?p=8038.

57 **"'themselves without embellishing'":** Roger Ebert, "Great Movies: *Rashomon*," *Chicago Sun-Times*, May 26, 2002, https://www.rogerebert.com/reviews/great-movie-rashomon-1950.

58 **April 23, 1896:** Jerry Roberts, *The Complete History of American Film Criticism* (Santa Monica: Santa Monica Press, 2010), 21.

59 **"Walt Disney productions":** Dennis McLellan, "Judith Crist Dies at 90; Film Critic 'Most Hated by Hollywood,'" *Los Angeles Times*, August 8, 2012, https://www.latimes.com/local/obituaries/la-me-judith-crist-20120808-story.html.

60 **a neck massage:** Daphnee Denis, "Tuesdays with Judith," *Slate*, August 8, 2012, https://slate.com/culture/2012/08/judith-crist-as-a-teacher-and-as-a-critic-she-was-both-loved-and-feared.html.

60 **"the fallout from Crist":** Mark Caro, "A Man of Influence," *Chicago Tribune*, February 22, 1999, https://www.chicagotribune.com/news/ct-xpm-1999-02-22-9902220139-story.html.

60 **"'to think of it'":** Judith Crist, "The Critical Years," *Silurian News*, May 1997, http://gos.sbc.edu/c/crist.html.

62 **in their entire lives:** James J. Kilpatrick, "My Gifted Counterpoint on *60 Minutes* Wrote Like an Angel," *Keene (NH) Sentinel*, July 5, 2005, https://www.sentinelsource.com/opinion/my-gifted-counterpoint-on-60-minutes-wrote-like-an-angel-by-james-j-kilpatrick/article_cf66570c-f7aa-5f2a-9b2f-b636f24420cd.html.

64 **"could be incubated":** Robert Feder, author interview, Brooklyn, NY, August 22, 2022.

64 **"were really wonderful":** Michael Loewenstein, author interview, Brooklyn, NY, April 6, 2022.

64 **"'to try it?'":** Thea Flaum, author interview, Brooklyn, NY, October 19, 2022.

65 **"had their credentials":** Josh Schollmeyer, *Enemies, A Love Story* (Now & Then Reader, 2012), ch. 1, Kindle.

66 **"a television program":** Nick Aronson, author interview, Brooklyn, NY, August 24, 2022.

67 **"at that lunch":** Aronson, author interview.

68 **"your part is":** *Tribute to Siskel & Ebert*, VHS, Museum of Broadcast Communications Archive, April 16, 1998.

68 **"of Ingmar Bergman":** Roger Ebert, "Special Provides Time for Two Movie Lovers to Play It Over Again," *Chicago Sun-Times*, June 11, 1989, E-3.

69 **"front of a camera":** *Tribute to Siskel & Ebert*.

69 **"but it's real":** Phil Rosenthal, "Bill Kurtis: 'There Was a Time When People Actually Watched Channel 2,'" *Chicago Tribune*, September 14, 2009, https://newsblogs.chicagotribune.com/towerticker/2009/09/bill-kurtis-there-was-a-time-when-people-actually-watched-channel-2.html.

69 **"with the movies":** *Chicago Tonight*, YouTube video, April 15, 1998, https://www.youtube.com/watch?v=SXCVZk__o48.

70 **"ever did professionally":** Jane Shay Wald, author interview, Brooklyn, NY, July 1, 2022.

70 **"for a pilot":** Ray Solley, author interview, Brooklyn, NY, August 31, 2022.

71 **"points of view":** Jane Shay Wald, author interview.

71 **"other on camera":** Jane Shay Wald, author interview.

72 **"into that approach":** Interview Archives Learning Objects, "Siskel & Ebert Advise Young Movie Critics," YouTube video, September 19, 2019, https://www.youtube.com/watch?v=__L9DzZIkwI.

72 **"I'm very pleased":** *Chicago Tonight*.

72 **"outside of his circle":** Nancy De Los Santos, author interview, Westerly, RI, February 23, 2022.

72 **"Roger would just talk":** Laura C. Hernández, author interview, Brooklyn, NY, March 15, 2022.

73 **"couldn't be trifled with":** Toni Schlesinger, "Best Enemies," *Chicago*, May 1987, 124.

74 **set dressings himself:** Jane Shay Wald, author interview.

74 **"We were just petrified"**: *Chicago Tonight*.

75 **"kind of droning"**: A. O. Scott, author interview, Brooklyn, NY, June 10, 2022.

75 **"commentary, and criticism"**: "Wednesday/Nov. 26," *Arlington Heights Herald*, November 22, 1975, 40.

76 **"the movie business"**: *Opening Soon . . . at a Theater Near You*, Pilot, SiskelEbert.org video, November 26, 1975, https://siskelebert.org /?p=4322.

77 **"from that meeting"**: Aronson, author interview.

CHAPTER FOUR: THE FIRST-TAKE SHOW

79 **"each other on TV"**: *The Tonight Show Starring Johnny Carson*, episode 5744, YouTube video, July 23, 1987, https://www.youtube.com/watch?v= 5J0Mn0kmLos.

79 **"disagree with your interpretation"**: *Siskel & Ebert*, episode 936, SiskelEbert.org video, June 10, 1995, https://siskelebert.org/?p=3485.

80 **"using the balcony"**: Michael Loewenstein, author interview, Brooklyn, NY, April 6, 2022.

81 **"a cushion, too"**: Mary Margaret Bartley, author interview, Brooklyn, NY, April 6, 2022.

82 **"lunch, dinner, and fights"**: Roger Ebert, "Remembering Gene," RogerEbert.com, February 17, 2009, https://www.rogerebert.com/roger -ebert/remembering-gene.

82 **"the *Chicago Tribune*"**: *Opening Soon . . . at a Theater Near You*, SiskelEbert.org video, December 21, 1976, https://siskelebert.org /?p=2528.

83 **"it *wasn't* a joke"**: John Davies, author interview, Brooklyn, NY, January 19, 2022.

83 **"to the editor"**: Ray Solley, author interview, Brooklyn, NY, January 24, 2022.

84 **"the newspaper is for"**: *Tribute to Siskel & Ebert* video, April 16, 1998.

84 **needed to stop**: Davies, author interview.

85 **"they were competitors"**: Solley, author interview, January 24, 2022.

86 **"in separate cars"**: *Sneak Previews*, episode 313, SiskelEbert.org video, November 29, 1979, https://siskelebert.org/?p=8249.

86 **"loving that about her"**: Solley, author interview, January 24, 2022.

86 **"did that for years"**: Thea Flaum, author interview, Brooklyn, NY, October 19, 2022.

87 **"want to talk about"**: Thea Flaum, author interview, Brooklyn, NY, January 14, 2022.

87 **"up with the idea"**: Joanne Harrison, "Two of a Kind," *Hollywood Reporter*, March 21, 1996, S-4.

88 **director called cut**: *Late Night with David Letterman*, episode 1399, YouTube video, March 14, 1991, https://www.youtube.com/watch?v= SS6O1AoGtAI.

88 **"he said '*Sneak Previews!*'"**: Solley, author interview, January 24, 2022.

89 **"that was that"**: Josh Schollmeyer, *Enemies, A Love Story* (Now & Then Reader, 2012), ch. 2, Kindle.

89 ***Ozzie and Harriet***: Flaum, author interview, January 14, 2022.

89 **"a bone of contention"**: Laura C. Hernández, author interview, Brooklyn, NY, March 15, 2022.

90 **"It was so crazy"**: Nancy De Los Santos, author interview, Westerly, RI, February 23, 2022.

90 **"we would use"**: Flaum, author interview, January 14, 2022.

91 **"had it in writing"**: Solley, author interview, January 24, 2022.

91 **"'can say yes'"**: Solley, author interview, January 24, 2022.

92 **"at the box office"**: Woody Allen, letter to *Siskel & Ebert*, 1983.

92 **"hadn't seen before"**: Flaum, author interview, January 14, 2022.

93 **"more weight than words"**: Solley, author interview, January 24, 2022.

93 **"of the clip"**: Davies, author interview.

94 **"and is very binary"**: Solley, author interview, January 24, 2022.

95 **a letter showed up at WTTW**: *Tribute to Siskel & Ebert*.

95 **"biscuits on this one"**: *Sneak Previews*, episode 501, SiskelEbert.org video, September 24, 1981, https://siskelebert.org/?p=7538.

96 **"'Marjorie Main of dogs'"**: Tom Shales, "Tom Shales Lunches with Siskel & Ebert," *Washington Post*, September 4, 1983, https://www .rogerebert.com/features/tom-shales-lunches-with-siskel-and-ebert.

97 **"sell it four times"**: Davies, author interview.

98 **"get it right"**: Ray Solley, author interview, Brooklyn, NY, August 31, 2022.

99 **"things getting easier"**: FoundationINTERVIEWS, "Roger Ebert Interview Part 1 of 3," YouTube video, September 4, 2009, https://www .youtube.com/watch?v=XHy05ZOHCss.

99 **finished the episode**: De Los Santos, author interview.

99 **"space of an hour"**: Solley, author interview, August 31, 2022.

100 **"talent is happy"**: Solley, author interview, January 24, 2022.

100 **"'have to do *this*'"**: De Los Santos, author interview.

100 **"done in real time"**: FoundationINTERVIEWS, "Roger Ebert Interview Part 1 of 3."

100 **"piss them off"**: Davies, author interview.

101 **"what that magic was"**: Hernández, author interview.

101 **"mad at each other"**: FoundationINTERVIEWS, "Roger Ebert Interview Part 1 of 3."

101 **"pick up the same frequency"**: Ebert, "Remembering Gene."

102 **"the same feeling"**: Jon Anderson, "Why Is *Movies* So Successful? It's Simple," *Chicago Tribune TV Week*, September 1–7, 1985, 11-3.

102 **"on the set with us"**: *Later with Bob Costas*, episode 1–114, SiskelEbert .org video, April 19, 1989, https://siskelebert.org/?p=5996 .

CHAPTER FIVE: ROMPIN' STOMPIN' FILM CRITICISM

103 **"having a bad time"**: *The Arsenio Hall Show*, YouTube video, March 26, 1991, https://www.youtube.com/watch?v=q5VOGKZOMBY.

103 **to confirm compliance**: Jason Zinoman, *Letterman: The Last Giant of Late Night* (New York: HarperCollins, 2017), 73.

104 **"movies to each other"**: *Late Night with David Letterman*, episode 17, YouTube video, March 1, 1982, https://www.youtube.com/watch?v=qfFG6YdayX4.

105 **"found so entertaining"**: Rob Burnett, author interview, Brooklyn, NY, February 9, 2022.

105 **"what they did"**: Jamie Bennett, author interview, Brooklyn, NY, August 30, 2022.

106 **"beautifully every time"**: Burnett, author interview.

106 **"with each other"**: Robert Morton, author interview, Brooklyn, NY, August 19, 2021.

106 **"part of their DNA"**: Morton, author interview.

107 **"when you spat"**: *Late Show with David Letterman*, episode 10, YouTube video, September 10, 1993, https://www.youtube.com/watch?v=ZDXtGhbxZmU.

108 **"was just livid"**: David Plummer, author interview, Brooklyn, NY, August 10, 2021.

108 **"their own with Dave"**: Don DuPree, author interview, Brooklyn, NY, August 16, 2021.

109 **"were scared shitless"**: Bret Watson, "They Still Like to Watch," *Entertainment Weekly*, May 17, 1996, 48.

110 **"With your help!":** *The Tonight Show Starring Johnny Carson*, episode 5647, YouTube video, December 12, 1986, https://www.youtube.com /watch?v=vlC_dnlc4Js.

110 **very much, either:** Roger Ebert, *Life Itself: A Memoir* (New York: Grand Central, 2011), 336.

111 **"think about the movies":** Brooks Egerton, "Citizen Ebert," *Capital Times*, November 14, 1987.

111 **"points of view":** Ben Mankiewicz, author interview, Brooklyn, NY, December 2, 2022.

111 **"complete basket cases":** Lawrence Grobel, "Playboy Interview: Siskel & Ebert," *Playboy*, February 1991, 61.

112 **"Real courageous, fellas!":** *Saturday Night Live*, "Saturday Night Live Film Festival," NBC, March 2, 1985.

113 **"picking the script!":** *The Tonight Show Starring Johnny Carson*, episode 5481, YouTube video, January 31, 1986, https://www.youtube.com /watch?v=DhzrnRLNCAU.

113 **"and not herself":** Gene Siskel, "Siskel Meets 2 of His Toughest Tests, Finds Them Easier to Take," *Chicago Tribune*, February 9, 1986, https:// www.chicagotribune.com/news/ct-xpm-1986-02-09-8601100771-story .html.

114 **"entertaining and fun":** Don DuPree, author interview, Brooklyn, NY, August 16, 2021.

114 **"*all* her fingers":** DuPree, author interview.

114 **"conversation about the movies":** DuPree, author interview.

115 **"I love you":** *The Tonight Show with Jay Leno*, episode 3189, YouTube video, October 20, 1994, https://www.youtube.com/watch?v= HReSLPfmpxc.

116 **"like children about it!":** Morton, author interview.

117 **supermodel Cindy Crawford:** DuPree, author interview.

118 **"standing right behind you":** *Late Show with David Letterman*, episode 189, YouTube video, June 30, 1994, https://www.youtube.com/watch?v= -NYARpevi-k.

119 **"celebrity totem pole":** Plummer, author interview.

119 **"That was Marlon Brando!":** DuPree, author interview.

120 **as objective critics:** Chaz Ebert, "Take a Bite: Roger's Love Affair with Apple Computers," RogerEbert.com, August 16, 2013, https://www .rogerebert.com/chazs-blog/take-a-bite-rogers-love-affair-with-apple -computers.

121 **"and anniversary parties":** Morton, author interview.

121 **"just pure silliness"**: Burnett, author interview.

122 **"got the world by the ass"**: *Tribute to Siskel & Ebert*, VHS, Museum of Broadcast Communications Archive, April 16, 1998.

122 **"and potentially exciting"**: Zinoman, *Letterman: The Last Giant of Late Night*, 92.

122 **"one-up each other"**: *Tribute to Siskel & Ebert.*

123 **"*certainly* couldn't have"**: *Late Show with David Letterman*, episode 109, YouTube video, February 10, 1994, https://www.youtube.com/watch?v= -NYARpevi-k.

123 **"on pressing ahead"**: Roger Ebert, "The Myth of the 'Spontaneous Exchange,'" *Chicago Sun-Times*, November 20, 1994, https://www .rogerebert.com/roger-ebert/the-mystery-of-the-spontaneous-exchange.

124 **"the fifth Beatle"**: *Late Show with David Letterman*, episode 1292, YouTube video, September 23, 1999, https://www.youtube.com/watch ?v=5hB2nOWslu8.

124 **"it's that simple"**: Morton, author interview.

125 **"and thumbs down"**: *Late Night with David Letterman*, episode 17, YouTube video, March 1, 1982, https://www.youtube.com/watch?v= qfFG6YdayX4.

CHAPTER SIX: TWO THUMBS UP

127 **"never say that"**: *At the Movies with Gene Siskel and Roger Ebert*, episode 322, SiskelEbert.org video, February 23, 1985, https://siskelebert.org/ ?p=5121.

128 **"professionally married couple"**: Ray Solley, author interview, Brooklyn, NY, January 24, 2022.

128 **"from the heart"**: Nancy De Los Santos, author interview, Westerly, RI, February 23, 2022.

129 **about $180,000**: "Ebert, Siskel Earning Big Bucks; Draw Trade-Wide Notices as Chicago's Improbable Celebs," *Variety*, May 6, 1981, 4.

129 **"$30,000 or so"**: Lewis Lazare, "Ebert and Siskel: How a Monopoly Covers the Flicks," *Crain's Chicago Business*, July 13, 1981, 36.

130 **$64,000 in 1982**: Josh Schollmeyer, *Enemies, A Love Story* (Now & Then Reader, 2012), ch. 4, Kindle.

130 **"of film reviewing"**: Chaz Ebert, author interview, Chicago, IL, August 15, 2022.

131 **"on commercial television"**: *Tribute to Siskel & Ebert*, VHS, Museum of Broadcast Communications Archive, April 16, 1998.

131 **"up at PBS!":** Liza Antelo, author interview, Brooklyn, NY, March 21, 2022.

132 **"wanted to syndicate us":** Joanne Harrison, "Two of a Kind," *Hollywood Reporter,* March 21, 1996, S-2.

132 **"just the hired hands":** Ted Joseph, "Ebert & Siskel Sneak into the Movies," *Illinois Entertainer,* November 1982, 25.

132 **they should be paid:** Harrison, "Two of a Kind," S-2.

132 **"where there is none":** Tom Shales, "Tom Shales Lunches with Siskel & Ebert," *Washington Post,* September 4, 1983, https://www.rogerebert .com/features/tom-shales-lunches-with-siskel-and-ebert.

132 **"You are not it":** Ray Solley, author interview, Brooklyn, NY, August 31, 2022.

133 **"sharpen your pencil":** Schollmeyer, *Enemies, A Love Story,* ch. 4.

133 **"are *we* making?":** Liza Antelo, author interview.

134 **"they called Thea":** De Los Santos, author interview.

134 **"been worth it":** Thea Flaum, author interview, Brooklyn, NY, October 19, 2022.

135 **"terrified about the move":** Harrison, "Two of a Kind," S-4.

135 **"about a movie?":** De Los Santos, author interview.

136 **"is the setting":** De Los Santos, author interview.

137 **"just sounds better":** De Los Santos, author interview.

138 **"I can guarantee you that!":** *Chicago Tonight,* April 15, 1998.

138 **"is not copyrightable":** Solley, author interview, August 31, 2022.

139 **"'Spin the skunk!'":** *Tribute to Siskel & Ebert.*

140 **"A turkey *vulture!*":** *Tribute to Siskel & Ebert.*

140 **"worthy of discussion":** Roger Ebert, "Special Provides Time for Two Movie Lovers to Play It Over Again," *Chicago Sun-Times,* June 11, 1989, E-3.

141 **"would be TV":** *At the Movies with Gene Siskel and Roger Ebert,* episode 248, SiskelEbert.org video, August 11, 1984, https://siskelebert.org/?p =4714.

142 **"more happening on-screen":** *At the Movies with Gene Siskel & Roger Ebert,* episode 210, SiskelEbert.org video, November 26, 1983, https:// siskelebert.org/?p=2064.

142 **up to 150 stations:** *Tribute to Siskel & Ebert.*

142 **working on *At the Movies*:** Carol Felsenthal, "A Life in Movies," *Chicago,* December 2005, 118.

142 **named Richard Roeper:** Richard Roeper, author interview, Brooklyn, NY, August 30, 2022.

143 **"do that show well"**: Shales, "Tom Shales Lunches with Siskel & Ebert."

143 **"if I do say it"**: Shales, "Tom Shales Lunches with Siskel & Ebert."

143 **viewers as *Sneak Previews***: Joseph, "Ebert & Siskel Sneak into the Movies," 26.

144 **"out of Roger's mouth"**: De Los Santos, author interview.

144 **"I don't remember"**: *20/20*, YouTube video, January 15, 1988, https://www.youtube.com/watch?v=qIqUH6nxOIs.

144 **"can't misquote that"**: Joshua Mooney, "Rule of Thumb," *Hollywood Reporter*, March 21, 1996, S-13.

145 **"people bothering me!"**: Liza Antelo, author interview.

145 **"help other people"**: Chaz Ebert, author interview.

146 **"has two edges!"**: Bill Zehme, "Out to Lunch," *Vanity Fair*, September 1985, 138.

146 **"death of unrisen dough"**: Marlene Iglitzen, author interview, Brooklyn, NY, September 18, 2022.

146 **"exactly the wrong approach"**: Roger Ebert, "Ebert Gets to the Crust of the Matter," *Chicago Sun-Times*, May 21, 1995, https://www.rogerebert.com/roger-ebert/ebert-gets-to-the-crust-of-the-matter.

CHAPTER SEVEN: ACROSS THE AISLE

147 **"that makes it mutual"**: *Siskel & Ebert*, episode 930, YouTube video, April 22, 1995, https://www.youtube.com/watch?v=v7o6CCw-rEs.

149 **"see what you think"**: *Siskel & Ebert*, episode 420, YouTube video, February 3, 1990, https://www.youtube.com/watch?v=6v4rCydxON8.

149 **"a half-hour show"**: Mary Kellogg, author interview, Brooklyn, NY, June 16, 2022.

150 **"was for optics"**: Robert Feder, author interview, Brooklyn, NY, July 6, 2022.

150 **"the other guy offstage"**: A. O. Scott, author interview, Brooklyn, NY, June 10, 2022.

150 **"how to use words"**: Pauline Kael, "Circles and Squares," *Film Quarterly* 16, no. 3 (April 1963): 16.

151 **"gave them a gift!"**: *Siskel & Ebert*, episode 729, YouTube video, April 3, 1993, https://www.youtube.com/watch?v=qIaN92lGmuM.

152 ***"I signed the picture!"***: Janet LaMonica, author interview, Brooklyn, NY, June 2, 2022.

152 **"it was from him"**: Lawrence Grobel, "Playboy Interview: Siskel & Ebert," *Playboy*, February 1991, 55.

153 **"the cruel one!"**: *Siskel & Ebert*, episode 835, YouTube video, May 7, 1994, https://www.youtube.com/watch?v=HpdmdqeAUJs.

154 **"not Kubrick's film"**: *Siskel & Ebert*, episode 136, YouTube video, June 20, 1987, https://www.youtube.com/watch?v=sMbdCqLfSmU.

155 **"about *one* couple?"**: *Siskel & Ebert*, episode 702, YouTube video, September 19, 1992, https://www.youtube.com/watch?v=j0xn AEHQ26U.

155 **"do you read?"**: *Siskel & Ebert*, episode 619, YouTube video, January 25, 1992, https://www.youtube.com/watch?v=uAjj5S9WIY4.

156 **"that explains it"**: *Siskel & Ebert*, episode 1031, YouTube video, April 6, 1996, https://www.youtube.com/watch?v=0Pxe9vhedVA.

156 **"how it stacks up!"**: *At the Movies with Gene Siskel & Roger Ebert*, episode 224, YouTube video, March 16, 1984, https://www.youtube.com/watch ?v=uAjj5S9WIY4.

156 **"did you, Roger?"**: Sid Smith, "The Show Goes On," *Chicago Tribune*, October 18, 1995, 5-1.

157 **"are fucking crazy!"**: Jim Murphy, author interview, Brooklyn, NY, May 26, 2022.

158 **"Not one word, fucker"**: John Davies, author interview, Brooklyn, NY, January 19, 2022.

159 **"he can't tell"**: Toni Schlesinger, "Best Enemies," *Chicago,* May 1987, 121.

159 **"he was interviewing"**: Laura C. Hernández, author interview, Brooklyn, NY, March 15, 2022.

159 **"throw him off the scent"**: Roger Ebert, "Special Provides Time for Two Movie Lovers to Play It Over Again," *Chicago Sun-Times*, June 11, 1989, E-3.

160 **"backpedal frantically"**: Stuart Cleland, author interview, Brooklyn, NY, September 19, 2022.

161 **"did the role"**: *Siskel & Ebert*, "If We Picked the Winners (1993)," YouTube video, uploaded June 27, 2021, https://www.youtube.com/watch?v= ncd8skPFlJM.

162 **"not enough motor coordination"**: "For *Crying* Out Loud," *TV Guide*, March 27, 1993, 4.

163 **"sticking to my guns"**: *Siskel & Ebert*, episode 1023, YouTube video, February 10, 1996, https://www.youtube.com/watch?v=gwQPddFeLeg.

163 **"the representation of that"**: Scott, author interview.

163 **"was so groundbreaking"**: Robert Thompson, author interview, Brooklyn, NY, May 31, 2022.

163 **"back-and-forth"**: Scott, author interview.

CHAPTER EIGHT: HOORAY FOR HOLLYWOOD

165 **"of the *Chicago Tribune*"**: *Siskel & Ebert*, episode 742, YouTube video, July 10, 1993, https://www.youtube.com/watch?v=CWRWB6SqYOQ.

166 **Award of the Year:** "Our History: Conference," NATPE, accessed December 4, 2022, https://www.natpe.com/about/about/our-history -conference/#.

166 **"grown-up Comic-Con"**: Richard Roeper, author interview, Brooklyn, NY, August 30, 2022.

166 **"you don't mean shit"**: Roger Ebert, "I'd Like You to Meet Your Best Friend," RogerEbert.com, November 12, 2009, https://www.rogerebert .com/roger-ebert/id-like-you-to-meet-your-best-friend.

166 **"Bozo the Clown!"**: Ebert, "I'd Like You to Meet Your Best Friend."

167 **"'they'll never leave'"**: Liza Antelo, author interview, Brooklyn, NY, March 21, 2022.

167 **"a big boo-boo"**: Carol Felsenthal, "A Life in Movies," *Chicago*, December 2005, 118.

168 **"the show under contract"**: Jamie Bennett, author interview, Brooklyn, NY, August 30, 2022.

169 **"picked his pocket"**: Bennett, author interview.

169 **"independence and autonomy"**: Lewis Lazare, "Ties to Disney May Oust Siskel as *Trib*'s Reviewer," *Crain's Chicago Business*, March 31, 1986, 51.

169 **"church and state"**: Mary Kellogg, author interview, Brooklyn, NY, June 16, 2022.

170 **"been very good"**: *Late Night with David Letterman*, episode 5101, YouTube video, September 11, 1986, https://www.youtube.com/watch ?v=qfFG6YdayX4.

170 **"any film Disney makes"**: Wendy Leopold, "Film Critic Ebert Backs Rival in Tribune Tiff," *Los Angeles Times*, April 22, 1986, https://www.latimes .com/archives/la-xpm-1986-04-22-ca-1667-story.html.

170 **"answer would be no"**: Bennett, author interview.

170 **"long term contract"**: "Tribune Entertainment's *At the Movies* to Introduce New Hosts, Format in Fall," press release from Robert Feder files, March 26, 1986.

170 **drivers wanted for it:** Morrie Gelman, "Critics Siskel and Ebert Move to Walt Disney," *Media*, March 31, 1986, 46.

171 **"box a little bit"**: Mary Margaret Bartley, author interview, Brooklyn, NY, April 6, 2022.

172 **"been used previously"**: Bennett, author interview.

173   **reality television shows:** Chaz Ebert, author interview, Chicago, IL, August 15, 2022.

174   **"they are in competition":** "Drop Siskel as Chi Trib Critic; TV Pact Cited," *Variety*, April 2, 1986, 94.

174   **"answer to that is yes":** *Late Night with David Letterman*, episode 726, YouTube video, September 11, 1986, https://www.youtube.com/watch?v=qfFG6YdayX4.

174   **"it was punitive":** Robert Feder, author interview, Brooklyn, NY, July 6, 2022.

175   **"for his film reviewing?":** Morry Roth, "Chi Film Critic Plot Thickens in Trib Circus," *Variety*, April 9, 1986, 2.

175   **"goddamn thing about the *Tribune*":** Frank Segers, "Siskel, Trib Still Talking; See Load Lighter by Summer," *Variety*, April 23, 1986, 266.

175   **years of loyal service:** Chaz Ebert, author interview.

176   **"keep Gene viable":** Robert Feder, author interview, Brooklyn, NY, August 22, 2022.

176   **"the golden egg":** Bennett, author interview.

177   **"in the theater":** Cliff Edwards, "Twentieth Century Fox: No More Previews for Siskel & Ebert," Associated Press, March 20, 1990, https://apnews.com/article/c78a9555535f49338cc5f212bcfbc67f.

178   **"when he gets home":** Larry Weintraub, "Fox Lets Siskel & Ebert Back into Balcony," *Chicago Sun-Times*, April 10, 1990, https://chicago.suntimes.com/pages/newsbank-archives.

179   **"another million every day":** Jeannie Williams, "Siskel Gives Thumbs Up to *Spy* Magazine Tally," *USA Today*, May 10, 1990, 2D.

179   **"shooting themselves in the toe":** "10: Gene Siskel & Roger Ebert," *Entertainment Weekly*, November 2, 1990, 23.

179   **"nightmares of depravity":** Bernard Weinraub, "Films and Recordings Threaten Nation's Character, Dole Says," *New York Times*, June 1, 1995, https://www.nytimes.com/1995/06/01/us/films-and-recordings-threaten-nation-s-character-dole-says.html.

180   **"been willing to do":** National Press Club, "National Press Club Luncheon with Siskel and Ebert," YouTube video, 1:02:58, August 17, 2012, https://www.youtube.com/watch?v=mK-Yiz8__bU.

182   **on their show:** Stuart Cleland, author interview, Brooklyn, NY, September 21, 2022.

182   **columnist Ann Landers:** Roger Ebert, *Life Itself: A Memoir* (New York: Grand Central, 2011), 362–63.

182 **Alcoholics Anonymous meeting:** *Life Itself*, directed by Steve James (Magnolia Pictures, 2014).

183 **"me and Roger":** Chaz Ebert, author interview.

183 **"bond between them":** Marlene Iglitzen, author interview, Brooklyn, NY, September 18, 2022.

183 **"it finally happened":** Feder, author interview, July 6, 2022.

184 **"one-stop shopping":** *Later with Bob Costas*, episode 1-114, SiskelEbert .org video, April 19, 1989, https://siskelebert.org/?p=5996.

184 **"at the hip":** Thea Flaum, author interview, Brooklyn, NY, January 14, 2022.

184 **"overcame a lot":** Jim Murphy, author interview Brooklyn, NY, May 26, 2022.

CHAPTER NINE: GET TO THE CROSSTALK

185 **"show is about the movies":** *The Museum of Television & Radio Seminar Series: Siskel & Ebert: Thumbs Up,* VHS, Paley Center for Media Archive, November 12, 1992.

185 **"that vicarious experience":** *The Museum of Television & Radio Seminar Series: Siskel & Ebert: Thumbs Up.*

186 **"start with that":** Interview Archives Learning Objects, "Siskel & Ebert Advise Young Movie Critics," YouTube video, September 19, 2019, https:// www.youtube.com/watch?v=__L9DzZIkwI.

186 **"show can understand":** *The Museum of Television & Radio Seminar Series: Siskel & Ebert: Thumbs Up.*

186 **about twenty sentences:** *The Museum of Television & Radio Seminar Series: Siskel & Ebert: Thumbs Up.*

188 **"And that's Roger!":** Gregory Paul Smith, "Siskel & Ebert Arguing— Retro Behind the Scenes Outtakes & Footage," YouTube video, June 23, 2020, https://www.youtube.com/watch?v=DqvsOAN-ii8.

189 **"compelling him to change it":** Angela DeCarlo, "Siskel & Ebert— Together 20 Years," *Disney Magazine*, Spring 1996, 37.

189 **"smartest and most clever":** *At the Movies with Gene Siskel & Roger Ebert*, episode 223, SiskelEbert.org video, March 9, 1984, https://siskelebert .org/?p=2366.

189 **"made me do that":** *At the Movies with Gene Siskel & Roger Ebert*, episode 403, YouTube video, September 28, 1985, https://www.youtube.com /watch?v=ah9yeD-MK2Q.

189 **"most pathetic movies of the year"**: *Siskel & Ebert*, episode 243, YouTube video, August 27, 1988, https://www.youtube.com/watch?v=vFtRMKi0Quw.

190 **"any year's worst"**: *Siskel & Ebert*, episode 1029, YouTube video, March 23, 1996, https://www.youtube.com/watch?v=my-kGkoXbI8.

190 **"wanted you to see"**: *Siskel & Ebert*, "The Worst Movies of 1986," YouTube video, January 10, 1986, https://www.youtube.com/watch?v=jqvWDj2YggY.

191 **more of their clichés**: *Siskel & Ebert*, episode 121, SiskelEbert.org video, February 14, 1987, https://siskelebert.org/?p=2857.

192 **"off the screen"**: *Siskel & Ebert*, episode 905, YouTube video, October 8, 1994, https://www.youtube.com/watch?v=eq3VDPoiS5s.

192 **"worst comedy ever made"**: *Siskel & Ebert*, episode 706, YouTube video, October 24, 1992, https://www.youtube.com/watch?v=5MOHHJJ64Rw.

193 **"we're defending it"**: Steve Kamer, "Gene Siskel and Roger Ebert," *American Focus*, December 11, 1983.

193 **"that *he's* flawed"**: *20/20*, YouTube video, January 15, 1988, https://www.youtube.com/watch?v=qIqUH6nxOIs.

194 **"I have for years"**: *Siskel & Ebert*, episode 207, YouTube video, October 31, 1987, https://www.youtube.com/watch?v=8fFBgaibl7o.

195 **"No kidding!"**: *Siskel & Ebert*, episode 333, YouTube video, May 6, 1989, https://siskelebert.org/?p=5620.

196 **"the word *hyperbole*?"**: Greg Stevens, "Rated K: For Kids by Kids #06 (Gene Siskel & Roger Ebert Special)," February 11, 2020, https://www.youtube.com/watch?v=XfKuCVhNmKg.

196 **hawking Stroh's beer**: Mike Gardner, "Yogi at the Movies: *Moonstruck*," uploaded October 12, 2010, https://www.youtube.com/watch?v=HFu3lZIxZZY.

196 **"the advertising begins"**: Patrick Goldstein, "Commentary: TV Film Critics Go for the Glitz. Roll Clip, Please," *Los Angeles Times*, January 3, 1988, https://www.latimes.com/archives/la-xpm-1988-01-03-ca-32442-story.html.

197 **"numbers, letters, or thumbs"**: Richard Corliss, "All Thumbs: Or, Is There a Future for Film Criticism?," *Film Comment*, March–April 1990, https://www.filmcomment.com/article/richard-corliss-all-thumbs-or-is-there-a-future-for-film-criticism.

198 **"the vulgar version"**: A. O. Scott, author interview, Brooklyn, NY, June 10, 2022.

199 **"mass-market entertainment"**: Roger Ebert, "All Stars: Or, Is There a Cure for Criticism of Film Criticism? Pt. 2," *Film Comment*, May–June 1990, https://www.filmcomment.com/article/roger-ebert-richard-corliss-cure-for-criticism-of-film-criticism.

199 **"take it seriously"**: Robert Thompson, author interview, Brooklyn, NY, May 31, 2022.

CHAPTER TEN: THE FUTURE OF THE MOVIES

201 **"we love movies"**: *Siskel & Ebert*, "The Best of '94," YouTube video, December 31, 1994, https://www.youtube.com/watch?v=DijuKlBPnDI.

201 **"the future of the movies?"**: Roger Ebert and Gene Siskel, *The Future of the Movies* (Kansas City, MO: Andrews McMeel, 1991), xi.

202 **"'not as a writer'"**: Chaz Ebert, author interview, Chicago, IL, August 15, 2022.

202 **"about the good ones?"**: Richard Roeper, author interview, Brooklyn, NY, August 30, 2022.

203 **"into an HDTV receiver"**: Ebert and Siskel, *The Future of the Movies*, 44.

203 **"on the screen"**: Ebert and Siskel, *The Future of the Movies*, 86.

204 **"*Sneak Previews* Take 2"**: Thea Flaum, author interview, Brooklyn, NY, January 14, 2022.

204 **"where they are headed"**: *Sneak Previews*, "Take 2: Midnight Movies," SiskelEbert.org video, October 4, 1979, https://siskelebert.org/?p=6642.

205 **"'in your place, women!'"**: *Sneak Previews*, "Take 2: Extreme Violence Directed at Women," SiskelEbert.org video, October 15, 1980, https://siskelebert.org/?p=6650.

205 **"focus on issues"**: *Tribute to Siskel & Ebert*, VHS, Museum of Broadcast Communications Archive, April 16, 1998.

206 **"for the demonstration"**: *Tribute to Siskel & Ebert*.

206 **an "abomination"**: Roger Ebert, "Movie Answer Man: Scorsese Shines Light on Stones," *Chicago Sun-Times*, April 17, 2008, https://www.rogerebert.com/answer-man/scorsese-shines-light-on-stones.

207 **"in part, successful"**: *Tribute to Siskel & Ebert*.

207 **"that he couldn't move"**: *Tribute to Siskel & Ebert*.

208 **"halfway decent right now"**: *Siskel & Ebert*, "Hail, Hail, Black and White," YouTube video, May 20, 1989, https://www.youtube.com/watch?v=WhdVVBnyvlM.

209 **"Shame on Disney!"**: *Siskel & Ebert & the Movies*, episode 143, YouTube video, July 10, 1987, https://www.youtube.com/watch?v=hRMVgqOKLTY.

209 **"their makers intended"**: Roger Ebert, "Special Provides Time for Two Movie Lovers to Play It Over Again," *Chicago Sun-Times*, June 11, 1989, 6.

210 **"the directorial imagination"**: *Sneak Previews*, episode 337, SiskelEbert .org video, July 16, 1981, https://siskelebert.org/?p=7481.

211 **"I loved them"**: Errol Morris, author interview, Brooklyn, NY, February 16, 2022.

211 **"aspects of our job"**: "Siskel Quizzes Ebert," *Chicago Tribune*, April 19, 1998, 15.

212 **"is like this"**: *Sneak Previews*, episode 611, SiskelEbert.org video, December 10, 1981, https://siskelebert.org/?p=2865.

212 **"The fact was"**: Wallace Shawn, author interview, Brooklyn, NY, January 31, 2023.

212 **"There was no question"**: Shawn, author interview.

212 **"of being a critic"**: Aaron Barnhart, "Remembering Gene Siskel," *TV Barn*, February 23, 1999.

213 **"then the door closed"**: Steve James, author interview, Brooklyn, NY, July 12, 2022.

214 **"'a theatrical film'"**: James, author interview.

214 **"It's rotten!"**: *Siskel & Ebert*, episode 924, YouTube video, February 18, 1995, https://www.youtube.com/watch?v=B0hxiwpoYaQ.

215 **"'I am outraged!'"**: James, author interview.

215 a **"find"**: *Siskel & Ebert*, episode 932, YouTube video, May 13, 1995, https://www.youtube.com/watch?v=tmYzI1FZCa4.

215 **"swarm"**: *Siskel & Ebert*, episode 1151, YouTube video, August 23, 1997, https://www.youtube.com/watch?v=jvRphaYyvnA.

215 **"breathtaking"**: *Siskel & Ebert*, episode 715, YouTube video, December 26, 1992, https://www.youtube.com/watch?v=UKimNFBVtXA.

216 **"the future of the movies"**: Ebert and Siskel, *The Future of the Movies*, 116.

216 **"Break the rule! Please!"**: *Siskel & Ebert*, episode 1021, YouTube video, January 27, 1996, https://www.youtube.com/watch?v= EMvwyRy4Myk.

216 **"And I like that"**: *Siskel & Ebert*, episode 712, YouTube video, December 5, 1992, https://www.youtube.com/watch?v=RSTnRzRdlgg.

CHAPTER ELEVEN: THE BALCONY IS CLOSED

217 **"you will never die"**: *Siskel & Ebert*, episode 601, YouTube video, September 14, 1991, https://www.youtube.com/watch?v=7AaG7TsH64ss.

217 **"the memories we leave"**: Roger Ebert, "Remembering Gene," RogerEbert.com, February 17, 2009, https://www.rogerebert.com/roger -ebert/remembering-gene.

218 **"happen to them"**: *Siskel & Ebert*, episode 330, YouTube video, April 15, 1989, https://www.youtube.com/watch?v=jMbO1eNQEtI.

219 **"get up and leave"**: Angela DeCarlo, "Siskel & Ebert—Together 20 Years," *Disney Magazine*, Spring 1996, 38.

219 **"overpaying for refreshments"**: *Siskel & Ebert*, episode 430, YouTube video, April 21, 1990, https://www.youtube.com/watch?v=RBub63iDjcU.

219 **"Gone. For. *EVER*"**: *Siskel & Ebert*, episode 1151, YouTube video, August 23, 1997, https://www.youtube.com/watch?v=jvRphaYyvnA.

220 **"very, very much"**: *Tribute to Siskel & Ebert*, VHS, Museum of Broadcast Communications Archive, April 16, 1998.

220 **didn't go away:** Carie Lovstad, author interview, Brooklyn, NY, May 23, 2022.

221 **"finish what we're doing"**: *The Tonight Show with Jay Leno*, episode 8125, YouTube video, March 24, 2000, https://www.youtube.com/watch ?v=aLpL3sKHZAY.

221 **"make it a schtick"**: Ebert, "Remembering Gene."

221 **terminal brain cancer:** *Life Itself*, directed by Steve James (Magnolia Pictures, 2014).

222 **"in the movies"**: "Siskel's Outlook Good after Growth Removed," *Chicago Tribune*, May 13, 1998, https://www.chicagotribune.com/news/ct-xpm -1998-05-13-9805130107-story.html.

222 **"next scheduled program"**: Roger Ebert, email to Robert Feder, May 13, 1998.

222 **hosting the show:** Josh Schollmeyer, *Enemies, A Love Story* (Now & Then Reader, 2012), ch. 7, Kindle.

223 **"didn't have them"**: Mary Kellogg, author interview, Brooklyn, NY, June 16, 2022.

223 **"was going on"**: David Plummer, author interview, Brooklyn, NY, May 24, 2022.

223 **"nothing on us"**: Sid Smith, "The Show Goes On," *Chicago Tribune*, October 18, 1995, 5-3.

223 **"for the next few minutes"**: *Siskel & Ebert*, episode 1237, YouTube video, May 30, 1998, https://www.youtube.com/watch?v=tu9JoJX5de0.

223 **"didn't feel any different"**: Jim Kirk, "Superfan Siskel Back for Bulls Fest," *Chicago Tribune*, June 17, 1998, 3-2.

224 **"what city he was in":** Transcript of Roger Ebert and Robert Feder interview, from Robert Feder files, retrieved August 13, 2022.

224 **"Keep them out":** *Siskel & Ebert*, episode 1237.

224 **"bump in the road":** Schollmeyer, *Enemies, A Love Story*, ch. 7.

225 **"make a bad movie":** *Siskel & Ebert*, episode 1240, YouTube video, June 20, 1998, https://www.youtube.com/watch?v=duvO4jn9HHI.

225 **"I can say it, enjoyable":** Peter Johnson, "Siskel Has Thumbs on Pulse of Movies Again," *USA Today*, June 23, 1998.

225 **"Good, great, fine":** Lovstad, author interview.

226 **"some other problem?":** "Walter Scott's Personality Parade," *Chicago Tribune*, January 17, 1999, *Parade*, 2.

226 **"bounced back so quickly":** Lovstad, author interview.

227 **"went about it":** Al Berman, author interview, Brooklyn, NY, August 25, 2022.

227 **"films of ideas":** *Siskel & Ebert*, episode 1238, YouTube video, June 6, 1998, https://www.youtube.com/watch?v=l5aWi0MeDMw.

228 **"take your life seriously":** *Siskel & Ebert*, episode 1310, YouTube video, November 14, 1998, https://www.youtube.com/watch?v=ixHV 06PWjcE.

228 **"in an instant":** *Siskel & Ebert*, "The Worst of '98," YouTube video, January 16, 1999, https://www.youtube.com/watch?v=6yKq6bIeDu0.

228 **"'as good as the book!'":** *Siskel & Ebert*, episode 1320, YouTube video, January 23, 1999, https://www.youtube.com/watch?v=oIiczMgS864.

229 **"the stunt double":** Eric Slater, "Gene Siskel; Gave Film Criticism Mass Appeal," *Los Angeles Times*, February 21, 1999, https://www.latimes.com /archives/la-xpm-1999-feb-21-me-10192-story.html.

229 **"speedy continued recovery":** Robert Feder, "Siskel Takes a Pause to Speed His Recovery," *Chicago Sun-Times*, February 4, 1999, 41.

230 **would be back in the fall:** Chaz Ebert, author interview, Chicago, IL, August 15, 2022.

230 **"knew no bounds":** Robert Feder, "Famed Film Critic Gene Siskel Dies at 53," *Chicago Sun-Times*, February 21, 1999, 2A.

230 **"that might result":** "Siskel and Ebert's Touching Last Chat," *Star*, March 9, 1999.

230 **"go see him now":** Chaz Ebert, author interview.

231 **"his back hurt":** Rick Kogan, "Farewell to Siskel Honors Private Side of Public Man," *Chicago Tribune*, February 23, 1999, https://www .chicagotribune.com/news/ct-xpm-1999-02-23-9902250002-story .html.

232 **"that we didn't"**: *Siskel & Ebert*, "Remembering Gene Siskel," YouTube video, July 8, 2022, https://www.youtube.com/watch?v=PvlTSxhWGqY.

232 **"Thank you"**: *Tribute to Siskel & Ebert*.

CHAPTER TWELVE: EBERT & ROEPER & LYONS & MANKIEWICZ & PHILLIPS & SCOTT & LEMIRE & VISHNEVETSKY

233 **"doesn't always provide that"**: *Siskel & Ebert*, episode 510, YouTube video, November 17, 1990, https://www.youtube.com/watch?v=Zi4Ab45opX4.

233 **"ending is arbitrary"**: Roger Ebert, "Reflections after 25 Years at the Movies," *Chicago Sun-Times*, April 8, 2016, https://www.rogerebert.com /roger-ebert/reflections-after-25-years-at-the-movies.

234 **"You don't need 'em"**: Richard Roeper, "Thumbs Up! 20 Years in the Balcony," *Chicago Sun-Times*, October 15, 1995, B-11.

235 **"I had to take it"**: Marlene Iglitzen, author interview, Brooklyn, NY, September 18, 2022.

235 **"continue in that tradition"**: *Siskel & Ebert*, episode 1347, SiskelEbert .org video, August 21, 1999, https://siskelebert.org/?p=3419.

235 **"*Siskel & Ebert* so original"**: Steve Brennan, "Sneak Preview of New Ebert," *Hollywood Reporter*, September 2, 1999, 11.

236 **"and the web"**: Roger Ebert, email to Robert Feder, June 7, 1999.

236 **"Good luck with that"**: Thea Flaum, author interview, Brooklyn, NY, October 19, 2022.

236 **of *the New York Times***: Carol Felsenthal, "A Life in Movies," *Chicago*, December 2005, 126.

238 **the *Tribune* at the time**: Richard Roeper, author interview, Brooklyn, NY, August 30, 2022.

238 **"*That's* what you need"**: Chaz Ebert, author interview, Chicago, IL, August 15, 2022.

239 **"so happy to be here"**: Roeper, author interview.

239 **"hottest movie deal"**: Robert Feder, "Seat Saved for Roeper," *Chicago Sun-Times*, July 11, 2000, 37.

240 **"'can't tell anybody'"**: Roeper, author interview.

240 **"all in the family"**: Robert Feder, "It's *Ebert & Roeper*," *Chicago Sun-Times*, July 13, 2000, 1.

240 **"not a complaint about Gene"**: FoundationINTERVIEWS, "Roger Ebert Interview Part 3 of 3," YouTube video, September 4, 2009, https://www .youtube.com/watch?v=fQq2bsNa_NQ.

241 **"so much easier!"**: Roeper, author interview.

241 **final year as cohost:** Felsenthal, "A Life in Movies," 126.

241 **"not very insightful":** Marisa Guthrie, "Thumbs Down: Siskel Is a Hard Act to Follow as Roeper Shows in His Debut as Ebert's Film Critic Sidekick," *Boston Herald*, September 2, 2000.

242 **"than in theaters":** Ken Tucker, "Rule of Thumb," *Entertainment Weekly*, September 22, 2000, 60.

242 **"good with that":** Roeper, author interview.

243 **"one recommended by Roger":** Northwestern Memorial Hospital Media Advisory, "Condition Update Re: Roger Ebert," February 22, 2002.

243 **"tonsillitis and ear infections":** Roger Ebert, email to Robert Feder, February 27, 2002.

244 **"cancer of the salivary gland":** Jim Ritter, "Once a Cure, Now a Threat," *Chicago Sun-Times*, March 3, 2002, 4A.

244 **"and Soupy Sales!":** Roger Ebert, email to Robert Feder, June 16, 2004.

245 **favorite pizza joint:** Don DuPree, author interview, Brooklyn, NY, August 16, 2021.

246 *"did the show!":* Roeper, author interview.

246 **"miss the Festival for anything!":** Roger Ebert, "It Wouldn't Be Ebertfest without Roger," RogerEbert.com, April 23, 2007, https://www.rogerebert .com/interviews/it-wouldnt-be-ebertfest-without-roger.

247 **"my angelic wife, Chaz":** Roger Ebert, "Ebert Announces His Return," RogerEbert.com, April 1, 2008, https://www.rogerebert.com/interviews /ebert-announces-his-return.

248 **"'two younger guys'":** Roeper, author interview.

248 **"continue its legacy":** "*At the Movies* New Hosts: Lyons, Mankiewicz," Associated Press, July 22, 2008, https://www.today.com/popculture /movies-new-hosts-lyons-mankiewicz-wbna25803407.

248 **"an entertaining product":** Ben Lyons, author interview, Brooklyn, NY, November 7, 2022.

250 **"long-term success":** Ben Mankiewicz, author interview, Brooklyn, NY, December 2, 2022.

251 **"down in Wisconsin":** Lyons, author interview.

251 **remove him from the show:** Chris Lee, "Dumbing Down the Film Critic," *Los Angeles Times*, December 28, 2008, https://www.latimes.com /archives/la-xpm-2008-dec-28-ca-lyons28-story.html.

252 **"on panels with him":** Lyons, author interview.

252 **"mistaken hiring decision":** Roger Ebert, "See You at the Movies," RogerEbert.com, March 25, 2010, https://www.rogerebert.com/roger -ebert/see-you-at-the-movies.

252 **"to the mouth-breathers"**: Roger Ebert, "Roger's Little Rule Book," RogerEbert.com, October 28, 2008, https://www.rogerebert.com/roger -ebert/rogers-little-rule-book.

252 **"hard to believe"**: Mankiewicz, author interview.

252 **"I just had to take it"**: Lyons, author interview.

252 **"needed Roger Ebert, period"**: Mankiewicz, author interview.

253 **"would happen in television"**: A. O. Scott, author interview, Brooklyn, NY, June 10, 2022.

253 **"what it looked like"**: Michael Phillips, author interview, Brooklyn, NY, July 18, 2022.

254 **"we *not* do that?"**: Phillips, author interview.

254 **"like, 'Well, okay'"**: Scott, author interview.

254 **"come to that realization"**: Phillips, author interview.

255 **"*something* at stake"**: Scott, author interview.

255 **"spell enormous change"**: Phillips, author interview.

255 **"no longer sustainable"**: Dave Itzkoff, "Final Season for *At the Movies*," *New York Times*, March 25, 2010, https://www.nytimes.com/2010/03/26 /arts/television/26cancel.html.

255 **"to get over it"**: David Plummer, author interview, Brooklyn, NY, May 24, 2022.

256 **"empty space it left behind"**: Roger Ebert, "The Balcony Is Closed," RogerEbert.com, July 24, 2008, https://www.rogerebert.com/roger-ebert /the-balcony-is-closed.

256 **"You bet I was"**: Ebert, "See You at the Movies."

256 **"instead of slowing down"**: Ebert, "See You at the Movies."

257 **"same old same old"**: Ebert, "See You at the Movies."

257 **"People were eager"**: Chaz Ebert, author interview, Chicago, IL, August 15, 2022.

257 **"to be a film critic"**: Christy Lemire, author interview, Brooklyn, NY, September 19, 2022.

258 **"why they approached me"**: Ignatiy Vishnevetsky, author interview, Brooklyn, NY, September 23, 2022.

259 **"*Mr. Popper's Penguins*?"**: Vishnevetsky, author interview.

259 **"We're just not them"**: Lemire, author interview.

259 **"get along really well"**: Vishnevetsky, author interview.

260 **"get the financing first"**: Chaz Ebert, author interview.

260 **one of his cable channels**: Chaz Ebert, author interview.

EPILOGUE: UNTIL NEXT TIME, WE'LL SEE YOU AT THE MOVIES

261 **"going to the movies"**: *Sneak Previews*, "Take 2 Revised: Going to the Movies," SiskelEbert.org video, August 6, 1981, https://siskelebert.org /?p=4845.

262 **"it's a great memoir"**: Steve James, author interview, Brooklyn, NY, July 12, 2022.

263 **"while we were filming"**: James, author interview.

264 **"see you at the movies"**: Roger Ebert, "A Leave of Presence," RogerEbert .com, April 2, 2013, https://www.rogerebert.com/roger-ebert/a-leave-of -presence.

264 **"just holding his hand"**: Chris Jones, "Oral Histories of 2013: Roger Ebert's Wife, Chaz, on His Final Moments," *Esquire*, December 24, 2013, https://www.esquire.com/entertainment/tv/news/a26606/roger-ebert -final-moments.

264 **"'at my memorial service'"**: Roger Ebert, "Go Gentle into That Good Night," RogerEbert.com, May 2, 2009, https://www.rogerebert.com/roger -ebert/go-gentle-into-that-good-night.

265 **"all at once"**: Jones, "Oral Histories of 2013."

266 **""Eh, what the hell?""**: Michael Phillips, author interview, Brooklyn, NY, July 18, 2002.

266 **"dialogue about the movies"**: Thea Flaum, author interview, Brooklyn, NY, October 19, 2022.

266 **"'something that has value'"**: Ramin Bahrani, author interview, Brooklyn, NY, August 8, 2022.

267 **"two competitive journalists"**: Marilyn Gill, author interview, Brooklyn, NY, March 23, 2022.

268 **"'had to go it alone?'"**: Chaz Ebert, author interview, Chicago, IL, August 15, 2022.

268 **"Time in a bottle"**: Roger Ebert, "Reflections after 25 Years at the Movies," *Chicago Sun-Times*, April 8, 2016, https://www.rogerebert.com /roger-ebert/reflections-after-25-years-at-the-movies.

270 **"passive consumers of escapism"**: Roger Ebert, "Special Provides Time for Two Movie Lovers to Play It Over Again," *Chicago Sun-Times*, June 11, 1989, E-3.

271 **"guys in the chairs was over"**: A. O. Scott, author interview, Brooklyn, NY, June 10, 2022.

271 **"had not yet emerged"**: Ignatiy Vishnevetsky, author interview, Brooklyn, NY, September 23, 2022.

271 **"no one can do it"**: Christy Lemire, author interview, Brooklyn, NY, September 19, 2022.

272 **"very well expressed"**: *Chicago Tonight*, YouTube video, April 15, 1998, https://www.youtube.com/watch?v=SXCVZk__o48.

272 **"'This is not'"**: Jamie Bennett, author interview, Brooklyn, NY, August 30, 2022.

273 **"makes film criticism better"**: *Tribute to Siskel & Ebert*, VHS, Museum of Broadcast Communications Archive, April 16, 1998.

273 **"where the growth comes"**: *Tribute to Siskel & Ebert*.

274 **to include television reviews:** Flaum, author interview.

274 **"kings of podcasts"**: Richard Roeper, author interview, Brooklyn, NY, August 30, 2022.

274 **"Two Thumbs Up!" merchandise:** Al Berman, author interview, Brooklyn, NY, August 25, 2022.

274 **bastions of cinephilia:** Jim Murphy, author interview, Brooklyn, NY, May 26, 2022.

274 **rival Rotten Tomatoes:** David Plummer, author interview, Brooklyn, NY, May 24, 2022.

274 **"talking about movies for sure"**: Chaz Ebert, author interview.

INDEX

Abbott, Bud, 121, 234

Academy Awards, 27, 42, 49, 91, 114, 139, 147, 160, 214–15, 229, 286

The Adventures of Ozzie and Harriet, 89

Airport (1970), 39

The Alcyon (movie house), 79–81

Aleandro, Norma, 283

Alexander, Shana, 62

All About Eve (1950), 249

Allen, Woody, 36, 91–92

All the President's Men (1976), 48–49

"All Thumbs: Or, Is There a Future for Film Criticism?" (Corliss), 197–200

Allyson, June, 41

Alston, Macky, 292–93

Alterio, Héctor, 283

Altman, Robert, 202

American Film Institute, 202

America's Got Talent, 142

Anarchy in the UK (1978, unreleased), 32

Andréi, Frédéric, 280

Annie Hall (1977), 36, 91

Antelo, Joe, 130–31, 133, 138–39, 142, 145, 167, 184, 220

Antelo, Liza, 131, 133, 167

Aroma the Educated Skunk, 138–39

Aronson, Nick, 65–67, 69–70, 77

Asimov, Isaac, 22

Associated Press, 24, 248, 257

Astounding Science Fiction, 22

Austin Powers: International Man of Mystery (1997), 32

Avildsen, John G., 284–85

Back to the Beach (1987), 284

Badham, John, 36–37

Bahrani, Ramin, 17–18, 266

The Balcony (set), 80–82, 102, 171, 250

Barrymore, John, 161

Bartley, Mary Margaret, 81, 171

Basch, Garrett, 262

The Beast Within (1982), 96

Beatty, Warren, 26, 224

Behan, Brendan, 19

Beineix, Jean-Jacques, 279–80

Benji the Hunted (1987), 154, 194

Bennett, Jamie, 41–43, 105, 167–72, 176, 272

Benson, Robby, 51

Bergman, Ingmar, 61

Berlinger, Joe, 289

Berman, Al, 50, 51, 226, 274

Bernstein, Carl, 48

Berra, Yogi, 196

Besser, Joe, 272

Beyond the Valley of the Dolls (1970), 30–33, 47, 197

"A Biased View" (Ebert), 23

The Big Easy (1986), 187

The Birth of a Nation (1915), 58

Blanc, Michel, 287

Bogdanovich, Peter, 61, 156

Bonham Carter, Helena, 228

Bonnaire, Sandrine, 287

Bonnie and Clyde (1967), 26–27

Boston Herald, 241

Bowman, Dick, 4

Branagh, Kenneth, 228

Brando, Marlon, 119

Bright Angel (1991), 288–89

Brody, Adam, 246

Broken Arrow (1996), 162

Brooks, Albert, 186

Brooks, Mel, 75

Brother's Keeper (1992), 289

Brubeck, Dave, 264

Bruckner, Don, 66

Buena Vista Television
  and acquisition of show, 167–69, 172
  and "buried treasure" films, 278
  and companion website for show, 268
  and *If We Picked the Winners* special, 160
  new hosts for show, 253
  and pilot episode of show, 75
  and popularity of show, 200
  and show after Ebert, 247–48, 253
  and show after Siskel, 235, 241
  and Siskel's health issues, 222
Bulworth (1998), 224
"buried treasure" films, 210–11, 277–95
Burnett, Rob, 105, 121
Burns, George, 159

Camelot (1967), 26
Cannes Film Festival, 19, 221, 222, 228–29,
    283
Capra, Frank, 289
Capshaw, Kate, 113
Carney, Art, 159
Carpenter, John, 205
Carson, Johnny, 108, 113, 114, 121
Casablanca (1942), 207
Casey, Frank, 26
Castro, Analía, 283
Cat People (1982), 158
CBS This Morning, 50, 51, 226, 227, 274
Chaplin, Charlie, 209
Chase, Chevy, 109–10, 113
Chicago Daily Herald, 234–35
Chicago Daily News, 2, 5, 16, 179, 210
Chicago International Film Festival, 6, 76
Chicago magazine, 158–59
Chicago Reader, 234, 258
Chicago Sun-Times
  current headquarters, 271
  and Ebert's background, 15–16, 18, 25–30
  and Ebert's film criticism, 64, 66–67, 82,
      84–85
  and Ebert's health issues, 243–44,
      246–47, 256, 264
  and film rating system for show, 94
  and hosts' talk show appearances, 123–24
  and "New Hollywood" renaissance, 61
  and origins of show, 64
  and popularity of show, 151
  and Roeper's addition to show, 237–40
  and show's final episode, 260
  and Siskel-Ebert rivalry, 2, 55, 85, 149,
      151, 272–73
  and Siskel's background, 45

  and Siskel's conflict at *Tribune,* 174–76
  and Siskel's health issues, 224, 229
  and twentieth anniversary of show, 234
Chicago Today, 2
Chicago Tonight, 69
Chicago Tribune
  current headquarters, 270–71
  film critics after Siskel, 235, 238
  and film rating system for show, 94
  and hosts' talk show appearances, 113
  and *At the Movies* guest hosts, 253
  and "New Hollywood" renaissance, 61
  ownership of, 130
  and popularity of show, 151
  and pranks between Siskel and Ebert, 159
  and salary/contract negotiations, 167
  and selection of Ebert's counterpart, 66
  and Siskel and Ebert's departure from
      PBS, 173–74
  and Siskel-Ebert rivalry, 2, 33, 85
  and Siskel's background, 36, 43, 45–48,
      51, 54–55
  and Siskel's film criticism, 68–69, 97, 110
  and Siskel's health issues, 221–22,
      225–26
Child, Julia, 272
cinéma du look, 280
Cinema Paradiso (1988), 147
"Circles and Squares" (Kael), 150
Citizen Kane (1941), 97, 249
Clark, Dick, 63
Clarkson, Lana, 31
Cleland, Stuart, 37, 41, 160, 182, 221–22, 224
Cleopatra (1963), 59–60
Close Encounters of the Third Kind (1977), 36
Close to Eden (1991), 216
Cohen, Leonard, 244–45
colorization of films, 206–8
The Color Purple (1985), 49
Coltrane, Robbie, 177
Conan the Barbarian (1982), 92
Connell, Evan S., 287
Cop and a Half (1993), 151, 153, 162, 265
Coppola, Francis Ford, 61, 158
Corliss, Richard, 197–200, 265–66
Corman, Roger, 282
Coro Foundation, 44
Costas, Bob, 119–20
Costello, Lou, 121, 234
Cowell, Simon, 50
Crain's Chicago Business, 129, 170
Crawford, Cindy, 117
Creative Artists Agency, 179

Crist, Judith, 58, 60
Criterion Collection, 32
The Critic, 231
"Critics Roundup" segment, 251
Crossfire, 267
Crowe, Cameron, 154
Crowther, Bosley, 26, 27
Cruise, Tom, 79
The Crying Game (1992), 160–62
Crystal, Billy, 112
Cuarón, Alfonso, 215
Cuban, Mark, 260
Curtis, Jamie Lee, 282
Curtis, Tony, 21, 41

Daily Illini, 23–25
Daley, Richard, 231
Dance Me to My Song (1998), 228–29
Daniels, Jeff, 181
Dante, Joe, 290
Danza, Tony, 217
Dargis, Manohla, 236
Daves, Delmer, 59
Davidson, Jaye, 160–61
Davies, John, 52, 83–84, 93, 97, 100, 158
A Day at the Races (1937), 20–21
Days of Heaven (1978), 93
Death Before Dishonor (1987), 191
De Los Santos, Nancy, 72, 90, 92, 98–100, 109,
        128, 133–37, 143–44, 171
Demme, Ted, 291–92
Dench, Judi, 282
Denny, Patterson, 89
DeRita, Joe, 272
Dettwiler, Glen, 226
DeVito, Danny, 295
Dieckhaus, Larry, 157
Disney–MGM Studios, 160. *See also* Walt
        Disney Company
Diva (1981), 279–80
Doctor Dolittle (1967), 30
Doctor Dre, 291–92
Dog Day Afternoon (1975), 73
Dole, Bob, 179–81
Donnelly, Patrice, 280–81
D'Onofrio, Vincent, 291
Douglas, Michael, 8–9
Dow, Tony, 284
Dr. Strangelove (1964), 154
Dumbo (1941), 40
Dunaway, Faye, 26, 27
DuPree, Don, 108, 113, 114, 119, 223
DVD market, 278. *See also* video recordings

Ebert, Annabel, 17
Ebert, Chaz
    on co-authored book proposal, 201–2
    and companion website for show, 268
    and documentary on Ebert, 263–65
    and Ebert and Roeper's relationship, 238
    on Ebert's job offers, 28
    engagement and marriage, 182–83
    on evolving entertainment market, 274
    on *Hoop Dreams* screening, 213
    on introspective personality of Ebert, 19
    and salary/contract negotiations, 130
    on serendipity in Ebert's life, 16
    and show's return to PBS, 257–58, 260
    on Siskel's health issues, 230
    on sitcom proposal, 173
Ebert, Roger
    atheism, 264–65
    background before show, 2, 6, 15–33
    "buried treasure" films, 277–95
    cancer diagnosis, 243–44, 264
    and co-authored book proposal, 201–5
    death, 264
    engagement and marriage, 182–83
    and evolution of debate format, 62
    fame and popularity of, 9–12, 89, 102,
        145–46, 195, 241
    on film criticism, 103
    and film preservation efforts, 202–3, 207
    film review format, 59–60
    final show, 247–48
    and Flaum's championing of show, 2, 5–7
    and format/dynamics of show, 82–102,
        127–46, 147–64
    influence of, 11
    on Kurosawa, 57
    legacy of life's work, 265–75
    life after television, 244–47, 252–53,
        256–60
    love of job, 261
    memoir and documentary, 261–64
    observation skills, 19
    and origins of show, 1–13, 59–78
    poor eyesight, 18
    post-graduate education, 25
    pranks, 151–52, 158–60
    primer on show production, 185–95
    Pulitzer Prize, 6, 16, 24, 28, 55, 82–83
    rivalry with Siskel, 2, 8–12, 115–18,
        128–29
    and set design for show, 80–82
    and Siskel's death, 230–32
    skepticism of film review shows, 7

Ebert, Roger (*cont.*)
  and talk show appearances, 108–25
  and thumbs up/down rating system, 9, 93,
      143–45, 250–51, 268–69
  website dedicated to work of, 256, 265
  writing style and influences, 16, 20, 22–23
Ebert, Walter, 17, 20
Ebert Presents: At the Movies, 257–60, 271
Ebert & Roeper Floating Film Festival, 243
Ebert & Roeper & the Movies, 240–41, 268
Ebert's Overlooked Film Festival
      ("Ebertfest"), 18
Ed Sullivan Theater, 124
Ehrlich, Ken, 64
Eisenstein, Sergei, 209
Eisner, Michael, 160, 168, 169–70, 179
Elliott, David, 2, 5
Emmy Awards, 68
E! News, 248, 249
Entertainment Tonight, 195, 249
Entertainment Weekly, 179, 242
Ephraim, Don, 131, 134
Esquire, 27, 28
Evans, Sonia, 264
Evil Under the Sun (1982), 281

Facebook, 256
Falk, Peter, 285
Family Name (1997), 292–93
Father & Son pizza chain, 146
Fear and Loathing in Las Vegas (1998), 223
Feder, Robert, 18, 64, 149, 174, 176, 183,
      239, 243
Federal Communications Commission, 63
Fellini, Federico, 61
Fields, Michael, 288–89
Film Comment, 197, 265–66
film preservation, 202–3, 207
Flaum, Thea
  on evolving entertainment market, 274
  and format of show, 76
  on legacy of Siskel and Ebert, 266
  on Museum of Broadcast Communications
      honors, 220
  and origins of show, 2, 4–7, 11–12, 64–65
  and production of show, 82–83, 86–88,
      91, 92, 94, 98–100
  on Siskel and Ebert's partnership, 184
  on Siskel's death, 236
  on "Special Edition" episodes, 204
  and syndication of show, 134
Fonda, Henry, 59, 207
Forman, Milos, 76

Foster, Jodie, 288
The Fourth Protocol (1987), 187
Free Willy (1993), 106
Frozen Assets (1992), 192
Full Metal Jacket (1987), 153–54, 194
The Full Monty (1997), 151
The Future of the Movies (show and book),
      203–5, 216, 227

Gabler, Neal, 142, 195
Gance, Abel, 209
The Garrett (popcorn shop), 274
Gates of Heaven (1978), 210–11
Geffen, David, 179
Gentlemen Prefer Blondes (1953), 48
Get Shorty (1995), 37
Ghosts of Mississippi (1996), 229
Gill, Marilyn, 267
Gire, Dann, 234–35
Give My Regards to Broad Street (1984), 49–50
Gleason, Jackie, 165–66
Glengarry Glen Ross (1992), 161
The Glenn Miller Story (1954), 41
Godard, Jean-Luc, 31, 61
Godzilla (1998), 223
Golden, Norman D., II, 151–52
Goldstein, Patrick, 196
The Gong Show Movie (1980), 97
Goodbye Solo (2008), 266
Goodman, John, 290
Gould, Elliott, 278
The Graduate (1967), 26
Gray, Joseph, 40
Gray, Mae, 40
Greene, Bob, 231–32
Greenfield, Jeff, 236
Greengrass, Paul, 228
Gregory, André, 211
Griffith, D. W., 58
Grobel, Lawrence, 40
Gronvall, Andrea, 171

Hacker, Don, 169, 170
Hackett, Buddy, 123
Hall, Arsenio, 221
Halliwell, Leslie, 148
Halloween (1978), 205
Hamilton, Guy, 281
The Hand That Rocks the Cradle (1992), 155
Hans Christian Andersen (1952), 21
Hanson, Curtis, 278
Happy New Year (1987), 284–85
A Hard Day's Night (1978-unreleased), 32

Hare, David, 282–83
Harper, Bob, 177
Harris, Bill, 171, 195
Harrold, Kathryn, 152
Hawks, Howard, 48
Heart Condition (1990), 148
Heaven's Gate (1980), 129
Hefner, Hugh, 47
Heinlein, Robert A., 22
Hemingway, Mariel, 280–81
Herman, Pee-wee, 284
Hernández, Laura C., 72, 89–90, 101, 159
Hersey, John, 45
Hobbs, Lyndall, 284
Hoffman, Dustin, 225
Hoffman, Norman, 104
Hoffmann, Bob, 96
Hoge, Jim, 25
Hollywood Reporter, 177, 235
Hollywood Walk of Fame, 244
Holm, Ian, 282
Home Alone (1990), 54
Hoop Dreams (1994), 182, 212–15, 262
The Horse Thief (1986), 236
Houdini (1953), 21–22, 41
Household Saints (1993), 290–91
Hughes, Wendy, 285
Hunter, Holly, 295
Hurt, John, 293–94

Idle, Eric, 177
Iglitzen, Marlene, 44, 47–48, 54, 72, 146, 183,
    224, 235
Iltis, John, 213
The Immediate Experience (Warshow), 27
The Immoral Mr. Teas (1959), 28–29
Indiana Jones and the Temple of Doom
    (1981), 140
Inherit the Wind (1960), 42
Internet Tonight, 236
Interviews with Film Directors (Sarris), 27
In the Land of Women (2007), 246
Ironside (1967), 75
Irving, John, 294–95
Ishtar (1987), 62
It's a Wonderful Life (1946), 289
Ivory, James, 287–88

Jackson, Michael, 142
Jacobson, Walter, 68–69
Jagged Edge (1985), 189
James, Steve, 213, 261–63
Joel, Billy, 75–76

Joffe, Charles, 91
Johnson, Mark Steven, 294–95
Johnson, Rian, 281
Jones, Amy, 281–82
Jordan, Michael, 119

Kael, Pauline, 150, 197
Katzenberg, Jeffrey, 168–70, 179
Kaye, Danny, 21
Keach, James, 282
Keen, Eleanor, 25
Kehr, Dave, 176
Kellogg, Mary, 149, 169–70, 222, 235
Kennedy, John F., 24–25, 208
Kilpatrick, James J., 62
King Kong Lives (1986), 190
Kinski, Nastassja, 158
Kirkpatrick, Clayton, 186
Knoblauch, Mary, 2
Knowles, Harry, 236
Kramer, Stanley, 42
Kubrick, Stanley, 153, 154, 218, 234
Kulhawik, Joyce, 236, 239
Kurosawa, Akira, 57, 61
Kurtis, Bill, 42, 68–69, 259
Kwietniowski, Richard, 293–94

Ladies' Home Journal, 61
LaGravenese, Richard, 295
LaMonica, Janet, 52
Landers, Ann, 182
The Larry Sanders Show, 107–8
The Last Picture Show (1971), 156
Late Night with David Letterman, 103–4,
    106, 108, 111, 113–14, 122, 124, 143,
    170, 174
Later with Bob Costas, 119–20
Late Show, 104–6, 114–16, 121–24
LA Weekly, 236
Leconte, Patrice, 286–87
Lederer, Eppie, 182
Lee, Spike, 179, 187, 266
Leigh, Janet, 21
Lelouch, Claude, 285
Lemire, Christy, 257–59, 265, 271
Lemmon, Jack, 122–23
Leno, Jay, 113, 115, 220–21, 245
Letterman, David, 103–8, 113–14, 116,
    120–24, 174
Letterman: The Last Giant of Late Night
    (Zinoman), 122
Lewis, Jerry, 234
Life Itself (memoir and film), 16, 19, 182, 261

Lisa (1990), 219
Little Indian, Big City (1994), 190
A Little Princess (1995), 215
Live with Regis and Kathie Lee, 168, 177
Living Out Loud (1998), 295
Loewenstein, Michael, 64, 79–82, 96,
        171–72, 257
London, Jason, 288
Looking for Comedy in the Muslim World
        (2005), 186–87
Lopez, Jennifer, 215
Los Angeles Times, 170, 196, 234, 251
Lost Angels (1989), 194
Love and Death on Long Island (1997), 293–94
Love Letters (1984), 281–82
Lover, Ed, 291–92
Lovstad, Carie, 38, 52–53, 222, 225–26
Lucas, George, 5, 113, 202–3
Lyons, Ben, 248–53, 255–56
Lyons, Jeffrey, 142, 195, 249–50
Lyons, Leonard, 249

MacArthur, James, 59
Macdonald, Dwight, 27
Made in Heaven (1987), 193
Madonna, 49, 179
Malcolm X (1992), 49, 187
Malick, Terrence, 93
Malina, Judith, 291
Maltin, Leonard, 195
Manhattan (1979), 91
The Man in the Moon (1991), 288
Mankiewicz, Ben, 111, 248–53, 255–56
Mankiewicz, Herman, 249
Mankiewicz, Joseph L., 59–60, 249
Man Push Cart (2005), 18, 266
Martin, Dean, 234
Marvin, Lee, 28, 76
Marx Brothers, 20–21, 28
Maslin, Janet, 236
Masterminds (1997), 219
Mathers, Jerry, 284
Matinee (1993), 290
Mazzello, Joseph, 294
McCarter, William J., 63–64, 66–67, 70, 74,
        77, 132
McCartney, Paul, 49–50
McLaren, Malcolm, 31–32
The McLaughlin Group, 267
Medved, Michael, 195
Meet Joe Black (1998), 227–28
Meet the Press, 62
Mellencamp, John, 245–46

memes, 265
Men Don't Leave (1990), 148–49
Merchant Ivory Productions, 287
Meyer, Russ, 28–33
Microcosmos (1996), 182
Midler, Bette, 148
The Mighty Quinn (1989), 286
Mimic (1997), 215
Minow, Newton, 63
Mister Quilp (1975), 4
Mitchell, Elvis, 234, 258
Mitchum, Robert, 28
Mommie Dearest (1981), 92
Monsieur Hire (1989), 286–87
Moonstruck (1987), 196
Moore, Michael, 215
Morgan, Al, 60
Morgenstern, Joe, 26, 27
Morris, Errol, 210–11
Morton, Robert, 106, 116, 120–21
Motion Picture Association of America
        (MPAA), 140, 209, 268
Mr. & Mrs. Bridge (1990), 287–88
MTV, 142, 196
Mulan (1998), 225
Mulligan, Robert, 288
Mulroney, Dermot, 288
Murdoch, Rupert, 175
Murphy, Eddie, 49
Murphy, Jim, 157, 184, 274
Museum of Broadcast Communications, 70,
        219–20, 232
music videos, 142
My Dinner with Andre (1981), 211–12
Myers, Mike, 32
Mystery Science Theater 3000, 95

National Association of Television Program
        Executives' (NATPE) annual
        conference, 165–67, 206
National Press Club, 180
NC-17 rating, 209
Netflix, 203, 269
The New 9:30, 52
Newcity, 234
Newley, Anthony, 4, 47
Newman, Paul, 287
News-Gazette, 23–24
Newsweek, 26
New York City Ballet, 64
New York Dramatic Mirror, 58
New Yorker, 197
New York Film Festival, 210

New York Herald Tribune, 59
New York Post, 210
New York Times, 26–28, 58, 163, 210, 236, 253, 258
Nicholson, Jack, 10
Nickelodeon, 195–96
Nielsen ratings, 170–71
Nightline, 107
Nixon, Richard, 45, 208
Norton, Edward, 156
"Notes on the Auteur Theory" (Sarris), 150
No Way Out (1987), 187
Nuns on the Run (1990), 177, 178

O'Brien, Conan, 113
The Odd Couple (1968), 172
The Official Story (1985), 283
"Oh, How They Watched" (Ebert), 23
O'Hara, Maureen, 59
Once Upon a Time . . . When We Were Colored (1996), 292
One Flew Over the Cuckoo's Nest (1975), 76
One from the Heart (1981), 158
One Trick Pony (1980), 279
On Movies (Macdonald), 27
Overlooked Film Festival, 246
Ovitz, Michael, 179
Oxford Pub, 2, 7–8, 11, 65

Pacino, Al, 73, 161
Paramount Pictures, 169
Parker, Bonnie, 27
Pataki, George, 42
Patch Adams (1998), 228
The Pat Sajak Show, 118–19
PBS
    and criticisms of Roeper, 242
    and Ebert's Pulitzer, 82
    and film rating system for show, 94
    and hosts' talk show appearances, 124
    and popularity of show, 88–89, 97, 102, 108
    and public perception of Siskel and Ebert, 233, 235
    and salary/contract negotiations, 130–32
    show's return to, 257–60
    and "Special Edition" episodes, 204
    and syndication of show, 135
The Pebble and the Penguin (1995), 191
Penn, Arthur, 26–27
Pereira, Michaela, 236, 239
Personal Best (1982), 280–81
"Personality Parade" column, 226

Peter Pan (1953), 41
PG-13 rating, 140
Philbin, Regis, 166
Phillips, Michael, 253–56, 266, 271
The Piano (1993), 114
Pickwick Theatre, 137–38
Pitt, Brad, 227–28
Platoon (1986), 9
Playboy, 47–48, 152
The Plot Against Harry (1970/1989), 285–86
Plummer, Christopher, 278
Plummer, David, 108, 119, 223, 255, 274
podcasting, 254, 270, 274
Poland, David, 236
"The Pot and How to Use It" (Ebert), 256
A Prayer for Owen Meany (Irving), 294
Preminger, Otto, 60
Pride, Ray, 234
Priestley, Jason, 293–94
Primal Fear (1996), 155–56
Princess Theater, 21
Pryor, Richard, 70
Puenzo, Luis, 283
Pullman, Bill, 289
Pulp Fiction (1994), 37, 192, 213–14

Queen Latifah, 295

Racing with the Moon (1984), 156
Radio City Music Hall, 59
Rashomon (1950), 57
Rated K: For Kids by Kids, 195–96
rating system. *See* thumbs up/down rating system
Redford, Robert, 48–49
Redgrave, Vanessa, 282
Reed, Rex, 171, 195
Reid, Tim, 292
Reiner, Rob, 229
The Return of Swamp Thing (1989), 194–95
Return of the Jedi (1983), 107
"Review of Late Films" (column), 58
"The Revolving Thumb" segment, 181
Reynolds, Burt, 151
Ridley, John, 245
Risky Business (1983), 79
Rivers, Joan, 113
Roemer, Michael, 285–86
Roeper, Richard, 142, 166, 237–48, 258, 274
Roger Ebert & the Movies, 235–39
Roger & Me (1989), 215
Rollins, Jack, 91
Rosenbaum, Jonathan, 234

Rotten Tomatoes, 268–69
Royko, Mike, 16
"Rule of the Suspicious Pedestrian," 191
Ryan, Meg, 246

Sales, Soupy, 166
Salvador (1986), 229
Sarris, Andrew, 27, 150, 197
Saturday Night Fever (1977), 35–40, 235
Saturday Night Live, 70, 109, 111–13
Sauter, Van Gordon, 69
Saving Private Ryan (1998), 187
Savoca, Nancy, 290–91
Say Anything (1989), 218
Schenkel, Carl, 286
Schindler's List (1993), 187
School Ties (1992), 54
Schrader, Paul, 158
Scorsese, Martin, 61, 202–3, 236, 254, 266
Scott, A. O., 75, 163, 198, 253–56, 271
Scott, Walter, 226
Screamers (1995), 216
Second City, 70
See No Evil, Hear No Evil (1989), 70
Selena (1997), 215
The Sender (1982), 152
Sesame Street, 120
Sex Pistols, 31–32
Shales, Tom, 143
Shalit, Gene, 61–62, 64, 267
Shawn, Wallace, 211, 212
Sheen, Charlie, 8–9
Shepard, Sam, 289
She's Out of Control (1989), 217
Shutter Island (2010), 254
Siegel, Joel, 236
The Silent Partner (1978), 278–79
Simon, Neil, 172
Simon, Paul, 279
Simon, Roger, 24
Simon Birch (1998), 294–95
Sinatra, Frank, 207
Singles (1992), 154
Sinofsky, Bruce, 289
Siskel, Arlene, 40
Siskel, Callie, 54, 220
Siskel, Gene
    background before show, 2, 6,
        35–55
    "buried treasure" films, 277–95
    candor and honesty, 46–51, 53–54
    childhood trauma, 39–41
    and co-authored book proposal, 201–5

competitive nature and rivalry with Ebert,
    2–3, 9–12, 42–44, 51, 55, 82–85,
    115–18, 128–29, 249, 272–73
and evolution of debate format, 62
fame and popularity of, 9–12, 89, 102,
    145–46, 195
and film preservation efforts, 202–3, 207
and film review process, 35, 60, 103
and Flaum's championing of show, 2, 5–7
and format/dynamics of show, 82–102,
    127–46, 147–64
and gambling, 37
illness and death, 221–32
influence of, 11
on interviewing style, 57
kindness and generosity, 51–53
last movie reviewed, 228
love of job, 261
marriage, 54
military service, 44–45
and origins of show, 1–13, 66, 69–78
pranks, 151–52, 158–60
and set design for show, 80–82
siblings, 40
and talk show appearances, 108–25
and thumbs up/down rating system, 9, 93,
    143–45, 250–51, 268–69
work style, 37–38
Siskel, Kate, 50–51, 54, 220
Siskel, William, 40, 54
Siskel-Ebert.com, 181
Siskel & Ebert on the Edge (sketch), 120
60 Minutes, 62
Smith, Anna Nicole, 234
Smith, Ian Michael, 294
Smith, Kevin, 245
Snow White and the Seven Dwarfs (1937),
    208–9
social media, 199, 249, 256
Solley, Ray, 50, 70, 83, 85–86, 88, 91, 93–94,
    97–100, 129–30, 132, 138
Soundstage, 63
Sparky the Wonder Dog, 95–96
Spectator, 23
Spector, Phil, 30–31
Spencer's Mountain (1963), 59
Spielberg, Steven, 4–5, 36, 107, 157, 179, 187,
    202–3
sportswriting, 23–24
Spot the Wonder Dog, 95–96
Spy magazine, 178
Squires, Jim, 173–74, 175
Stanton, Harry Dean, 12

Stanwyck, Barbara, 147–48
Star magazine, 230
Star Trek, 200
Star Wars (1977), 36, 93, 203
State-Lake Theater, 55
Stealing Home (1988), 189
Stella (1990), 147–48
Stewart, Jimmy, 41
Stewart, Kristen, 246
Stone, Oliver, 229
Strasberg, Lee, 159
Strathairn, David, 294
Stymie (sci-fi fanzine), 23
Suddenly (1954), 207
"Summer Vacation" (opening credits song), 89
Sundance Film Festival, 17–18, 213–14
Susann, Jacqueline, 30
Synagogue Beth El, 231

Talbot, Dan, 212
Tarantino, Quentin, 213–14
Taulbert, Clifton, 292
Taylor, Lili, 288, 291
Terry, Clifford, 46
Teshigahara, Hiroshi, 42
The Theory of Flight (1998), 228
"They'll Do It Every Time" segment, 209
This Is Spinal Tap (1984), 189, 279
Thompson, Robert, 163, 199
Three Amigos (1986), 109–10
3 Ninjas Kick Back (1994), 153
Three Stooges, 272
Thriller (music video), 142
thumbs up/down rating system, 9, 93, 143–45, 250–51, 268–69
Tian, Zhuangzhuang, 236
Time, 28, 45
Today show, 60, 61–62, 64, 267
Tomei, Marisa, 152
The Tonight Show, 103, 108–10, 113–16, 168, 220–21, 245
Torn, Rip, 279
Toro, Guillermo del, 215
Touch of Evil (1958), 218
The Towering Inferno (1974), 39
Towne, Robert, 280–81
Toy Story (1995), 215
Tracy, Spencer, 42
Travolta, John, 35–39, 162
Tribune Entertainment, 130, 133–37, 143, 164, 168, 170, 173, 235, 278
The Truman Show (1998), 227
Turan, Kenneth, 234

Turner, Ted, 179, 207
Turner Classic Movies, 111, 248, 274
TV Guide, 88, 160–61
20th Century Fox, 30, 174, 175, 177
20/20, 193
Twitter, 249, 256
2001: A Space Odyssey (1968), 218, 265
Two Weeks in the Midday Sun (Ebert), 19
Tyler, Aisha, 245

Ullman, Tracey, 291
University of Chicago, 25–26, 66, 274
University of Chicago Review of the Arts, 66
University of Chicago Roundtable, 62
University of Illinois, 24, 66
US Department of Defense Information School, 45
U.S. Farm Report, 130
US Patent and Trademark Office, 145
Ustinov, Peter, 281

Valley of the Dolls (1967), 30–32
Vampires (1998), 229
Varecha, Bob, 139
Variety, 129, 173–75
vaudeville, 20
video recordings, 91, 140–41, 154, 202–3, 214, 278
Village Voice, 197
violence in film, 205–6
viral clips, 187, 265
Virginia Theatre, 20
Vishnevetsky, Ignatiy, 20, 257–59, 271
Vital Signs (1990), 178
Vixen! (1968), 29–30
von Hoffman, Nicholas, 62

Wald, Eliot, 70, 71–73, 77, 99, 111, 220
Wald, Jane Shay, 70–71
Wall Street (1987), 8–9
Wall Street Journal, 29
Walt Disney Company
    and acquisition of show, 167–72
    and book proposal, 201
    and criticism of show, 175–76
    and show after Ebert, 245, 247, 249–51, 253, 255–57
    and show after Siskel, 239–40
    and Siskel and Ebert's film reviews, 208–9, 225
    and Siskel and Ebert's influence, 179, 206, 208–9
    and Siskel's background, 40–41